# International Stability and Progress

**United States**

**Interests**

**and Instruments**

The American Assembly

Graduate School of Business

Columbia University, New York, N.Y.

June, 1957

*PRINTED IN U.S.A.*

*LIBRARY OF CONGRESS*

*Catalog Card No. 57-11284*

# Preface to the final edition

On May 2-5, 1957, sixty-two Americans drawn from a wide range of activities, interests, and areas gathered at Arden House, Harriman, New York, for the Eleventh American Assembly. The subject was *International Stability and Progress: United States Interests and Instruments*—a consideration of United States military assistance programs, world competition with the Soviets, and economic and technical aid as instruments of foreign policy.

During three days of discussions the Assembly was divided into three panels. They worked on common agenda, formed from the background papers of this volume by its editor, Professor Lincoln Gordon of Harvard University. The panel leaders were Philip C. Jessup, Hamilton Fish Professor of International Law and Diplomacy at Columbia University; Paul H. Nitze, President of the Foreign Service Educational Foundation, Washington, D. C.; and George W. Ball, Attorney and Counsellor at Law, of Washington, D. C.

In a plenary session at the close of their discussions, the participants considered a draft of findings and recommendations, which after discussion and modification was issued as the final Assembly report. It appears in this volume on page 171.

Formal addresses were delivered at the Assembly by Douglas Dillon, Deputy Undersecretary of State for Economic Affairs; and Eric Johnston, Chairman of the International Development Advisory Board.

The essays in this volume reflect the attitudes and experiences of the individual authors; and the conclusions are those of members of the Eleventh Assembly. The American Assembly as such takes no position.

The Eleventh American Assembly is to be followed by three regional meetings on the same topic, making use of the chapters in this book and of the Assembly conference techniques. The Arden House and regional meetings on *International Stability and Progress* are all made possible by a generous Ford Foundation grant, which the Assembly hereby acknowledges with thanks.

The American Assembly
Henry M. Wriston
*Executive Director*

# Contents

# 5. American aid and economic development:

International
Stability
and
Progress

*Introduction:*

# Foreign assistance in perspective

by Lincoln Gordon

The process of "Great Debate" concerning the ends and means of foreign policy has in recent years become a chronic feature of American public life. However strongly our natural instincts and our traditions may impel us to concentrate our energies on domestic concerns, the problems of our relationships with the world outside thrust themselves insistently on our attention. They determine the major shape and magnitude of our national budgets, the plans and careers of our young men,

Lincoln Gordon, William Ziegler Professor of International Economic Relations at the Harvard Graduate School of Business Administration, has had extensive experience in the field of foreign affairs. In 1946, he was a member of the United States delegation to the United Nations Atomic Energy Commission; in 1947, Consultant to the State Department for the European Recovery Program; in 1948, Director of the ECA's Trade Policy and Program Coordination Division; in 1940-50, Director of the Program Division, ECA European Headquarters; in 1950-51, Economic Adviser to the Special Assistant to the President; in 1951-52, Assistant Director for Mutual Security; and in 1952-55, Director of the U. S. Operations Mission and Minister for Economic Affairs, American Embassy, London. In 1956 Professor Gordon was consultant to the Ministerial Committee of the North Atlantic Council on Nonmilitary Functions of NATO.

1

the employment of much of our scientific and engineering talent, an important and increasing share of our economic life, and our sense of confidence in the future of our institutions and our most strongly held values.

The focus of debate, however, shifts continuously. There are hardly more than sporadic rear-guard actions on the question of whether we are to work out our destiny in either splendid or wretched isolation. There is a clear national consensus that the United States is actively concerned with the outer world. For present purposes, it matters little in what proportions the roots of that consensus are to be found in the technology of transportation and communication, the development of weapons which make absolute physical security impossible, the menace of Soviet communism as a world force, the increasing reliance of our economy on imported fuels and raw materials, the decline of Western European and especially British power as a shield for our way of life, or simply increased national maturity which tells us that the would-be isolationism and neutrality of the 1930's was in fact an illusion irreconcilable with our basic national interests.

The national consensus, moreover, extends not only to the existence of an active concern with external relationships but also to the global dimensions of that concern. For well over a century, there has been little domestic challenge to the concept of an active American interest in the whole of the Western Hemisphere; even the most enthusiastic exponents of neutrality between the wars were really hemispheric rather than national isolationists. On the other hand, despite our long-established national interest in the Far East, the experiment in Southeast Asian imperialism in the Philippines was never wholeheartedly accepted. On the European side, our intervention in World War I led to the bitterly isolationist reaction of the 1920's and 1930's.

In the past ten years, however, almost every region of the globe has become a theater of active American foreign policy, in most cases symbolized by major actions taken with overwhelming Congressional and popular support. In the Eastern Mediterranean and Europe, there have been the Truman Doctrine, the Marshall Plan, and the North Atlantic Treaty; in the Far East, our alliances with Japan and the Chinese Nationalists on Taiwan and our major intervention in the Korean War; in Southeast Asia, our sponsorship of SEATO and the ANZUS Treaty; and now in the Middle East, the Eisenhower Doctrine. While most of Africa has been *terra incognita* for all but a few Americans, Vice President Nixon's trip early in 1957 is only one evidence of our growing affirmative interests there, especially in the territories emerging from European colonial rule into national independence. The Mutual Security Program, with its provisions for military, economic, or technical assistance to almost every country in the world not subject to communist control, is one striking symbol of this global interest.

Within this basic consensus, the terrain of debate is now shifting to more precise definitions of objectives and especially to the merits of various possible instruments of foreign policy. Few will be found to quarrel with the desirability of international stability and progress—the key words of our title. What, however, do these noble objectives mean in practical application? By what means are they to be pursued? What risks shall be run and what costs assumed in their pursuit?

As Professor Jessup makes clear in his present essay, and as the National Security Council has repeatedly discovered, the effort to define national interests in terms more precise than resounding platitudes is no easy task. One approach to greater precision is to catalogue objectives as Professor Jessup does. Another is to emphasize certain basic assumptions. In another connection, I have attempted this in the following terms:

It is assumed that American interests will best be served in a world in which free institutions predominate and popular aspirations for material improvement and other social change are met by such institutions without recourse to force. Communist expansionism is the most obvious threat to such a world—a global and potentially mortal threat. There are also conceivable challenges from other forms of totalitarianism, perhaps based on the frustrated nationalism of newly independent peoples in Asia or Africa. It is likewise assumed that the indicated national strategy must pursue three broad lines: (a) maintenance and strengthening of free world alliances among all nations recognizing the common danger; (b) action to harmonize the interests of neutralist underdeveloped countries with the free world in the short run and to secure their identification with the cause of freedom in the long run; and (c) action to contain Soviet expansionism in whatever form and to weaken the cohesion of the Soviet bloc.

Such approaches, however, hardly do more than give broad direction to policy. They are of only limited usefulness in coming to grips with the specific decisions of which actual policy is made. Moreover, whatever the definition of objectives, it is important to free ourselves of certain easy illusions. American public thinking on foreign policy suffers occasionally from two great contrasting myths: that of omnipotence and that of impotence.

Our wealth and power, great as they are, do not give us unlimited ability to dispose of the world as we might like. In the critical realm of the conflict with world communism, we have learned that we cannot simply will the liberation of the Eastern European satellites or the unification of Germany, Korea, or Vietnam. Quite apart from the problem of communist-dominated areas, it has been painful for many Americans to learn that we cannot create by fiat a United States of Europe, or secure ready Indian adherence to the system of anti-communist alliances. Patient negotiation with American help did produce an amicable settlement of the Italian-Yugoslav dispute over Trieste, but neither this nor other instruments of policy have yet found the means to resolve the problems of Cyprus, Kashmir, the Arab-Israeli conflict, or racial tensions in South and East Africa. Nor can our resources bring us absolute physical security, which is unobtainable in today's world.

The opposite myth of impotence is less in tune with the general

3

American outlook, but still not wholly unknown. This view holds that the main currents of international life are beyond our power to influence and that the best we can do is to adapt ourselves to the historic tides. One manifestation of this attitude is the notion that underdeveloped countries are bound to fall under communist control sooner or later, because the process of development itself upsets the old structure of social power and only communism offers the necessary combination of popular appeal and autocratic discipline required to limit consumption, force the pace of investment, and secure rapid industrialization by pulling at the bootstraps.

This view is suspiciously reminiscent of the notion of a Fascist "wave of the future," which deluded so many leaders of opinion in this and other free countries on the eve of World War II. Believers in the myth of impotence might well be asked whether they deny that the Truman Doctrine prevented a communist conquest of Greece or at best another partition on Indo-Chinese lines. Do they seriously question the role of the Marshall Plan in making possible the restoration of the European economy as a going concern? Do they doubt the significance of the United Nations action in Korea, not only in preventing communist control of South Korea but also in down-grading overt international aggression as a major instrument of communist strategy? Are they prepared to say that foreign aid can make no difference to the prospects of success or failure for India's efforts at accelerated economic development under democratic institutions?

There is, in short, very great room for maneuver in foreign policy, but not an unlimited choice of specific achievable objectives or workable instruments. The use of certain conceivable instruments is foreclosed by our basic military and political inhibitions; we simply will not resort to preventive war or use force to build an American empire. Our resources are not unlimited, and we are not happy with the economic and social consequences of large security expenditures and heavy involvement in various forms of overseas aid.

Specific policies, each apparently compatible with our basic objectives, may contain contradictions among themselves. There is the dilemma of reconciling our European alliances with our general opposition to colonialism. There are the literally dreadful problems of allocating military resources between instruments of massive retaliation and lesser weapons required to deter or fight the limited conflicts which the super-weapons cannot be certain of preventing. There is conflict between our desires to dispose of agricultural surpluses and to avoid disrupting the markets of other friendly countries. The Northern Tier defensive alliance in the Middle East may seem strategically sound, but if it encourages Soviet arms aid to Egypt and Syria, or a bending of Indian neutrality in the Soviet direction, the net effect may be counter-productive. With a vast legislative and executive apparatus involved in foreign policy-making and execution, there is a formidable task of integrating the instruments of policy into a consistent whole.

The areas of current debate on policies to promote international sta-

4

bility offer many topics for fruitful discussion. The Tenth American Assembly considered our relations with the Far East. Others that come readily to mind include the relative emphasis on the role of the United Nations as compared with regional collective security alliances and bilateral negotiation; the merits of the alliance system as against independent international action; the problem of effective substitutes for the use of force as a means of achieving international adjustments; the likelihood of limited war and means of dealing with it; the problem of European security and the attitude toward quasi-satellites in Europe; disarmament; the basic posture of the United States toward declared neutrals in the struggle with communism.

The central focus for consideration by the Eleventh American Assembly is on one of the principal instruments of foreign policy: the programs of military, economic, and technical assistance to other countries. This topic has been selected because it is the subject of unusually intense current debate and because it touches on a wide range of today's outstanding foreign policy issues. It is the theme of a series of official executive and legislative reviews comparable only to the many inquiries of 1947 which preceded adoption of the Marshall Plan. They include the President's Citizen Advisers on the Mutual Security Program (the Fairless Group); the International Development Advisory Board (the Johnston Board); the House Foreign Affairs Committee; and the Senate Special Committee to Study the Foreign Aid Program. In addition, numerous private groups and individuals are participating in the open general debate.

The American Assembly obviously cannot engage in the compilation of massive data on individual country programs or the intensive review of detailed issues of programming or operations in the field which are among the subjects of the extensive official inquiries. It can, however, seek to place the instrument of foreign aid in the perspective of basic national policy objectives and review the key issues of its proper role in relation to other major instruments of foreign policy.

This endeavor appears especially timely because it is only in the last year or two that the Administration has come to advocate, and the Congress and the public to appraise, the concept of foreign assistance as a policy instrument of indefinite duration. The only avowedly permanent legislation in this field to date has been the Act for International Development of 1950, which was designed to implement President Truman's "Point Four" proposal for expanded multilateral and bilateral technical assistance to underdeveloped countries. In its orginial concept, however, this program was limited to the provision at low cost of expert advisers coupled with efforts to expand the flow of private capital. It was not intended to include any substantial volume of publicly financed developmental capital. All the other programs of economic and military assistance were, when adopted, expected to meet specific needs over a few years and then to be dismantled. To be sure, the explicit terminal date was a major feature only in the case of the Marshall Plan, but the legislative history of the other programs

5

frequently stressed their limited objectives. The Mutual Security Program, which since 1951 has gathered together all the foreign aid activities except for Export-Import Bank lending, requires annual Congressional authorization as well as appropriation.

The effort to place foreign assistance programs in a wider perspective is also timely because certain of their aspects have only recently come into prominence, while others appear to be still flowing from the momentum of Korean wartime impulses in directions which may no longer be appropriate. The idea of capital assistance for economic development, for example, has appeared in Mutual Security legislation for several years, but its merits as an element of foreign policy have yet to be explicitly accepted. Agricultural surpluses have come to play a very important practical role, but there is not yet a recognized doctrine concerning their use. Much of our military assistance is still devoted to meeting equipment deficiencies for military establishment targets worked out for various countries in the light of Korean War conditions; it is not well adjusted either to changing political and strategic concepts or to the technical necessities imposed by subsequent and prospective weapons developments. More broadly, there is a widespread feeling that aid programs are now being carried on from year to year as much from inertia as from conscious design, without a clear-cut philosophy, a purposeful sense of direction, or a conviction of the relationship of particular means to given ends.

This focus on foreign assistance should not be taken to imply a view that it is either an end in itself or a panacea for securing international stability and progress. There are many critical issues of foreign policy to which aid can make little or no contribution: witness the problems of disarmament, of German unification, or of liberation of the Soviet satellites. Nor can it be divorced from other aspects of foreign policy, as the problem of developing the river valleys of the Middle East makes eminently clear. Foreign assistance does, however, play an important role over a wide range of foreign policy, and the questions of its proper role are among the most critical issues now requiring consideration by the American public.

To assist in the American Assembly's deliberations, the following chapters have been prepared by authors of recognized distinction in their respective fields. They are designed not primarily as factual expositions, but rather as thought-provoking essays to help crystallize the issues of major concern in shaping the future place of the foreign assistance programs in the total framework of American foreign policy.

Professor Jessup's chapter provides a broad background discussion of the ends and means of foreign policy, emphasizing the historical development of both our objectives and our policy instruments. He shows the predominant role of security considerations and of the communist menace in contemporary policy-making, but also the need for taking fully into account other policy objectives and relations with states other than the communist bloc. He weighs the relative importance of the traditional instruments of diplomacy and the tools of the new diplomacy, including the United Nations, regional alliances, and the foreign assistance programs. He points to the major influence of domestic factors, institutional and other, in setting a part of the framework in which realistic policy must be conducted.

Professor Grossman describes the evolution of the Soviet economy as a basis of Russian influence in world affairs, with its bearing on military potential, foreign economic policy, and possible attractiveness—or unattractiveness—of the Soviet Union as a model of rapid industrialization for other countries bent on accelerated economic development. There emerges from his chapter a picture of the USSR as a formidable antagonist, but one also experiencing severe strains from a combination of labor shortages, elemental pressures for increased consumption, continued domestic industrialization, a huge military effort, demands from its bloc partners, and increasing commitments to the underdeveloped regions of the world. He raises the critical question of interaction between Russian and American policies and the opportunities open to us for influencing their future course in ways conducive to our own long-range purposes.

Dean Mason's chapter, while focused mainly on Southern Asia, also deals with the general question of the nature of our national interest in foreign economic assistance. He finds the answer predominantly in security, rather than economic or humanitarian, factors. At the same time, he emphasizes a concept of security sufficiently broad to encompass several of the additional points of Professor Jessup's catalogue of objectives. Dean Mason describes the new lines of Soviet foreign economic activity and sketches the developmental position and prospects of five of the leading Southern Asian countries, indicating both the limitations and the potentialities for accelerated development and the possible role of foreign capital and technical assistance in this process. He concludes with an analysis of certain contrasting views on the possible range and conditions of American assistance.

Mr. Nitze's chapter lays the foundation for fundamental political and strategic analysis which must underlie any intelligent review of our military assistance policies. Against the historical background of the development of military assistance, which has for several years constituted the bulk of our aid programs, he sketches the main alternative lines of strategy open to us, suggests certain conclusions as to the strategic alternatives, and draws from these conclusions a number of basic issues on the future of military assistance in Europe, the Middle East, and the Far East.

Professor Schelling's chapter presents an analytical summary and review of the principal recent official and unofficial appraisals of the aid programs, including all the materials available up to Secretary of State Dulles' major policy pronouncement of April 8, 1957. The central focus of this chapter is the most novel and controversial segment of the Mutual Security effort—assistance in the economic development of underdeveloped countries. After a brief statement of the actual record

7

in this area, Professor Schelling examines in some detail eighteen out-standing issues, indicating the range of proposals for their resolution and bringing to the fore the critical implications of alternative policy choices among them.

Taken as a whole, the papers provide a background for consideration of all the major problems around which the current debates are focused and on which an informed public opinion is especially necessary. Without attempting a comprehensive listing, the principal questions can now be briefly formulated.

In present and prospective world conditions, do the national interests and foreign policy objectives of the United States require programs of foreign military, economic, and technical assistance for the indefinite future? If so, is this conclusion exclusively a result of the struggle with communism, or would there be sound grounds for foreign assist-ance of any type even if the communist menace were greatly reduced? In what circumstances could there be envisaged a substantial reduction *or* a termination of foreign assistance programs?

On the military side, does a sound American strategy clearly require collective security alliances or can some or all of them be dispensed with? Are such alliances designed simply to reinforce the weight of the " Great Deterrent," or do they also have a role in combatting possible limited aggression or internal subversion? Is military assistance an indispensable part of such alliances? What broad lines of adjustment in the character of military assistance appear called for by weapons developments and by current evidence as to Soviet intentions or capa-bilities? Does military assistance have any proper role in connection with possible conflicts other than those arising from communist ag-gression?

With respect to technical assistance, does experience confirm the assumption of our present legislation that technical advice, training, and demonstration in such fields as public health, agriculture, public administration, industrial development, and business administration are appropriate long-run activities for the United States government? Is the present division of responsibility between United Nations and bilateral programs satisfactory? What are the strengths and limit-ations of technical assistance as a means of fostering development or promoting other American foreign policy objectives? Is technical as-sistance a satisfactory instrument unless it is coupled with some effective means of stimulating the simultaneous transfer of capital, private or public?

What is the nature of the United States foreign policy interest in eco-nomic assistance? Is it solely a part of national security policy, or are there important economic, humanitarian, or other nonsecurity ob-jectives to be served by such assistance? Apart from our direct economic interests, is there a derived American interest of major importance because of the greater dependence of our industrialized allies in Western Europe and Japan on expanding world trade and out-side sources of energy and raw materials? Is it a proper purpose of economic assistance programs to reduce this dependence or to promote greater stability in their, as well as our, sources of supplies, markets, and investment outlets?

Should assistance for economic development in underdeveloped countries now be explicitly accepted as a well-defined objective of American foreign policy? How would such an objective be related to the other main foreign policy interests of the United States? What would be the magnitude and time periods of such a program? If accepted, should the program of development assistance be based on a comprehensive general approach with standard criteria for the various classes of potential recipients, or should it be developed country by country in the light of specific political, economic, social, and other conditions? What standards of self-help should be required?

What should be the policy concerning assistance for declared neutrals in the cold war? Should they be ruled out, given a deferred position in relation to allies, or treated on a basis of equality? As a leading test case, should the United States make a greater contribution to closing the external gap in the second five-year development program of India? Should assistance programs exclude or include countries which have communist regimes but are not responsive to the control of Moscow?

What are the appropriate magnitudes of foreign assistance? Do current magnitudes place a severe strain on the United States? Is there a proper balance among the broad categories of direct military, defense support, economic development, and technical assistance? How should the various components of the assistance program be divided between loans and grants? If loans are employed, should they be exclusively "hard" dollar loans, or should they also include provision for unusually low interest rates, long periods of repayment, waivers of interest and principal in certain circumstances, or possible repayment in local currency rather than dollars? What is the appropriate role of agricultural surpluses in assistance programs?

Should the foreign assistance programs or some part of them be established on a longer range basis than can be provided through annual congressional authorizations and appropriations? Should military, economic, and technical assistance continue to be combined in a single program, or should they be separated? By whom should they be administratively controlled?

What are the opportunities for greater private participation in advancing a national policy of promoting economic development? Are there possibilities for a major shift from public to private capital supply? Could more of the technical assistance be privately organized? Could effective arrangements be worked out for joint private and public ventures?

Are the general objectives of the foreign assistance programs better served by giving aid bilaterally or by channeling it through such international instrumentalities as the United Nations Technical Assistance Programs and the International Bank? Should the United

9

States support the proposed Special United Nations Fund for Economic Development? Is the possibility of Soviet participation in such international efforts a controlling factor? Should economic development assistance be organized in whole or in part through regional instrumentalities? Are there means available for encouraging the participation of other advanced countries, and if so how should their efforts be coordinated with those of the United States?

What conditions should be established for the various forms of foreign assistance? Should offers of aid or threats to withdraw aid be used as inducements to secure the support of other governments for United States policies? Can a valid distinction be drawn between "political strings" and economic or other conditions designed to ensure the success of the immediate program objectives?

Underlying many of these questions is the broader one of whether the current concepts, objectives, and administration of foreign assistance are playing their proper part in the totality of foreign policy. The evident malaise in the Congress on this topic and the spate of current official and unofficial reappraisals suggest at a minimum the need for clarification of purposes and methods, and possibly the need for a wholly fresh approach in some or all segments of the program. It is hoped that the Eleventh American Assembly can contribute substantially to a sound resolution of these vital questions.

# 1. Ends and means

# of American foreign policy

by Philip C. Jessup

Foreign policy is influenced by both heredity and environment. No one concerned with United States foreign policy is free to act without reference to the past. He would be a fool to ignore the future. He can never escape the present.

## The objectives of foreign policy

### The lessons of history

To say that one should be guided by the "lessons of history" does not mean that one needs to imitate under the different conditions of

Philip C. Jessup is Hamilton Fish Professor of International Law and Diplomacy at Columbia University. His career of teaching at Columbia since 1925 has been interspersed with periods of service in foreign affairs. In 1929 he assisted Elihu Root in negotiations at Geneva for United States participation in the World Court. In 1930 he was legal adviser to the American Ambassador to Cuba. From 1943 through 1945 he held official positions connected with the establishment of UNRRA, the International Bank and Monetary Fund and the United Nations. From 1948 to 1953 he served as a representative of the United States in the United Nations Security Council, the Interim Committee of the General Assembly and several sessions of the General Assembly. Dr. Jessup was United States Ambassador at Large from 1949 to 1953. He has written widely on international law and is also the author of a biography of Elihu Root.

today the actions taken at some earlier period. The contrasts are just as important as the comparisons. In earlier periods of our history, the United States was sufficiently free from responsibility for the peace of the world to enable us to indulge in statements or actions which if imitated today would represent an irresponsibility fraught with the most dangerous consequences. Burdened as we now are with power, our freedom of choice is limited by our responsibilities. We should not be surprised, however, if smaller states do not have the sense of sharing the responsibility and therefore act in a way which seems to us to be irresponsible. One of the problems of foreign policy is to make a fair appraisal of the attitudes of other governments and it is perhaps in this respect that a re-examination of our own history is particularly useful. A convenient point of departure may be provided by some considsideration of the labels which are popularly attached to foreign policies.

## The use of labels

If one looks back over even small segments of American history, one finds that our foreign policy frequently was known by general substantive labels rather than by regional labels. Thus up to our entry in World War II—subject to some belligerent interludes—the United States followed a "neutrality policy." Coupled with neutrality was the policy known as the "freedom of the seas." There was also the policy of the Monroe Doctrine, which had a particular regional impact in terms of Latin America but which was very much broader than the Western Hemisphere and which contained the reciprocal doctrine of isolation from European entanglements. Similarly we had a tariff policy and an immigration policy. During the Taft Administration, our policy of economic and financial expansion went under the then not invidious name, "Dollar Diplomacy."

On the other hand there were contemporaneously policies which could be described regionally. Certainly from the end of the nineteenth century we were quite conscious of having a Far Eastern policy which was identified in the public mind with the Open Door. This policy, of course, had its roots in an earlier period but was dramatized by John Hay's Open Door notes. Moreover the dramatic events of the Boxer Rebellion served to sharpen our interest in the Far East, which came to an even higher pitch with the events of the Russo-Japanese War and President Theodore Roosevelt's action in bringing about the peace conference at Portsmouth. From this time on Japan loomed as a strong power threatening our interests and safety. Probably President Theodore Roosevelt exaggerated, but in July 1907 he wrote to Secretary of State Root: "In France, England, and Germany the best information is that we shall have war with Japan and that we shall be beaten. My own judgment is that the only thing that will prevent war is the Japanese feeling that we shall not be beaten, and this feeling we can only excite by keeping and making our navy efficient in the highest degree."

But the danger of war with Japan was not sufficiently imminent to become an obsession, and it did not crowd out of consideration foreign policies directed particularly to other areas. For example, we undoubtedly had a regional policy which revolved around Latin America. As already indicated, our Latin American policy was in part merely a reflection of the Monroe Doctrine. But it had its dramatic phases, as for example Olney's famous pronouncement over the Venezuelan incident and the Roosevelt corollary which arrogated to the United States the role of policeman in the Caribbean. Our interest in the Panama Canal was in a sense a part of this regional policy and in part a link between it and policies with other countries of the world. It is fair to say that this policy continued until it evolved into the " Good Neighbor Policy" of President Franklin D. Roosevelt, which had been initiated by Secretary of State Root and developed—subject to some interludes —by intervening Administrations.

It can hardly be said that in the early decades of this century we had a Middle Eastern policy. When the American minister to Persia fifty years ago asked for instructions regarding his joining in representations by the diplomatic corps to the Shah, urging that he compromise his dispute with the Persian Parliament, Secretary Root sent a note to President Roosevelt marked " Personal, Confidential and Foolish":

The enclosed dispatch from Jackson shows the serious results to the State Department of your yielding to your admiration for him and making him Minister to Persia purely as a matter of favour. So far as I am aware, this is the first time that the State Department has ever been called upon for instructions from Persia. We already have trouble enough. I have drafted a reply which Mr. Adee thinks too serious. I shall be glad of your instructions.

The draft reply read: " Continue quarrels with missionaries as usual."

This characteristic " kidding" of Roosevelt by Root brings out by contrast the lack of interest of the United States in the Middle East fifty years ago and our interest today, when the Secretary of State is forced to be so much concerned with the problems of that area that such a pleasantry would scarcely be amusing.

One might generalize by saying that various glances at American foreign policy in the past show that we have necessarily developed a particular foreign policy to meet any threat to our safety and have developed other policies as means of developing our general economic interests and the position of our investors abroad. It would distract us too much from our present inquiry to examine the various other historical aspects of American foreign policy—for example, to analyze the expansionist policies going back to the War Hawks of 1812 on through the period of Manifest Destiny into the Spanish American War and its immediate aftermath. If one were making a complete catalogue, of course one would also signalize the relapse into isolationism after the defeat of Woodrow Wilson's efforts to bring the United States into cooperation with the rest of the world through the League of Nations.

13

## Contemporary regional labels

The tendency of many analyses today is to put the emphasis on regional policies and in fact to assume that if we are doing our foreign policy business properly we must have a special foreign policy for each area of the world. Thus it has become the cliché of condemnations of the Department of State to say that it has "no Middle Eastern policy" or "no Far Eastern policy." Whether the criticism is well founded or not at any particular time, the assumption is that there must be a policy bearing a regional label.

To be sure, the United States should act in all situations in conformity with some plan, but the regional designations may be inappropriate. It is possible, for example, to think of "an African policy," but at the present juncture the policy in regard to the North African fringe of the Mediterranean is necessarily influenced by factors other than those which would influence policy in regard to the still colonial or emerging regions of Africa south of the Sahara. Egypt is geographically located in the continent of Africa, but generally one considers the policy toward Egypt to be part of what is described as a Middle Eastern policy. It might well be that a policy regarding Africa south of the Sahara would be part of a general policy on the colonial question; and such a policy is related just as much to Western Europe, where the administering powers are located, as to the continent or regions in which the colonies are located.

Similarly as one looks at a globe, the question is what is the size of the geographic segment for which one should have a separate policy? One may have a Far Eastern policy which perhaps would be concerned particularly with China or Japan, or one could think in terms of an Asian policy including not only those two countries but also the states of South East Asia and even the subcontinent with India and Pakistan. If, however, one approached the problem from the other side of the globe and marked out the area to which a Middle Eastern policy would apply, Pakistan would be included with Iran and the Arabian states instead of with its great Indian neighbor to the east. The difficulty has been abundantly illustrated of late in the discussions of the definition of the general area of the Middle East to which the Eisenhower Doctrine is to apply.

## The influence of State Department organization

The tendency to emphasize the geographical divisions of foreign policy may be due in part to the fact that the now traditional organization of the State Department is along geographic lines despite various fluctuations and the separation from time to time of functional areas such as economics. It is true that over a considerable period of time the Assistant Secretaries of State charged with responsibility for certain geographic areas have exercised a strong influence on the formulation and execution of foreign policy, with a predominant role in recent times going to the bureau dealing with Western Europe. It is a far cry to the days when this system of geographical organization was inaugurated in the State Department under Secretary Knox. The first State Department order setting up a geographical division is dated March 20, 1908, and reads as follows: "Mr. William Phillips, a clerk of the $900 class, is hereby designated Chief of the Division of Far Eastern Affairs (correspondence, diplomatic and consular, on matters other than those of an administrative character, in relation to China, Japan, Korea, Siam, Straits Settlements, Borneo, East Indies, India, and in general the Far East)."

Inevitably as policies develop in regard to geographical areas, they clash as particular problems are presented for solution. Thus the United States, speaking broadly, has had a policy of support for Western Europe and our NATO partners and also a policy of cultivating friendly relations with the nations of the Middle East and of Asia. When questions concerning Tunis and Morocco and Algeria have arisen in the United Nations, it is natural that the Assistant Secretary of State for European Affairs should present the point of view that it is necessary to support our ally France, while his colleague, the Assistant Secretary for Near Eastern, South Asian, and African Affairs, would present the importance of maintaining our stand in favor of the independence of peoples and the right of self-determination. It is impossible to have some neat catalogue which in advance will provide an automatic resolution of such clashes of interest.

It is particularly true in the years since 1945, when statements are constantly made to the effect that the United Nations is the cornerstone of our foreign policy, that it has been quite impossible to reconcile that very broad and vague concept with the demands of particular regional policies. We have seen this very strikingly illustrated in the recent events when the policy of support for the United Nations and the principles of the Charter led us to take a stand against other members of the Grand Alliance of NATO and to oppose in the General Assembly France's and Great Britain's action in Egypt.

Thus broad labels such as "a United Nations policy" or a "peace policy" are no more helpful than the labels cast in terms of geographic regions. Setting aside the labels for the moment, one may then look at some of the more basic facts underlying foreign policy.

## The problem of concentration on the maximum menace

If regional labels on foreign policy are misleading, so also is the customary concentration on the Soviet Union. There is a common tendency to assume that all American foreign policy is directed toward our relations with the Soviet Union or more broadly with the communist powers. One therefore finds broad generalizations, which may be apt so far as our relations with the Soviets are concerned but which are not applicable to our relations with other countries of the world.

15

It is possible to say that our foreign policy is focused on our relations with the Soviet Union because it is from that quarter that the one threat to American survival can now be seen. National survival, or more broadly the question of defense against threatened danger, must always be the central factor in foreign policy. Looking from this point of view, one can properly say that all of our other policies are related to and dependent upon our policy in regard to the communist powers. Yet this oversimplification does not lead to the most intelligent analysis of many of the individual problems which confront the policy-makers. For example, one issue now confronting the United States is the question of membership in the new proposed Organization for Trade Cooperation, designed to provide general organizational support to the accepted policy embodied in the General Agreement on Tariffs and Trade (GATT). Only in a very general sense could this issue be considered part of our policy with relation to the Soviet Union. It is true that if those charged with developing a foreign trade policy are met by an objection that their plans would conflict with some overall policy concerning the Soviet Union, the particular policy might have to yield or be modified to fit in with the general underlying objectives. Thus, in connection with restrictions on East-West trade, those government officials concerned with the general liberalization and expansion of trade might pay more attention to the needs of Western Europe to trade with the Soviet area, whereas those who were particularly mindful of the strategic factors and the development of Soviet power, might insist upon restrictions. Congress in enacting the Battle Act was more concerned with the latter than with the former problem. The question of recognition of the Chinese Communist regime is directly connected with our general concern with the expansion of communist power, but the question of our relations with the Peron dictatorship in Argentina had only a remote connection with the central problem.

Even, however, if we take our Soviet policy as the focus because of its relation to national survival, we are bound to look at it not only from the point of view of the dangers of the moment but in terms of the long pull. The immediate dangers were perhaps uppermost in the minds of policy-makers from the time when the Soviet policy in its true colors became apparent as the war drew to a close. We were then confronted by a series of issues which were definitely the result of the aggressive Stalinist policy. This situation resulted in such vigorous moves in American foreign policy as the announcement of the Truman Doctrine in 1947 to halt the Soviet drive against Greece and Turkey; the Berlin Airlift to meet the Berlin Blockade in 1948; and the formulation of the Marshall Plan and the creation of NATO. A new emphasis in these policies came with the attack on Korea in June 1950. With the momentary changes in at least the tactics of the Soviet Union itself after the death of Stalin, a renewed awareness of the importance of long-range factors required us to pay more attention to our relations with some of the other parts of the world.

16

# The memorandum of Eyre Crowe

It is worthwhile to reread in these days the famous 1907 memorandum on German foreign policy before the war, which was written for Sir Edward Gray by Sir Eyre Crowe, who was then in the British Foreign Office. It was a time when the Prussianized German Reich was so strong militarily and so obviously interested in expansion that the situation created great anxiety in England. While there are striking comparisons between Sir Eyre's analysis of German intentions and potentialities on the one hand and our views of the Soviet Union today on the other hand, the notable point is that Sir Eyre begins his analysis by referring to some of the very broad long-range considerations which must underline British foreign policy. He points out that England was the great sea power and that the very fact of British maritime supremacy naturally inspired "universal jealousy and fear." There was always the danger, therefore, of a general combination of powers of the world against which England could not stand. The memorandum continues:

The danger can in practice only be averted—and history shows that it has been so averted—on condition that the national policy of the insular and naval State is so directed as to harmonize with the general desires and ideals common to all mankind, and more particularly that it is closely identified with the primary and vital interests of a majority, or as many as possible, of the other nations. Now, the first interest of all countries is the preservation of national independence. It follows that England, more than any other non-insular Power, has a direct and positive interest in the maintenance of the independence of nations and therefore must be the natural enemy of any country threatening the independence of others and the natural protector of the weaker communities.

Sir Eyre Crowe then continues to say that second to the ideal of independence, nations cherish the right of free intercourse and trade and that the British policy of promoting free trade was an essential element of its position.

The appositeness of Sir Eyre Crowe's observations to the present position of the United States is clear, even if one must then distinguish his analysis of the balance of power system from the present situation of bipolarity.

One may be attempting to gild the lily in going beyond Sir Eyre Crowe's masterful simplicity in defining the objectives of foreign policy. Part of the difficulty of framing a definition of the objectives of American foreign policy is that at first blush they seem so obvious. One is apt to slip into the complex confusion of Dr. Samuel Johnson's *Dictionary* definition of a net as a "reticulated mesh with interstices between the intersections." It helps but little to say that the objectives of foreign policy are to protect and advance the national interest of the United States. Skillful writers have described the "national interest" to little avail. We do move further along if we turn to Professor Lin-

17

coln Gordon's descriptive statement that "American interests will best be served in a world in which free institutions predominate and popular aspirations for material improvement and other social change are met by such institutions without recourse to force." Along the same line, it might be suggested that the objective of American foreign policy is to secure a world environment in which all countries share the same sense of values and which would therefore permit us to devote our talents to the continued raising of man's standard of living and the pursuit of other nonmaterial values, acting on the principle that we ourselves will rise higher if the rest of the world rises with us. But it might be said in reply that if other statements are oversimplifications because of their obsession with the Soviet danger, such descriptive statements as these do not sufficiently emphasize our concern with our security and national survival.

A half century ago Secretary of State Root could say that "to keep the country out of trouble... in the right way is the main object of diplomacy." The problems of today are too varied for such a negative approach to satisfy. In current jargon, such an approach is not sufficiently dynamic. Perhaps one may usefully substitute for a definition a brief catalogue. One would include in the catalogue those desiderata toward the attainment of which a successful foreign policy can contribute. There may be some overlap in the items in the catalogue and there may be some argument as to which are means and which are ends. If it be said that another catalogue would serve as well, it may be true that this catalogue will serve as well as another.

## Catalogue of foreign policy objectives

### *Security*

There is no doubt that foreign policy must have as an objective—a prime objective—the defense of the United States from devastation by an enemy or defeat in war. There have been times in our history when the danger was not so acute as to lead us to put this objective in the first place. Other countries—let us say Uruguay or Venezuela for example—may be in that same happy situation today. For the United States, however, the danger is very real. The problem is to prevent this danger from driving out of our minds other long-range objectives. During World War II, concentration upon the objective of winning the war in some instances prevented our paying due heed to the problems of the postwar era. The United States must not permit concentration upon the necessity of winning the Cold War to obliterate other objectives or to cause it to subordinate them so that they are merely considered means to this one end. Perhaps the problem is most easily envisaged if one assumes that the communist menace is removed and if one then asks what are the other objectives of our foreign policy.

## Economic prosperity

Despite some echoes from our isolationist past and despite occasional plaints inspired by self-interest, it is hardly necessary any longer to argue that the American economy is affected by foreign trade and by economic conditions in other parts of the world. It is clear that international economics problems fall within the scope of our foreign policy even though as a matter of our governmental organization the decisions are not all made in the Department of State but are shared with, for example, the Treasury, Commerce, and Agriculture Departments, and the Export-Import Bank; and such international agencies as the International Bank of Reconstruction and Development, and the International Monetary Fund. Our foreign aid programs are, or should be, definitely linked to the general problem of maintaining international economic and financial stability and to promoting world-wide economic development in the benefit of which we will share. The fact that the aid programs may serve other ends as well cannot obscure this consideration.

## Opportunity for self-improvement

This objective is closely related to security and to economic prosperity but it contains other elements. We would like to be able to devote ourselves to various domestic reforms such as slum clearance, better education, care for the aged and disabled, better hospitals, more recreation facilities. We are aware—sometimes rather vaguely—that a successful foreign policy, which diminishes the danger of war, can contribute to these ends. If we succeed in evolving a workable plan for the limitation of armaments, this contributes not only to security but also to the reduction of the national defense budget so that more of our resources can be devoted to these domestic goals. It is less often appreciated that progress toward these goals is also a contribution to the foreign policy of a great power. As George Kennan said in his Stafford Little Lectures:

Blighted areas, filthy streets, community demoralization, juvenile delinquency, chaotic traffic conditions, utter disregard for esthetic and recreational values in urban development, and an obviously unsatisfactory geographic distribution of various facilities for homelife and work and recreation and shopping and worship; these things may not mark all our urban communities in conspicuous degree; but they mark enough of them to put a definite imprint that leads others to feel that we are not really the masters of our own fate, that our society is not really under control, that we are being helplessly carried along by forces we do not have the courage or the vitality to master . . . . . Peoples of the world are not going to be inclined to accept leadership from a country which they feel is drifting in its own internal development and drifting into bad and dangerous waters.

19

## An environment conducive to freedom

This objective is also closely related to the three already described, but it suggests a positive American interest in the fruitful development of free institutions elsewhere in the world. It is sought not only to avoid the constrictions on our own lives of a "garrison state," but also because it permits our society to benefit from the healthy interchange of ideas, peoples, and values with other societies. It is in a sense the international counterpart of our faith in the domestic ideal of an "open society."

## Prestige and influence

It may well be argued that prestige and influence are sought merely because they are means to other ends. Unquestionably they are such means, but they are something more. In one degree or another almost every state seeks these ends just as individuals do, nor is this reprehensible. One sees constantly in the United Nations the intense rivalry for positions of prestige which have only a remote connection with the advancement of other national interests. A small state, member of the United Nations, is eager to have one of its nationals chosen as a judge of the International Court of Justice for example, not because it expects to be a litigant before the Court and hopes to have a sympathetic member on the bench, but because of the general prestige factor. As a state grows in power and influence it may well disregard some of the minor insignia of prestige, but the prestige factor itself is not cast aside. This is not to say that United States foreign policy should be directed toward the absurd goal of winning a popularity contest as if Uncle Sam were competing for selection as "The Man of the Year." It is one of the popular fallacies, for example, that our foreign aid programs are designed to "buy friends," bound to us by ties of gratitude and affection. Millikan and Rostow have dealt effectively with this misconception. It is doubtful whether any responsible United States official has ever labored under the delusion that such a policy could ever achieve such a result. The prestige of a nation is not based on popularity; it rests far more upon respect. To be respected and to have the prestige and influence which flow from such respect is a natural and legitimate objective of foreign policy.

## Satisfying a sense of justice

Many will challenge the inclusion of "satisfying a sense of justice" as an objective of foreign policy, but it represents something substantial from the point of view of the American people. The American people are not likely to consider a foreign policy successful if it secures some material gain at the expense of principles which they consider part of their heritage. Here looms the whole debate over the proper role of morality in the making of foreign policy. The names of Kennan and Morgenthau are usually associated with the "realist"

20

theory that morality should not enter into foreign policy decisions; Louis J. Halle has sketched a somewhat different thesis in articles in the *Virginia Quarterly Review* and the *Yale Review*.

Without rearguing here the dilemma of the policy-maker, it is asserted that there is such a thing as an American national conscience, which does not rest easy if it feels that the United States has failed to show a "decent respect to the opinions of mankind." There is a persistent uneasiness about the justification for the use of the atom bomb on Hiroshima and Nagasaki. The anti-imperialists were able to build on a like uneasiness in opposing McKinley's Philippine policy. Congress has reflected this call of conscience in resolutions adopted on such occasions as the Jewish pogroms in Russia and the massacre of Armenians in Turkey. The reception of Kossuth in Washington a century ago, like the reception of the Hungarian refugees today, is further illustration. In framing its policy on the issues of colonialism today, it is clear that the Department of State feels the necessity of taking into account the sympathies of the American people for groups which are seeking independence. Whether or not the policy-maker be influenced by expediency or necessity in deciding upon a certain course of action, the results of the policy will be judged by the American people at least partly in terms of whether they feel they can look the world in the eye and say, "This was the right thing for the United States to do."

## Some specific problems in foreign policy

The objectives of foreign policy which have been suggested, no matter how they are phrased, must be in the back of the minds of those who frame foreign policy. But they do not provide an easy litmus-paper test for decisions on specific problems. Repeated quotation has not dulled the truth of Mr. Justice Holmes' dictum that general principles do not decide concrete cases. A general policy paper approved by the President on the recommendation of the National Security Council can not be fed into an IBM machine to turn out an answer to a particular question. A general policy of countering Soviet efforts to woo the "uncommitted" nations does not supply the answer to the question whether the United States should supply $ x——— to Egypt to build the Aswan dam. When, on a Saturday evening in June 1950, word reached the State Department that the communists had attacked the Republic of Korea, one could not pull out a file card marked "Korea" and find what should be done. But the decision when reached was in accordance with general lines of policy on the containment of Soviet expansion, on the defense of the Pacific area, on support for the United Nations. Different weightings may have been attached to various points in the minds of the President's several advisers, but there was unanimity in the conclusion that the United States must react immediately, must react with force, and must act through the United Nations.

Let us turn then from general objectives to certain types of problems with which American foreign policy today must deal.

## Policies directly related to international communist power

The Soviet Union is militarily powerful and politically hostile. So long as this is true, United States foreign policy must concern itself with the need for protecting this country against the possibility of Soviet attack. It must envision all-out direct attack, indirect attack through "nibbling" at the periphery of the free world, and the erosion of the free world through propaganda and subversion.

The maintenance of our own military strength is thus an essential part of foreign policy. No one can question the necessity for maintaining SAC, our stockpile of A- and H-bombs, some form of ground and naval forces, and unceasing progress with the perfection of new weapons such as the intercontinental ballistic missile. Many of the incidental decisions about types and numbers of weapons, aircraft, or naval craft, are based on technical considerations, and the maker of foreign policy may have little to say about them. But in other respects the military can not provide the necessary implements of foreign policy unless they know what the national foreign policy is in regard to meeting the so-called brushfire wars, to stationing troops abroad, to supporting possible United Nations actions.

The military strategist may desire certain foreign bases, but it is the task of foreign policy to negotiate base agreements with the countries where such bases would be located. Since a large part of the value of the base may depend upon the friendliness or hostility of the government and people of the country in which it is located, foreign policy has the task of keeping them well disposed. Soviet foreign policy may include the brutal suppression of Hungarian opposition; American foreign policy, in part due to the sixth objective stated above, is compelled to use other means. The problem of the use of force to attain national objectives will be considered in more detail later. It suffices to stress here that aid programs, cultural missions, information services and all the normal processes of diplomacy are intimately related to the problem of defense.

Foreign policy must plan and conclude desirable alliances like NATO. It must equally provide some viable arrangement short of an alliance with such countries as Saudi Arabia, Lybia, and Morocco, where bases are located. United States foreign policy fails when the Soviet Union gets a foothold in some state which has hitherto been at least among the uncommitted nations. Preoccupation with these elements in the international situation may, however, lead to over-emphasis upon the need for military pacts and may exceed the range of the possible. While it has been said that politics is the art of the possible and that to broaden the area of the possible is the art of statesmanship, too zealous attempts to practice that art may well be self-defeating. If Indian neutralism falls short of the desires of some strategists, it can nonetheless prove a distinct asset to the United States. On the other hand, to insist that neutralism is an unfriendly posture can actually make it so.

The military technician must constantly revise his plans in the light of changing technical developments. The political or diplomatic technician must constantly revise his plans in the light of other changes. Nothing can be more disastrous to a successful foreign policy than a lack of flexibility—unless it be wavering inconsistency. The key European problem of German unity presents a good example. The policy which led to the restoration of German sovereignty and the inclusion of Germany in NATO was soundly based upon considerations emerging from the posture of the Soviet Union and the condition of Western Europe eight or nine years ago. It does not follow that it will continue to be the best policy. When the eastern satellite armies had to be counted as a definite part of the Soviet fighting strength, the withdrawal of actual Russian forces within the Soviet frontiers would not have left Western Europe with a sense of security. If it be true that changes in Poland and Hungary and perhaps in other satellites alter this picture, the frequently suggested plan for a demilitarized belt in central Europe requires reexamination. The outsider, who necessarily lacks much vital information, should hesitate to be dogmatic in suggesting the answer, but he is justified in refusing to assume that it must be the same today as it was before.

## Initiative versus reaction

A certain amount of confusion has been created in the American mind by slogans which enjoy a certain vogue during our periodic political campaigns. Just as it is a convenient beating stick to say that an Administration has "no" policy in regard to a certain area, so it is easy to assert that policy should be "dynamic" and should not be merely a "reaction" to Soviet initiatives. This palaver at one point reached the stage where it was said that it was impossible to tell whether the United States was following a policy of "dynamic containment" or of "static liberation."

It is certainly true that in war or peace, in sports or diplomacy, it is well to have the initiative. On the other hand, one cannot avoid the fact that a powerful state like the Soviet Union—expansionist, aggressive, and not limited by public opinion or by notions of morality or law— may initiate actions, such as the attack on Korea, which a country like the United States is inhibited from initiating. If the enemy does take such an initiative, of course the United States must react. The Soviet Union in turn reacted in a variety of ways to the positions of strength developed by the United States with our NATO allies. The Soviet Union also reacted to the obviously successful policy of the United States which in Europe took the form of the Marshall Plan and in the so-called underdeveloped countries took the form originally of the Point Four program, which has continued in the general program of foreign aid. Naturally when the Soviet Union reacted to our aid policy, the United States was faced with the problem of meeting these counter moves. Soviet moves in Egypt and Syria led to the announcement of the

"Eisenhower Doctrine," which in turn evoked the Chou-Bulganin statement of January 18, 1957.

All of this does not mean that possible moves by the enemy should not be anticipated or that deterrents should not be provided. Here those charged with the collection and analysis of intelligence play a vital role. Nor is it merely changes in communist policy which must influence United States foreign policy. A revolution in Iran or Egypt or a change of government in the United Kingdom or France may require adjustment in our policies. It is not so much that the foreign policy itself changes in response to changing circumstances on the world scene. What does change is the adaptation or application of the foreign policy which, if soundly conceived, should be applicable in spite of many alterations in the international picture.

## Disarmament

Directly related to international communist power today, although it has been a hardy perrenial in the garden of foreign policy for over fifty years, is the question of disarmament. This misleading short term actually refers to plans for the reduction or limitation of armament, although plans for complete national disarmament also have their enthusiastic advocates. It is true that the key difficulty at this time is the supreme lack of confidence in Soviet paper-promises, a difficulty to be met only by fool-proof inspection schemes (which human ingenuity has not yet been able to devise) which would meet the test of negotiability. But even in eras of less international tension, when the Czar proposed disarmament as a function of the Hague Peace Conference of 1899 or when the League of Nations struggled with the problem, the technical difficulties seemed as insuperable as the political ones. The only genuinely successful step in this direction, at the Washington Naval Conference of 1921, has been widely denounced, with the advantage of hindsight, as a bit of political folly.

The efforts must, of course, continue, and if they be crowned with even a modicum of success they should contribute both to security and to economic prosperity. Should this result be achieved, it may well confront the United States government of the day with a serious problem, for we have repeatedly indicated since the late Senator Brien McMahon first suggested the idea, that savings from an agreed reduction of armament would be applied to aid the underdeveloped countries. Many American taxpayers are likely to feel that the savings should be utilized on the principle that charity begins at home.

## Policies directed toward relations with states other than the communist bloc

It has already been suggested that we cannot afford to allow the focal attention on national security and the source of the threat to that security to lead us to neglect or subordinate other facets of United States foreign policy. Granted the inescapable interrelationship of security and alliances and of cold war contests for the sympathies of uncommitted nations, we may still consider some of the problems apart from our watchfulness of the communist world. The so-called colonial problem brings to mind many of the factors.

## The "colonial" problem

Like other labels, the term "colonial problem" is misleading. Broadly considered, it involves much more than the question of overseas dependencies. Indeed, the "salt water myth," which would put into a special separate category territories separated from the metropolitan country by salt water, is an absurdity which beclouds the fundamental issues and is used by our opponents for that purpose.

Looked at from one point of view, the fundamental issue is self-determination. This doctrine, which played such a large role in Woodrow Wilson's philosophy, is a part of the democratic ideology. It assumes that a people should and can govern itself. It leaves unanswered what is a "people." Few would seriously push the concept to its logical extremes and support the recent demand of Bretons for independence from France or insist that the United States should recognize the sovereignty of the Hopi Indians. But the so-called Belgian thesis in the United Nations makes an effective argument in calling attention to the many instances in which the vehemently anti-colonial states are outraged at the suggestion that they should heed the demands for independence from various alien groups within their own borders. Obviously, there is no more—and indeed much less—reason why the Russians should rule great numbers of Asian peoples located in various Soviet Republics than that the United States should administer Hawaii or Alaska.

Soviet hypocrisy aside, the gist of the matter is that the spearhead of the opposition to colonialism is the states which have recently emerged from a colonial status and which in large part are swept by ardent nationalism. In the "revolution of rising expectations" these states have not yet gained the satisfactions or the self-assurance which they anticipated would flow at once from political independence. They are not and can not yet be economically independent, and they resent the fact. With considerable irresponsibility they insist that other peoples shall at once receive the same political independence whether or not they are in a position to enjoy it.

On the other hand, the administering powers have been slow to adjust to the new forces which make impossible a continuation of a nineteenth-century order. In some instances they have poured out blood and treasure in a hopeless struggle which, even if successful, would have left them with only a few more splotches of color on the map. Eventual withdrawal under various compulsions has left both them and their former subjects embittered. The bold British policy of liberation after the end of World War II has paid much greater dividends. Yet many

25

subject areas remain, each with its own particular characteristics. The British problem in granting independence to the Gold Coast, where there were practically no white settlers, can not be compared to the French problem of finding a solution for Algeria with its more than a million *colons* of European origin whose settlements there date back a century.

## The American dilemma

The United States is impaled on the horns of a dilemma. The dilemma is still the same as that which Cordell Hull described in his *Memoirs*, speaking of the latter days of World War II:

Our prime difficulty generally with regard to Asiatic colonial possessions, of course, was to induce the colonial powers—principally Britain, France and the Netherlands—to adopt our ideas with regard to dependent peoples . . . . But we could not press them too far with regard to the Southwest Pacific in view of the fact that we were seeking the closest possible cooperation with them in Europe. We could not alienate them in the Orient and expect to work with them in Europe.

But today the non-European horn of the dilemma is much sharper. It is no longer just a question of the dependent peoples themselves or of American sympathies for their aspirations. Today there is the problem of our relations with a large group of Asian, Arab, African, and Latin American states which have made themselves the champions of the dependent peoples and to a large extent identify the fate of those peoples with their own. As already mentioned, we have far more than a mere platonic interest in the friendship of these champions; our interests are closely tied to theirs both positively and in the negative sense of blocking communist penetration. Moreover Secretary Hull was not confronted with the recurring necessity of taking a stand in the United Nations, where the issue is constantly raised either in connection with trusteeships, or with the debates on non-self-governing territories in the Fourth Committee of the General Assembly, or with the more dramatic instances in which such cases as those of Morocco, Tunis and Algeria arise in the Security Council or in the Assembly's Political Committee.

There is no real escape from the dilemma, and the United States will probably continue to perch uncomfortably between the horns, being pricked first by one and then by the other. Yet our position might be eased somewhat by a kind of frankness which might gain respect even though it still failed to make us popular. The United States might make clear that it adheres to the Wilsonian doctrine of self-determination but believes that in every specific case there is a question of timing and of orderliness in the process of evolution. We might emphasize that there is no point in lifting a nonviable community out from under the administration of one state and then insisting that the United States, through the United Nations or directly, should cover the inevitable deficit. Members of the United Nations who insist upon immediate independence must be ready to assume some responsibility, financial and otherwise, for the newborn states. In addition, it ought to be explained at a very high level to the governments of both the administering states and to the persistent champions of independence that we shall be bound to differ with them on these issues from time to time but that we hope they will cooperate with us in cushioning the outraged clamor of the press, in the realization that our common interests are much greater and of longer duration than our momentary differences.

The "colonial problem" typifies the difficulties for United States foreign policy when the interests of the states of Asia and the Middle East and Africa clash with those of our Western European partners. The type of problem illustrated by the Suez Canal question will be examined later, but here it is useful to consider issues which arise between and among non-European states.

## The Kashmir problem

The problem of Kashmir is illustrative. This is an issue upon which both India and Pakistan feel very deeply indeed. On the other hand, from the point of view of the United States it is not *per se* of great importance whether Kashmir belongs to one state or the other. It is important to the United States that the two countries involved should reach an amicable adjustment of their differences and that this potential danger to the peace of the subcontinent should be eliminated. True, Pakistan is a member of both the Baghdad Pact and the Southeast Asia Treaty Organization and is thus linked to the general system of Western defenses against the Soviet Union. We have therefore supplied Pakistan with arms to the great annoyance of India. But it is certainly not in the interest of the United States to encourage or to support Pakistan in any belligerent stand against her neighbor. Mindful of our own long historic devotion to a policy of neutrality, we have no reason to chide Nehru for his neutralism. We may well think that he is mistaken, that he fails to realize the acuteness of the danger from aggressive communism, but we may remind ourselves that our Canadian, British, and French friends felt even more bitter about the stupidity, and even what they considered the cowardice, of the United States from 1914 to 1917.

It is abundantly clear that Nehru's fundamental sympathies are with the democratic way of life, and no government has been more rigorous than his in checking local communist trouble-makers. Largely because of Nehru's personal prestige, India exercises great influence over other Asian governments. India is and can be extremely useful in checking the spread of Chinese Communist influence in Asia, not because India is a "running dog" of American imperialism, but because Chinese expansionism is a direct threat to India itself. Just as we have sound reasons for giving support to Pakistan, we would do well to recognize the important position of India and to seek a working partnership on all questions on which it would be reasonable to hope for agreement, without requiring India to depart from her basic policies.

Just as we formed and, hopefully, are resuming the habit of close consultation with London and Paris on all matters of common concern, so we would do well to make consultation with New Delhi a normal stage in the evolution of any policy or decision affecting Asia and the Middle East. India and Japan, at the two ends of a crescent skirting an area of very real danger, are countries with great potentialities and inherent elements of strength. Our foreign policy on matters of direct concern to them should be anchored on close and friendly relations with them both.

Nevertheless, the Indian government can not expect that any such close rapprochement would require us to become their partisan on the Kashmir issue any more that we would expect India to take a position favoring the United States in the unlikely event that we were again involved in a bitter territorial dispute with Canada as we were fifty-five years ago over the Alaskan boundary.

## The Palestine question

For a variety of reasons, the United States is much more closely concerned with the Palestine problem. In addition to the facts that the Arab states control vast oil resources, that as a great maritime power we are interested in the Suez Canal, and that Soviet penetration of this strategic area must be a matter of deep anxiety to us, United States foreign policy is bound to be affected by the fact that an influential part of the American electorate has a strong sentimental attachment to Israel. We would play a much more active part in the Kashmir case if our population included the descendents of large numbers of Kashmiris. This is a delicate issue, but there is no reason why it should not be faced as frankly as historians can now deal with the Irish question and its occasional impact on Anglo-American relations.

It remains true that from a broad view of the interests of the United States we should be more interested in *a* settlement than in the advantage which one side or the other might gain from some particular part of the settlement. Naturally, the United States is concerned to see a settlement which will be permanent because it responds basically to the demands of fairness and reason. No settlement will be wholly satisfactory to either Israel or to the Arab states, but almost any decent settlement would be to the advantage of both sides.

The United States still has great influence with both sides despite past inconsistencies and waverings in our policy. The situation is not one in which it is possible to impose a solution by force, but there must be what is in effect an imposed solution. It is a situation in which a firm and continuing and reasonably specific policy supported jointly by India and the United States in the United Nations would have a good chance of success. A purely "Western" solution has no such chance. From the outset in 1947, the United Nations General Assembly has played a role in the Palestine question which stretches the original conception of its function and authority. Some "realistic" analyses of foreign policy refuse to take into consideration the potentialities of evolution of the United Nations Charter, guided by the same type of basic constitutional development which has characterized our own history.

## Latin America

In an earlier period, when we were not burdened with the responsibilities of world power, Latin America occupied a prominent place in our foreign policy. Again preoccupation with issues which seem more immediately to affect our very survival has tended to crowd into the background the importance of our relations with our neighbors in this hemisphere. We have tended to coast along on the new friendliness inspired by the Good Neighbor Policy. We have not even followed the sound business practice of setting up a reserve for depreciation.

Our foreign aid programs have their actual roots in our Latin American relations prior to World War II. When the communist threat became paramount after the war, it necessitated a contribution first to Western Europe and then to other areas across the seas. The limit of Congressional tolerance was being reached and priorities had to be established. Latin America did not present a case for a high priority in the cold war. It was not ignored, but it properly had the feeling that it was no longer in the forefront of our minds. Again the general principle of the importance of Latin America does not tell the officers of the State Department or of ICA or the Budget Bureau how many dollars to allot to Chile, Brazil, or Peru, but it does dictate a continuing concern.

Once more it should be emphasized that it is folly to assume that one can "buy" friends through a foreign aid program. On the other hand, so long as such a general program is being undertaken it is possible to engender hostility through indifference to the needs of a particular area or of individual states. It may well be that we are somewhat protected by a longer tradition of private investment in Latin America and that military defense budgets in those countries do not present as acute a need as they do in other countries. We may recall that in the 1957 Mutual Security program, one-tenth was earmarked for economic development and nine-tenths for direct or indirect military aid. Nor should one write off the value of certain intangibles, as when Secretary of State Root wrote in 1905: "The South Americans now hate us, largely because they think we despise them and try to bully them. I really like them and intend to show it." Fortunately, on the political side, the Organization of American States has been developed intelligently by an evolutionary process which now enables us almost as a matter of routine to take joint instead of separate action on issues arising between two or more of our neighbors to the south.

29

# Instrumentalities of foreign policy viewed procedurally

## *The new diplomacy*

Persons skilled in the traditional art of diplomacy are apt to look down their noses at what seem to them the vulgar and futile debates in the United Nations. Sir Harold Nicholson, skillfully and with great literary charm, has presented the case for the old diplomacy, as for example in his Chichele lectures on "The Evolution of Diplomatic Method." He paints a fascinating and rather nostalgic picture of the good old days before diplomacy was uncontaminated by the "egalitarian illusions of the Americans." Those were the days when Europe was "the center of international gravity," and the Great Powers were really great enough to disregard the small states, which did not merit the appelation "powers" even when qualified by the adjective "small."

It is no doubt true that the old diplomacy was the best way of dealing with international problems in that eighteenth or nineteenth century world just as our forebears could not have a better vehicle for courtship than a surrey with a fringe on top. But that world has been replaced by another just as the carriage has been replaced by the automobile. The United States has to drive its foreign policy through the committees and councils of the United Nations and runs the risk at least of denting a fender if it ignores the smaller policies driving along the same highway. Even a Cadillac, if it collides with an old jalopy, may land in the ditch.

The processes of multilateral diplomacy have come to stay, at least for the foreseeable future. Bipolarity and communist techniques have enhanced instead of diminishing the importance of the smaller powers. Instead of bemoaning the past and castigating the present, it is more profitable to understand the new procedures and to seek to improve them.

It is of course also a fallacy to assume that the new methods of diplomacy have wholly eliminated the old. No one with any experience in the United Nations would underestimate the continuing importance of what Secretary General Dag Hammarskjold has called "quiet diplomacy," which is practiced daily in and around the United Nations. It was no doubt more titillating to pick up bits of political information in the boudoirs of the eighteenth century, but the gathering of information still continues in the couloirs of the United Nations. Nor have bilateral negotiations lost their importance, and it is therefore still vital that the United States have adequate diplomatic representation abroad, as the American Assembly recognized in its study of that question in 1956. But the American Assembly also recognized the present necessity for a body of officials skilled in the new technique.

Multilateral diplomacy seems particularly irritating when it is observed that decisions are taken by votes in which the vote of the smallest member is equal to that of the United States. But multilateral diplomacy is also practiced—although with marked differences—in such organs as the council of NATO, where no votes are taken but where it is also necessary to get the concurrence of the smaller powers. Since modern diplomacy is not confined to matters of high politics but includes economics and finance, it is also well to keep in mind that weighted voting is by no means unknown, as in the case of the thirty-one per cent vote of the United States in the International Bank for Reconstruction and Development or in the case of the International Sugar Council, where Cuba casts 245 votes as against the 100 votes of the Soviet Union.

Much of the irritation over the necessity for debating the world's troubles in the General Assembly of the United Nations stems from a misconception of the nature of the organization and the proper scope of its functions. The Great Powers are partly to blame for this misconception. Back in the days of the League of Nations, the Great Powers often found it convenient to blame their inaction upon the failure of the League Council to act. They would deferentially cloak themselves in the mantle of respect for their obligations under the Covenant, while the fact was that they themselves were the Council or at least its motivating force. So today there is a tendency to say we must sit back and wait for the United Nations to do something, although we know perfectly well that the United Nations is its membership and acts as its most influential members inspire it to act. As Mr. Dean Acheson recently told the House Committee on Foreign Affairs: "It will not do to say that the United Nations will determine policy, make decisions, and enforce them. The United Nations is not a supranational entity with a mind, a will, and power. It is a forum, and no more than the nations which meet there. Nothing more comes out of it than is put into it."

It may be that the courageous and skillful new activities of the Secretary General and some future evolution of the United Nations Emergency Force foreshadow a new type of organization, but the day is not yet. The supranational model of the European Coal and Steel Community has not yet been put on the political production line.

There are advantages in international group action as is shown by the successful operation of voting blocs in the United Nations. But the technique has not been perfected and the "Wise Men" of NATO have not yet succeeded in expanding the non-military functions of that close-knit Alliance to a point where all conflicting interests of its generally like-minded member states can be reconciled in joint conference. The case of Cyprus, with the divergent interests of Greece, Great Britain and Turkey, points the lesson today.

## Instrumentalities of foreign policy
## viewed substantively

### The use of force

Force, or military power, was a prime instrument of foreign policy in earlier periods. Its role has changed today.

31

Military power is still a dominant reality in the relations between near equals. As already shown, it is the keystone of that essential part of our foreign policy which is directed toward the containment of the Soviet Union. It is a reality in the relations between the Arab States and Israel. Speaking in terms of Soviet-American relations, military power is a prime factor because of the realization that it will be used under certain circumstances. Though not clearly defined, the circumstances under which it will be used are, in a general way, mutually appreciated. The present epitome of military power, the nuclear weapons and the means for delivering them, represent the most important factor in this equation.

But the possession of the H-bomb is not a prime factor in our relations with, let us say, Saudi-Arabia or Chile, because those states justifiably reason that we will not use it against them to compel their acceptance of our will. Mexico no longer needs to anticipate that if the United States disapproves of actions of its government, the marines will land to prove that "our fiat is law upon this continent." Great Britain and France tried the old traditional methods at Port Said and ended in ignominious disaster. There were many reasons for the disaster, including poor military execution and the breakdown in their relations with the United States, but there are also more fundamental reasons which United States policy-makers must keep in mind.

In the earlier period when the use of force for the vindication of rights or the promotion of interests was a normal aspect of international relations, the propriety of the method was not challenged. If Germany took the Shantung Peninsula and England took Hong Kong, did not the United States also "take" Panama? The United States did not concern itself if Germany, France or England found it expedient to appropriate a bit of Africa, nor did those powers interfere when we landed marines in Haiti. True, there were recognized spheres of influence (our own being marked by the Monroe Doctrine), but this was a device for minimizing conflicts among the larger powers themselves and not any acknowledgement of the rights of the smaller countries. If there were complaints from a China, a Persia, or a Haiti, they were scarcely audible. To be sure, even in this era there were moral crusades, but they had other targets, largely humanitarian and not in protest against the usual methods of Great Power foreign policy: thus the British-led crusade against the slave trade and joint protests against atrocities in the Congo.

## The change in the international atmosphere

The change in the international atmosphere has been gradual. The emergence of the United States—fresh, vigorous, inexperienced and somewhat moralistic—played a part. The Second Hague Peace Conference of 1907 marked the first occasion when the Latin American states, sponsored by the United States, were received as equals around the international green-baize-covered table. With the advent of the

League system the small states found that they had a voice in international decisions and as a consequence a measure of power. Able statesmen—a Branting of Sweden, a Titulesco of Rumania, a Politis of Greece—were influential even though their countries were weak. Great power politics still dominated but the changing temper of opinion could be measured by the widespread indignation which greeted the Hoare-Laval Agreement. Then the military dictatorship of Japan, Italy, and Germany strutted to the front of the stage, the League with its new egalitarianism faded, and the war came.

The postwar stage saw the world's characters in new roles. Great Britain was seriously crippled. France, divided, did not resume her place until she had passed through the humiliation, as at Bretton Woods, of having her representatives denied the right to be listed as "France" and labelled merely as "French Delegation." Germany, Japan and Italy were impotent. The United States and Russia were the two Great Powers. States which had been dimly seen as supernumeraries in choruses backstage were now named in the international dramatis personae.

Japan had lost the war, but not until it had ended the era of white supremacy in Asia. An informed observer at the time marked the end of that era when he watched British residents evacuating Penang, carrying their own suitcases through lines of silent brown-skinned people. Had the Japanese won, they would have had their own troubles with the Asian nationalism they helped to awaken, but in the event they left the problem to the West. The Soviet Union, following Lenin's prescription for the ultimate conquest of Asia, used it as an asset.

It seems to be the thesis of some who profess to be realists to deny the twentieth-century reality of anything which does not fit into a nineteenth-century mold. Nothing could be more unrealistic. The old mold is broken, and a realistic twentieth-century policy can not be poured into it. The fanaticism of nationalism in the Asian-Arab-African world can not be equated to the reasoned logical reactions of a nineteenth-century European Foreign Office. It is a basic error of those who have not escaped from the pattern of the past to fail to take into account the irrationality of their adversaries. If your adversary does not regard national suicide as an unmitigated evil, there is no effectiveness in a logical demonstration that a certain course of conduct is suicidal. Nor can you deter a country from a course of conduct by proving that such a course will cause it to lose everything, if the country thinks that it has not yet acquired anything to lose.

## The establishment of the United Nations system

The decision to organize the United Nations and the ratification of its Charter marked the adoption of something more than a new institutional form. The members, including the Great Powers, accepted the rule that they would no longer make unilateral determinations concerning their use of force to secure their rights and interests. They made the mistake of thinking that they had provided an adequate substitute which, through the coherence of the Great Powers with permanent seats on the Security Council, would enable collective force to be used under the aegis of the world organization. The Soviet Union broke its promises and the coalition and so destroyed the effectiveness of the new substitute. The United States, among others, both felt the obligation of its plighted word and was reluctant to scrap the new institution. That situation still obtains; it has sunk into the consciousness of peoples so deeply that it was inescapable that the Franco-British attack on Egypt should arouse widespread indignation. Lord McNair, former President of the International Court of Justice, was delivering more than a judicial opinion when in the Suez debate in the House of Lords he called attention to the fact that England had lost her nineteenth-century freedom to use such means of self-help.

It is no answer to say that if Britain and France had carried out their attack successfully their sins would have been forgiven and forgotten. How could the Britain and France of today be successful in such a venture? A perfectly timed and executed attack might have prevented the blocking of the Canal; it could not have prevented the sabotoge of the pipelines or further sabotage of pumping stations and refineries and at the wells themselves. It is a complete miscalculation of current forces to assume that the local military success would have left a quiescent and cooperative Egypt and that other Arab governments would then have feared to cancel base agreements and oil concessions. Neither the French nor the British economy could have supported the inevitably necessary military occupation of many strategic points. Sooner or later a distressed and tax-burdened electorate would have demanded a withdrawal, and the loss of prestige and of material benefits would have been the greater for being somewhat deferred.

Nor is it conceivable that the United States is ready to scrap the new system, the new mores, unsatisfactory and frustrating as they may be. Self-interest, including the realization that the NATO alliance must be rebuilt, dictated aid in supplying Europe with oil to meet the emergency precipitated by the Franco-British (and Israeli) action. But it was a necessary part of the argument that many smaller European states which were guiltless, were equal sufferers with those whose ill-timed action had cut the lifeline. It is hard to believe that the United States would have supported a continued military occupation of the Middle East by France and Great Britain. Had we done so, there would have been nothing but war to prevent the communist states from "protecting" themselves by occupations in such areas as those of South East Asia. The long struggle for the uncommitted world with all our expenditures and efforts would have gone down the drain, and the holders of the super-weapons would have been poised in far more threatening posture, with "brush fires" heating our tempers and their smoke clouding our eyes.

In the face of public condemnation registered through the United Nations, the Soviets merely poured more tanks and Asiatic troops into

Budapest whereas England and France "had yet that grace of courtesy in them left" which made them yield. Such a result was naturally so exasperating that it turned many against the United Nations. Perhaps the trouble was that while the weakness of the United Nations was well known, its possible influence was not appreciated. Surely, Britain and France would not want to be heard to say that they wished to accept the Soviet standards as the model for their conduct.

## The missing alternatives

The difficulty which all of this poses for American foreign policy is that we have not yet perfected alternatives to the outright use of force. The communists have been more successful. Their system of penetration and subversion, their riding of the wave of nationalism, has given them the advantage. It is doubtful that we could outdo them in the use of the same methods. It is not inconceivable that the less dramatic methods of persuasion, supported intelligently by a well-conceived aid and information program, can attain results. I hope I do not misrepresent the views of one of our ablest diplomatists in saying that George Kennan relies heavily on the fact that the seeds of their own decay infest the totalitarian communist world rather than our own. The defects and deficiencies in our own society, to which he draws urgent attention, are remediable within the framework of our democracy. The weaknesses inherent in their dictatorship can not be remedied without a change in their system. Meanwhile, there is the world in-between, which as he says, looks to us "for positive and imaginative suggestions as to how the peaceful future of the world might be shaped and how our vast economic strength in particular might be so adjusted to the lives of other peoples as to permit a fruitful and mutually profitable interchange, without leading to relationships of political dependence and coercion." All the objectives of our foreign policy would be served by an answer to this appeal.

# Domestic factors conditioning foreign policy

## The Congress

The American constitutional system entrusts to the President the formation and control of foreign policy. The judiciary refrains from intruding upon his domain when it is confronted by a political question the decision of which by the courts might embarrass the executive in our relations with other countries. The Congress wields the power of the purse and, through the Senate, may refuse to confirm appointments and may prevent the ratification of treaties. But a Congressional direction to the President as to what foreign policy he should pursue has only such power of persuasion as may stem from the extent to which it genuinely reflects an aroused public opinion. If it merely reflects a jealousy of prerogatives or a desire to enhance Congressional power at the expense of the executive, a vigorous President can and will ignore it. So the Congress may provide for a National Security Council to coordinate foreign policy, but it cannot dictate what the Council recommends nor compel the President to accept its recommendations.

Obviously, cooperation between the President and the Congress is desirable and when obtained presents the most efficient mobilization of the resources of the government for the execution of foreign policy. A statement of a Congressional attitude passed in support of a Presidential attitude can be helpful, as was the Vandenberg Resolution of 1948. It is too near the event to appraise the value of the resolution on the Middle East, which is still being considered as this is written.

It is true that American foreign policy may be swayed or even controlled by Congress when appropriations are essential to its execution. It is therefore necessary that there be a meeting of minds between the executive and legislative branches on a foreign aid program. The Executive does have the responsibility for framing the policy and " selling" it to Congress. The " sales campaign" may be direct or through the media of public opinion and the pressure groups which represent important segments of informed opinion. Unfortunately, it seems often to be necessary to obtain Congressional approval by stressing the self-interest of the United States to such an extent that the potential recipients are estranged. If an aid program is defended on the ground of the military defense of the United States, a "neutralist" nation may feel compelled to decline the proffered assistance lest it be thought to signify membership in the Western alliance. Even the kind of normal programming and accounting which Congress usually insists upon strikes the sensitive nerves of some newly independent states as constituting "political strings" or masking some new kind of "colonial" domination. In at least some instances it has been true that the International Bank for Reconstruction and Development, as an international agency, can exact information and insist upon financial reforms which will not be yielded on the demand of the United States. Yet Congressional distrust of the United Nations may restrict the extent to which the United States can operate through the United Nations technical assistance programs.

The extreme position which at times demands that practically every grain of American wheat contributed abroad should be stamped " Gift of the American People," is indicative of the old fallacy that aid programs are designed to purchase gratitude. It is vital that Congress should be led to see the objectives instead of concentrating on the methods. Most of the objectives of American foreign policy which have been listed above are served by foreign aid programs but in different degrees in different areas. Obviously military support for our NATO partners is not to be put in the same category with economic and financial aid to India in its task of demonstrating that it can build up its economy without resorting to the methods used in Communist China.

# The problem of secrecy

Our difficulties are often enhanced by the fact that in making our government decisions we whisper out loud. When an official of the State Department goes before a Congressional committee to justify a request for foreign aid funds, he naturally makes the best case he can and will try to answer questions in such a way as to disarm opposition. He may ask that he be allowed to testify in executive session so that he can explain confidentially to the committee why x dollars are budgeted for State A, and x plus 2 for State B. Unfortunately, testimony in executive session is frequently published afterwards, even if the gist of the testimony is not immediately communicated to the press either deliberately or by inadvertence. The case has occurred, for example, where post-publication of such confidential testimony has come into the hands of a United Nations delegate from another country just before an important vote and where the bare printed record looked as if his country had been treated somewhat disparagingly. The value of an aid program can easily be destroyed by such a mischance.

This is a field in which the dictatorships have an advantage. They can pitch the tone of statements to some foreign audience and prevent the text from being distributed to their own people, even though some distribution of the news is subsequently achieved through foreign broadcasts. On the other hand, an American President or Secretary of State is apt to think that he is speaking to the audience before him or at most to the American people. It is an almost—but not quite—impossible task for the official speech writers to have constantly in mind that the speech is going to be appraised in Delhi and Karachi as well as in Duluth and Kansas City. A well-turned phrase designated to tickle the ears of a Congressman may rasp the nerves of a European. The only remedies are eternal vigilance and a large degree of coordination among officials who are attuned to the probable reception on distant shores.

The United States is also often hampered in its foreign policy by unfortunate statements made by persons in American official life, whether in the legislative or in the executive branch. Many such damaging statements are the product of our peculiar institution of the press conference, which responds to an American demand but often not to our requirements as a world leader. Sometimes it is merely an ill-chosen word or expression; sometimes it is the statement of an opposition leader or party maverick which, with the ever present aid of alert communist propagandists, is widely published as an official statement of American policy.

Still another difficulty—not peculiar to the American scene—is that of preserving the secrecy of official correspondence or decisions. There may be very good reasons indeed why a particular paper or decision should not have publicity at a particular time, but everyone can recall instances in which a zealous press has unearthed and published the information. It is very doubtful in many such cases whether the interests of the American people are really served by prematurely sharing the secret not only with their own officials but with all the world. The trouble is no doubt partly due to the exaggerated system of classification preventing the release of information which might well be made public. Sporadic efforts to eradicate this evil have not met with success.

Even where there has been no direct leak of information, the readers of the press and the radio listeners are daily being informed, with a good deal of dogmatic assurance, just what is in the minds of their leading officials in Washington. This is not a charge that all columnists and commentators are irresponsible, but again the impact abroad may be unfortunate and require official " corrections" which do not always serve their purpose. In some other countries the relations between a foreign office and at least parts of the press is well-established, and the press item can be rather accurately evaluated as a trial balloon or as a bit of official propaganda. Our tradition of a free press necessitates a somewhat less formal relationship, and it is left to the reader to form his own conclusions as to the extent to which the particular journalist has the " inside track."

## Bureaucracy

Even when a foreign policy is intelligently conceived and has been duly approved by the President on the advice of the National Security Council, the officials charged with its execution often find themselves tangled in a bureaucratic web which makes the execution of the policy well-nigh impossible. The multiplicity of departments, bureaus and agencies involved in foreign policy seems to require a resort to numerous coordinating committees in which differences of opinion on detail may be sharpened rather than reconciled. Most policy decisions are broadly framed and can not provide the answer for the concrete case. If there are differences of opinion at a lower level, they must be taken back to the top for resolution, and " the top" is already overburdened. There are many important foreign policies which can not be carried out by the Secretary of State alone without the cooperation of his colleagues in Defense, Treasury or elsewhere. Some of these difficulties are inherent in the governmental process; some can be removed by skillful administrative organization and good staffing.

## Conclusion

There are undoubtedly characteristics of United States foreign policy which are shared in other countries. Some of the difficulties faced by American officials are faced by their opposite numbers in other countries. But many of the problems discussed above are peculiarly American or have their peculiarly American aspects. Particularly in regard to aid programs one may summarize some leading characteristics.

The rescue of the war-torn economies of Europe through the Marshall Plan was easily seen as necessary to prevent gains by the local communist parties. The Truman Doctrine, first enunciated for Greece and Turkey, had established the principle of military aid to states threatened by communist aggression. NATO further emphasized the need for concerted military defense in Europe. Appropriations for the necessary armaments were forthcoming.

It was soundly argued that in the underdeveloped countries the communists found easy converts among illiterate and poverty-ridden populations. Actual demonstration by the West of improvements in agriculture, village life, and industrial development could offset unfulfilled communist promises. To satisfy Congress, it was necessary to emphasize that countering communism in the underdeveloped countries was part of American defense against Soviet expansion. Thus the Economic Cooperation Administration became the Mutual Security Agency carrying on the aid program of the Marshall Plan in Europe as well as the Point IV Program in other regions. The name " International Cooperation Administration" is a return to a sounder approach.

The attack on Korea in June 1950 supported in the Congressional mind the Administration's emphasis on Asia. The situation in Indo-China showed the dangers and it was not hard to prove the importance of Southeast Asia.

Meanwhile the Arab-Israeli conflict also drew attention to the Middle East, but the aid program was slow in developing from the eastern shore of the Mediterranean to the Bay of Bengal. This was due in part to British initiative in the Colombo plan and to Washington's unwillingness to devote the resources necessary to take over the traditional British responsibility for peace in the Arab world. The United States, continuing the lead of the Truman Doctrine, did continue to give substantial economic and military aid to Turkey which, in 1952, became also a NATO partner. For reasons obvious from the history of the " China Tangle," substantial aid continued to be given to Formosa. Aid programs for Germany and Japan began with the responsibility for occupation costs and continued in the light of the policy to turn these former enemies into friends and allies against the Soviet Union. Clearly friends and allies should be as strong as possible, economically and militarily.

Latin America aid programs seemed less closely related to the communist menace but had begun before it and were continued on a relatively modest scale.

Again it may be asserted that these programs of foreign aid have contributed toward the attainment of at least five of the six objectives of foreign policy suggested above: Security, Economic Prosperity, an Environment Conducive to Freedom, Influence or Prestige, and a Sense of Justice. But clearly aid programs are merely one of many instruments for the attainment of foreign policy objectives. They are not ends in themselves to be pursued at the expense of a fundamental objective. But the objectives and the ways in which the programs contribute to them must be widely understood or the programs will not be supported.

It is not to be expected that the American people will soon master all the intricacies of statecraft or be alert to all of the international political eddies and whirlpools through which our foreign policy must steer. Of those charged with the conduct, some will merit approbation and some will not, but all will share misunderstanding and a measure of public indifference and disdain. This is not a static or eternal condition and it has improved greatly in recent years as foci of interest in international relations have multiplied in the churches, clubs and other organizations across the land. Not every problem in foreign policy defies definition and clarification. Public support can be obtained and can be a strong bulwark.

United States foreign policy must be self-reliant without disdain, responsive to the call for leadership without yielding to the temptation to dominate. If it accepts national security and national well-being as its main goals, it must realize that these can not be obtained merely by blocking the counter-policies of an adversary, but by affirmative contributions to the building of a world environment in which our way of life will prosper and its advantages extend to all the far corners of the earth.

# 2. Soviet economy and Soviet world power

by Gregory Grossman

## Problems of definition and measurement

How strong is the Soviet economy? How far behind ours is it? How soon might it catch up?

Questions of this sort unhappily do not permit of concise and elegant answers, if they can be answered unequivocally at all. The dimensions of world economic power are numerous; the applications many. The specific nature of Soviet ideology and institutions further compounds the traditional variables of national power, while propaganda and secrecy combine to resist fair appraisal.

There are at least three major areas of Soviet national power in which the economic element predominates. First and perhaps foremost, there is the economic basis of military might. Secondly, there is the political attraction exerted by the flow of commodities and capital. Until recently this was a minor weapon, except within the Soviet orbit. And thirdly, in a world shopping around for models of economic

Gregory Grossman, Assistant Professor of Economics at the University of California (Berkeley), was for several years associated with the Russian Research Center, Harvard University. He is the author of a number of studies of the Soviet economy, particularly in the fields of national income, planning, and finance.

development, some prestige and power accrue to the Soviet Union in that it represents a definite, and in certain ways highly successful, prototype of industrialization. To identify these three areas of economic power is not to isolate them. Clearly, they interact in many ways and supplement each other and other elements of power within the armory of Soviet foreign policy. But they also compete among themselves for resources—*e.g.*, steel manufacturing equipment shipped to India is not available for installation in Siberia. And in some ways they are mutually conflicting—*e.g.*, autarky may be welcome to the military strategist but is a hindrance to the travelling salesman.

No simple yardstick can measure Soviet economic strength, and no single figure or even set of figures express it adequately. To any attempt to quantify the problem the statistician will add his own reservations. Every aggregate measure, such as total industrial output or gross national product, is in a sense a fiction, for it purports to reduce to a single figure a multitude of diverse and not always commensurable things. Its meaning is therefore always relative to the weights ascribed to the components and the mathematical formula employed. Nonetheless, even fiction may be useful and instructive, so long as we remember that fiction it is.

## Comparing United States and Soviet outputs

Much computational effort has recently gone into comparing rates of growth of the national product, or of industrial production, in the USSR and in the West. Other attempts have tried to measure the lag in time between Russian and American industry, and the change in the lag since the beginning of Soviet industrialization. When performed by competent hands and with a healthy dose of "acute methodological discomfort" such exercises are perhaps not entirely idle, although their interpretation requires all the caution at our command. For instance, in a very interesting article on "The Pace of Soviet Economic Development" (*Lloyd's Bank Review*, April 1956), Alec Nove, one of the ablest and best-informed western students of the Soviet economy, suggests that "the USSR, though still well behind the United States, may have reached America's *present* [1956] industrial output by about 1963." (Total—not *per capita*—output is meant here.) Such sobering glances into the future—apart from the correctness of the specific computation, which in this case was made before the downward revision of the Sixth Five-Year Plan was announced—are welcome for the shock effect they have on us at a time when complacency may be costly indeed.

In the article cited, Nove does not venture an estimate of when the USSR may *catch up* with the United States in industrial output, although arithmetically it would not have been difficult for him to do so. Others are not always as careful. In fact a certain fascination attaches itself at first glance to this problem of when and whether the one will catch up with the other. This fascination unfortunately may easily lead us into a fallacy. Parity of output, total or *per capita*, is only a convenient numerical benchmark; it is little else. The composition of the output, its allocation to different uses, the efficiency of its utilization, the purposes to which it is being applied—all of these mean more in the international conflict than do questionable aggregate magnitudes. In some relevant sense the economic power of the Soviet Union may have outstripped that of the United States long before its total industrial production has reached our level. Or it may fail to do so even after Soviet industrial output exceeds that of the United States, should that happen.

Current American industrial output is perhaps roughly two to three times the Soviet output, and two and one-half to three and one-half times on a *per capita* basis. Yet this does not of itself tell us very much with regard to the three areas of economic power mentioned above. Witness on the one hand the MIGs, submarines, and nuclear weapons that imbue our military planners with healthy respect; and on the other hand the fact that the hourly real earnings of the Soviet worker or employee (as recently estimated by Norman Kaplan) are less than one-fifth of the earnings of his American counterpart—a fact that, one hopes, will imbue economic planners in the underdeveloped countries with healthy skepticism toward Soviet claims. Why then should parity of industrial output at some future date, if ever attained by the Soviet Union, be especially meaningful, other than attesting to progress of Russian industry in some very general sense?

Only a little more meaningful and less hazardous are comparisons of levels of output (total or *per capita*) of individual "key" commodities, such as steel, cement, coal, oil, electric power, etc. Here at least one can be more selective and purposive, though too often the selection if not the purpose is severely limited by the availability and trustworthiness of Soviet data.

## Stalin's yardstick

Yet it should be noted that the Soviets themselves have done much to clothe sheer numerical comparisons with political significance. Speaking before the XVIIIth Party Congress in 1939, Stalin made it the "fundamental economic task of the USSR" to surpass the most advanced capitalist countries in the *per capita* output of industrial products. This, he assured his audience (while at the same time delivering an unintended accolade to the capitalism of the nineteen-thirties) would enable the transition of the Soviet Union from socialism to full blown communism, *i.e.* to an economy of unlimited abundance. He allotted ten to fifteen years to the completion of the task. While the war and postwar reconstruction raised other goals to greater urgency, recently the theme has reappeared. Witness Khrushchev's similar but more cautious words at the XXth Congress in early 1956.

The great advantages of the socialist economic system, the high rate of development of social production, enable us to carry out in a historically very brief

43

period the main economic task of the USSR—to catch up and surpass the most developed capitalist countries in per capita output.

This criterion, therefore, whatever its substantive merit as a relative measure of power, has by now assumed a considerable propaganda and political content. Perhaps for this if for no better reason can some of the statisticians' exercises be excused.

## Soviet economic growth and its prospects

### *The recent record*

The general outlines of Soviet economic growth since the inauguration of the Five-Year Plans in 1928 are well known by now and need no repetition here. It may be worth reiterating, though, that Russia's domestic resources in 1928 were more adequate for the launching of rapid industrialization than are those of most major underdeveloped countries today.

Of greater interest here are the current trends, but since wartime damage to plant and equipment was not repaired, by and large, before the end of 1950, our attention must be restricted primarily to the period of the Fifth Five-Year Plan, which ran from 1951 through 1955. Admittedly this is not long enough for an appraisal of the dynamic of Soviet economic growth. Nor were the years particularly "normal": they witnessed the Korean conflict, Stalin's death and the change in leadership, and several major revisions in domestic and foreign economic policy. Yet to fall back on a longer period, especially one which includes the war and the ensuing reconstruction, might be even more misleading.

The creation of the implements of war and of the sinews of industry, both products of "heavy" industry and of construction, continues to enjoy foremost priority in Soviet development. Such indirect economic evidence as exists is not inconsistent with the general public impression that the production of munitions has been large and has made rapid progress in recent years. But in an autarkic economy growing as fast as the Soviet the production of civilian capital goods must be large and increasing rapidly too. The output of many important products of basic industry—fuel, power, metals, basic chemicals, and building materials—increased by 50 to 90 per cent over the period, or at the average rate of $8\frac{1}{2}$ to $13\frac{1}{2}$ per cent per year. Construction activity and the output of civilian machinery increased to approximately the same degree. The output of major industrial consumers' goods—processed foodstuffs, textiles, and footwear—rose by some 30 to 60 per cent, or $5\frac{1}{2}$ to 10 per cent per annum on the average, although production of certain consumer durables, still largely in the luxury class, grew much more rapidly. Bracketing together all industry and construction we might find an overall increase of, say, 60 to 70 per cent over the five years or 10 to 11 per cent per year.

Although the total population increased by almost 9 per cent, and the urban population by 20 per cent, *per capita* consumption levels improved considerably, chiefly by virtue of increased availability of manufactured consumer goods. The supply of foodstuffs increased only moderately. There was hardly any improvement in the urban housing situation. It continued to be very tight even by Soviet standards, with a density of about 1.7 persons per room, including kitchens. And lastly, activity in the fields of science, education, and medical care expanded greatly.

The same trends continued into 1956, the first year of the Sixth Five-Year Plan, with the exception that the very favorable weather conditions in the grain-growing eastern part of the country in that year and in the livestock-raising western part in the preceding year combined to brighten the food picture considerably.

Estimating roughly, the rate of growth of Soviet national product since the beginning of the nineteen-fifties has been some 6 to 7 per cent per annum. Probably this is about the same as that which prevailed on the average during the first two Five-Year plans—from 1928 through 1937. However, the recent rate of expansion of industrial output has been lower, some 10-12 per cent per year as against 13-14 per cent then. But the now higher weight of industry in the economy largely compensates for this with regard to the effect on the growth of the national product as a whole. These rates are independent western estimates, not Soviet claims, and generally are weighted by some approximation to the real costs of the country and period in question: they are what I have elsewhere called "own rates of growth."

While the rate of growth of the Soviet economy over the last six years has been very high by general standards, it is not altogether without parallel in the postwar experience of non-communist countries. Such western countries as the German Federal Republic, Brazil, Colombia, and Mexico have shown approximately the same over-all rates of economic expansion. Yet in drawing the comparisons one must keep in mind the very much higher diversion of resources to military end-use in the postwar Soviet economy than during the first two Five-Year Plans or in the western countries just mentioned.

## The beginning of retardation

It has been argued for some time by western economists that the near future is likely to bring some retardation in the rate of Soviet economic growth. And indeed, the events of the past year, and especially of late 1956 and early 1957, seem to be bearing this prognosis

45

out. In early 1956, the Party's Directives for the Sixth Five-Year Plan provided for a somewhat lower relative increase in industrial output than was claimed to have been achieved during the Fifth Five-Year Plan. Then, at the very end of 1956, but before the full version of the Sixth FYP had yet been drafted, a downward revision of its targets was decreed. The results of the revision are still unknown at this writing, but the reasons for it are not hard to deduce.

They are, most probably: (a) an original overestimation of the available resources; (b) failure to provide in the initial Directives for the promised reduction in the length of the work-week and certain other welfare measures announced in 1956; and (c) the unexpected turn of events in Eastern Europe, which is likely in the near term to increase the demands on Soviet agriculture and to reduce the supplies of consumers' goods from the satellite countries.

Finally, when the plan for 1957 was announced in early February, it called for an increase in industrial output of 7 per cent in comparison with the preceding year, as against 11-13 per cent officially claimed to have been attained in several previous years, or the 10.5 per cent per annum that the Directives for the Sixth FYP originally envisaged. Yet it would be incautious to assume on the basis of the 1957 plan that the pace of Soviet industrial expansion in a longer-run sense has declined by as much as 25-50 per cent, as the above figures suggest. For one thing, primary attention seems to be devoted this year to the breaking of bottlenecks in the supply of fuel and metals.

## *Reasons for retardation*

If the rate of Soviet economic growth is to slow down in the near future it will hardly be due to any relapse in the determination of the regime to industrialize with the utmost speed—"to carry out the fundamental economic task of the USSR in a historically very brief period." Nor will it be because of any decline in the rate of gross investment, which probably averaged a quarter or more of the gross national product during the first half of the fifties. (In our much richer country this proportion has varied in recent years between one-sixth and one-fifth, and a comparison of *net* investment rates would be even more favorable to the USSR.) Barring a sharp upward turn in military outlays, the stress on heavy industry points to at least a similar rate of investment in the foreseeable future.

However, some shifts in the distribution of this investment may take place. Soviet investment in the past has been marked by great emphasis on heavy industry and other growth-inducing branches. The contrast with the distribution of American investment, in both instances during the postwar period, has been well summarized by Kershaw in *The Annals of the American Academy of Political and Social Science*

(January 1956):

|  | USA | USSR |
|---|---|---|
|  | in per cent of total | |
| Industry | 25 | 50 |
|    Metal and metal products | (10) | (21) |
| Agriculture | 10 | 16 |
| Transportation | 10 | 10 |
| Housing | 25 | 15 |
| Other | 30 | 9 |
| Total (rounded) | 100 | 100 |

Greater investment in transportation and housing in the USSR has been heretofore avoided by overloading pre-existing capital plant in both of these sectors in order to economize on capital outlay. This most important loan from the past is now falling due. The share of transportation and housing in the investment total may be expected to increase moderately in the near future, and perhaps the share going to industry will decline slightly. This, together with the growing need to replace obsolete equipment in industry, may have an adverse effect on the rate of industrial expansion.

Such advance in agriculture as took place in the last few years has been due largely to the one-third increase in sown acreage since 1950. This process is coming to an end. Apart from organizational reforms further gains in agricultural production depend primarily on the flow of material resources into the village and, for a while, on holding back the outflow of manpower from the village, both clearly at the expense of industrial growth.

## The labor shortage

This brings up a most important factor, labor supply, where the picture is now radically different from the past. During the First and Second Five-Year Plans, when nonagricultural employment increased two and one-half times and the urban population two-fold, perhaps about one-half of the increase in real national product was due to the transfer of millions of men and women from rural to urban employment, from less productive to more productive work. Even by the end of the thirties this process had greatly slowed down, and now comparable resources no longer exist.

The war cost the country some 40 million persons (in the sense that had the rate of natural increase during the forties been what it was shortly before the war and then again in the fifties, the population in

47

1950 would have been that much greater than it actually was). Postwar reconstruction pulled another 10 million or so into nonagricultural employment and into the cities. Thus in a sense, the whole demographic damage of the forties, and more, was borne by the village, particularly so with regard to males in the working age groups. It is not impossible, incidentally, that this drastic and tragic "solution" of the traditional rural overpopulation problem may have helped more than hindered immediate postwar reconstruction. Be this as it may, agriculture was soon to pay the price; its production levelled off even before prewar output was reattained. Since 1950 the rural population has stayed virtually stable and is likely to remain so for some time while the agricultural problem remains acute.

This means that new additions to nonagricultural employment must come primarily from the natural increase in the working population, for the moment overlooking demobilization of the military and other non-demographic factors. More specifically such additions must come from the age group born during and shortly after the war. This age group being an exceptionally small one, however, the net annual additions to the labor force between now and the middle sixties, allowing for deaths and retirements, will be very small by past standards. For example, N. Jasny has estimated that the annual net addition will decline from 2.1 million in 1956 to 0.3 million in 1959 and 1960.

## Renewed emphasis on productivity

In the original Directives the sixth Five-Year Plan accordingly envisages only a 14 per cent increase in the nonagricultural labor force, and only a 10 per cent increase in industrial employment proper, for the whole period. Further, should the work-week be shortened as promised—which is not at all certain in view of the pending revision of the Plan—there may be no increase in *man-hour* input in the nonagricultural sector or in industry over the five years. It should be noted that, unlike the labor force, the total population continues to increase rapidly—over three million, 1.7 per cent, per year. The number of mouths is growing and the ratio of workers to dependents is falling.

And yet the "fundamental economic task of the USSR" is to be pursued without respite! The solution offered is rapidly rising productivity per worker, in industry and elsewhere. More specifically this calls for continuing enlargement in the volume of capital investment—by two-thirds from the last Five-Year Plan to this, according to the unrevised version of the plan. It also calls for rapid technological advance; automation and mechanization; replacement of obsolete equipment; and expansion in the already vast scale of training in scientific, professional, and industrial skills.

The ability of Soviet industry to turn out machinery in large amounts, and of Soviet schools to turn out specialists in large numbers, is therefore crucial for the maintenance of a respectable rate of industrial growth at this juncture in Soviet history. This ability has been demonstrated in recent years. But emphasis on the expansion of heavy industry does not slacken. Shall we witness a great spurt in Soviet economic growth in the later sixties, when the many children born since 1950 reach working age, and after a giant capital-goods-producing industry has been created and a huge army of specialists trained?

It will be recalled in this connection that the United States manpower outlook is just the reverse of the Soviet: the annual accretions to the working population will rise markedly in the mid- and later fifties as our post-depression "baby boom" begins to be felt. Hollow as the phrase may ring amid the anxieties of the day, are we entering upon a decade's breathing spell in the contest of our age? Shall we employ it wisely?

The picture just sketched goes far, if not all the way, to explain some of the Kremlin's recent moves: the so-called unilateral reduction of armed forces by 1.8 million men announced on two occasions in recent months, the pressure for disarmament, and the "peaceful co-existence" theme. To these we shall return after taking a brief look at some structural and institutional characteristics of the Soviet economy.

## Some institutional problems

### Our "economocentric" bias

We may fall prey at once to overestimating and underestimating Soviet strength and capabilities, as William Benton perceptively and persuasively argued before a conference of "Soviet experts" in New York in April 1956. If we do, the reason is perhaps only in part the paucity and bias of the information at hand. In part the fault lies with our own "economocentric" bias—our propensity to transfer to another economy the values and structural proportions that we take for granted in our own. Judging by our own standards we have time and again resisted believing that performance can be as uneven, priorities as one-sided, and achievements as varied as we have later discovered to have been the case. Thus there is a definite pattern to our past erroneous appraisals of the USSR: we have generally tended to underestimate *both* its successes and its failures on the economic and technical fronts. Many serious American students of the Soviet scene underrated the ability of the USSR to resist the German attack, the speed with which it would reconstruct its heavy industry, the pace at which it would progress in the development of nuclear weapons and modern means of their delivery, the achievements of some branches of Soviet pure science, and perhaps most recently its ability to conduct a large program

49

of "foreign aid." In some of these cases our underappraisals derived comfort if not conviction from Soviet secrecy, until the secrecy was shattered by a dramatic event such as a nuclear explosion or a jet "fly-past." In general, however, we almost instinctively failed to appreciate the emphasis and priority that the Soviet leadership was willing and able to place on programs of highest urgency to itself.

But at least we have been consistent. Where Soviet performance has been very poor we have tended, if anything, to disbelieve the full magnitude of the failure. Once again our ingrained sense of economic balance may have played handmaiden to Soviet secretiveness. Often not until more ample information came to light have we quite fully appreciated the stagnation of Soviet agriculture after the war, the gap between the best and the average, not to say the worst, in Soviet industry, and the inefficiency of use of labor and equipment where it is at its less creditable. It is no more proper to be over-impressed by these elements of "weakness" in the Soviet economy than to be over-awed by the elements of "strength." The two are opposite sides of the same medal.

## Progress by pressure and "campaign"

Neglect of many things is, after all, the inevitable price of feverish concentration on a few, especially where the goals constantly strain the resources at hand, and where all pressure comes from above and little initiative rises from below. By conducting a quasi-military campaign, redeploying men and goods, cutting red tape, and manipulating the numerous levers of a dictatorship, the regime has more than once in the past closed an important breach on the economic front or performed an urgent task of great priority. There is little reason why it cannot do so again. For instance, should the Soviet leaders set their minds on large-scale economic and technical assistance to the underdeveloped countries of their choice, one would be foolhardy to discount their ability to do so. The success of such "campaigns" rests fundamentally on the domestic power of the regime, on its ability to order its subjects about and to elicit obedience. Needless to say, a dictatorial regime enjoys substantial advantages over a democracy when resolute and sudden action is in order.

Nor should we blindly repeat the credo that "free labor will always outproduce slave labor." Although labor productivity in Soviet industry is still on the average probably less than half the American, it compares very well with the West European level, and has been rising faster than either. Much of the productivity that we tend to ascribe to our free institutions rests in truth on technical maturity, high provision with capital equipment, and good training—all of which are with time not entirely out of reach for the USSR. And labor unfreedom has its beneficent effects on productivity too: incentive pay systems that no free trade union will stand for, speed-ups, absence of strikes, and so forth.

## Weaknesses in managerial incentive

It is not in the effectiveness of the country's leadership, nor in the potential of the rank and file worker, but in the motivation and incentives of the middle layers of the Soviet administrative pyramid that the major weaknesses from the point of view of productivity and economic growth lie. Technological advance, frantically pushed from above, is often resisted from below. Decades of extreme centralization of planning and decision-making, coupled with severe penalties for failure, have placed a premium on the avoidance of responsibility and initiative by the individual. An incentive system which compares actual performance with a pre-determined "norm" breeds preference for the familiar routine, resists innovations, and does not encourage quick adjustment to environmental changes. Constant pressure for quantity of output and a continuous "seller's market" lead to disregard for quality and cost. The planning machinery is cumbersome and tardy, and the supply system is inefficient. And so, wherever things are left alone they tend to stagnate if not to deteriorate, until perhaps pulled up by a "campaign" from above.

In sum, as the economy is now organized and as incentives are now structured, rapid economic progress is largely predicated on constant pressure from above. The Party's own economic function is to be the whip and the goad as well as the checker and controller. In this function it is too often delinquent, for the good reasons that the Party and the bureaucracy—the would-be whip and the would-be whipped-on—have largely merged.

The political implications of this are significant, for given the self-imposed furious race with the West and the present institutional character of the Soviet "command economy," serious limits on any liberalization of the Soviet polity may be imposed hereby. And conversely, any significant domestic political liberalization through a process of evolution, if such a development is possible, may entail enough relaxation of the pressure from above, not to mention reduction in the rate of investment, to dampen appreciably the pace of economic growth.

At this time, when technological progress has assumed especial significance for Soviet economic growth, the regime has become seriously concerned with the inertia and inefficiency of the planning machinery and the managerial apparatus. A vigorous campaign is currently being waged against bureaucratic faults in general, and against resistance to the adoption of new methods and techniques in particular.

On the positive side, a radical change in the organizational structure of industry and construction is being advanced by Khrushchev as these lines are written (spring 1957). The overgrown and overcentralized ministries are to be abolished, and enterprises are to be grouped under regional "economic councils." It is thus hoped to reduce the cumbersomeness and inflexibility of economic administration, and particularly to break the tendency toward ministerial self-sufficiency and compartmentalization which entail much waste. Whether this reform,

51

if carried through, will significantly alleviate the problem remains to be seen. Since the ills arise from deeply ingrained institutional causes, such as the system of planning and the " seller's market," we may now expect strong tendencies toward regional autarky.

## Trend toward "economic rationality"

A more fundamental reform has to take place before decentralization of the Soviet economy can be successful. If decision-making is to be dispersed, and if it is to serve the interests of the national economy, then the people on the spot, from the ministries down to the factories and farms, must possess the necessary information for decision-making (i.e., prices and costs). The information must be meaningful from the national-economic point of view, and there must be definite rules as to its use in making decisions. While there are still many areas of the Soviet economy where this is not yet the case, some significant steps to make economic calculation possible and more meaningful have been taken in recent years.

There is no space here to describe in detail these steps in the direction of " economic rationality." They comprise a variety of means, such as the introduction of business accounting where it has not been hitherto applied (*e.g.* in the machine-tractor stations); elimination of subsidies (*e.g.* on state farms); and extension of profit incentives (*e.g.* in construction). Other important measures are under inquiry and discussion—such as the introduction of cost calculations in the collective farms, where they have been completely lacking, and rules for the replacement of obsolete equipment in industry. Still more fundamental questions addressed to the rationality of the whole price-cost structure are being raised and presumably thought about. So far, the significance of these steps lies more in the trend that they foreshadow and in the willingness to compromise ideology for the sake of efficiency that they suggest than in the actual achievements. (A few of the measures in question have been ably discussed by Robert W. Campbell in *World Politics*, October 1956.)

Only if the trend toward " economic rationality" is carried far enough—of which there is as yet no assurance—can managerial incentives be so restructured as to elicit initiative and flexibility on the spot and to render functional decentralization successful. And only then, if then, can one expect any substantial diminution of the constant pressure from above on a half-willing economy that has been so characteristic of the Soviet way of doing things for over a generation. That such a change may have a profound impact on every facet of Soviet economy and polity, even on foreign relations, goes without saying. At the moment, however, it would certainly not be wise either to foretell its arrival or to blueprint its effects.

# The allocation of economic resources

The position of the USSR as a world power is closely related to its pattern of resource utilization, and vice versa. While the reconstruction of Soviet national income accounts is anything but conceptually simple or statistically easy, and is subject to controversy even among the specialists themselves, a rough picture of the allocation of the Soviet national product to major uses will suffice for present purposes. One such attempt, based essentially on Professor Bergson's pioneering methodology, depicts the following pattern of allocation of the Soviet gross national product in 1953, a pattern which may be taken as fairly representative of the situation since at least 1948: (in per cent of total at " adjusted ruble factor cost")

| | |
|---|---|
| Private consumption | 47 |
| Health and education services | 8 |
| Government administration | 3.5 |
| Defense and related expenditures | 15 |
| Gross investment | 26 |
| Total GNP (rounded) | 100 |

(82nd Congress. 2nd Session, Joint Committee on the Economic Report, *Trends in Economic Growth,* Washington 1955, p. 284; the actual estimates are attributed to Dr. Herbert Block, U.S. Department of State. The expenditures "related" to defense are those on internal security, and atomic and other special weapons.

Soviet secrecy being what it is, the figure for defense outlay is probably the least reliable of the lot, and is perhaps an underestimate. Thus, the diversion of resources to military and related end-use in recent years has very likely been more than half as large as the outlay on gross investment, and possibly approaching *net* investment in volume. Interestingly, while the shares of both defense and gross investment in total GNP have been lower in the United States in recent years—about 10-12 and 17-20 per cent, respectively—the *ratio* between the two has been approximately the same as in the USSR.

## *Obstacles to expanding consumption*

This pattern of allocation of the Soviet GNP can be seen as a political compromise, a moving equilibrium charted by a set of conflicting forces. Not the least among these forces is the continuous and almost elemental pressure from below for a better and easier life, for more and better housing and consumers' goods, for a larger share of the fruit of the individual's labor. Unorganized but nonetheless very apparent.

53

this force is probably not without its spokesmen even among the leadership. At times it may find vent in a Malenkovian "New Course," only to be thwarted again by a reassertion of "the primacy of heavy industry." Yet even a very drastic turn of policy in its favor is not likely to raise the *share* of consumption in the GNP by more than a few percentage points, that is, by more than a small fraction of itself, in the near term.

The reasons for this are several: (1) the intractability of the raw materials base, particularly of agricultural production, on which any expansion of the supply of consumers' goods must rest; (2) the defects of the organizational and institutional structure in the production and distribution of consumers' goods, which could be remedied but only in conjunction with a radical, and hence not very likely, overhaul of the economy's institutions; and (3) the fact that the physical nature of the resources now tied up in serving other sectors is frequently such that they cannot be quickly converted to serve consumption. It is perhaps in part for these reasons that Malenkov's "New Course" was such a resounding flop, though other factors may well have hastened its demise. This does not mean that in a longer run the share of consumption could not conceivably be raised very significantly.

Of the three events that could alter suddenly and drastically the pattern of resource allocation in the Soviet economy, two—a radical change in the regime, and outright war, or sharply stepped up preparations therefor—fall outside the tacit assumptions of this essay. The third such event is large-scale disarmament, which is presumably predicated on a diplomatic understanding of some sort with the United States.

## Likely effects of disarmament

What are the likely effects of large-scale disarmament on the Soviet economy, on its structure and dynamics, in the near and medium terms? Surely this is a significant question for our policy planners to ask. The answer undoubtedly in part depends on the precise degree and form that the disarmament takes. Let us assume for the sake of argument that the share of defense in GNP is cut down, immediately or more likely by stages, from 15 to 5 per cent, thus releasing resources equivalent to 10 per cent of GNP for other uses. Where will this enormous volume of resources be channeled? Let us assume further that the number of men in uniform, the current production of munitions and armaments, the production of nuclear weapons, and the construction of new military facilities, are all sharply reduced and in some cases perhaps even eliminated, but that military research and development is perhaps reduced more moderately if at all.

In two instances in the past the reverse happened, that is military preparations were stepped up. At the end of the thirties, when military preparedness was greatly intensified and a local war was fought against Finland in 1939-40, the sharp increase in defense outlays was almost entirely at the expense of investment. By Bergson's computation (in "adjusted prices") the share of defense, excluding internal security forces, rose from 7.7 to 15.6 per cent, and that of gross investment fell from 22.9 to 16.6 per cent, between 1937 to 1940. Military preparedness in those years was "financed" by an over-all increase in the national product and by a diversion of resources from investment. Total consumption was not cut into though *per capita* consumption declined considerably.

We are only beginning to learn what happened in the Soviet economy during the Korean conflict. In seems, however, that the expansion of production of civilian machinery and equipment as a whole was held back, and the output of some individual items was sharply cut back, presumably to permit the production of military hardware to be stepped up. Once again investment seems to have borne the main brunt of the military emergency.

These experiences, if not conclusive, are suggestive of the direction of reallocation of resources in the event of large-scale *dis*armament in the foreseeable future. Investment, that is, is likely to be the chief beneficiary of the reshuffle. The same can be argued on *a priori* terms as well. The physical nature of the resources that are now committed to the defense effort—the heavy industrial plant and the metals, chemicals, etc., and the associated manpower and skills—is such that most of them can much more easily be redirected to building civilian investment goods than to producing consumers goods. True, some of these investment goods may in turn be designed for the expansion of consumers-goods industry; but this still qualifies as investment, and the attendant consumption effect will be at best delayed. Moreover, the capacity of many consumers-goods industries to absorb additional resources and manpower is in the near-term largely limited by the ability of agriculture to provide the raw materials.

It is also likely that some of the released capacity and materials will be devoted to solving the agricultural problem. For instance, they may be put to the production of agricultural machinery and implements and mineral fertilizers, in part to raise farm output but in part also to release more labor from the village for nonagricultural employment. Similarly, recalling our discussion of the labor shortage, we may expect that most of the manpower taken out of uniform will be channeled, directly or indirectly, to non-agricultural employment, and particularly to help break the present bottlenecks in basic industry.

It is quite likely that a portion of the large volume of resources released by disarmament will be channeled beyond the borders of the USSR: for additional economic assistance to China and other "friendly" countries on the one hand, and to the "uncommitted" nations of the world on the other. The reduced strain on the Soviet economy and the change in the international political climate following large-scale disarmament may well make it at once more difficult for the Soviet government to resist requests from its "friends" and more tempting to make overtures in order to win new ones. Since foreign economic assistance now takes a relatively small slice of total Soviet resources, one can easily visualize a considerable increase in its volume, given the availability of the resources and the willingness of the regime to commit them in this direction. While any substantial program of foreign economic assistance would certainly be at the expense of domestic investment, the latter is of so much greater an order of magnitude than the former that the adverse effects on the rate of growth of the Soviet economy need not be very serious.

We may conclude that, in the near run, investment will most likely be the main beneficiary of large-scale disarmament. The setting in of some retardation in economic growth, and especially the downward revision of the targets of the Sixth Five-Year Plan now in process, would seem to make this conclusion particularly plausible. This of course does not exclude some immediate concessions to the consumer as well. Again for purposes of argument, let us say that of the ten percentage point reduction in defense outlay we have postulated, six to seven percentage points are allocated to investment and the remaining three to four to consumption and perhaps to "leisure" (the promised reduction in working hours). Then the volume of gross investment would be raised by about a fourth, and the volume of *net* investment, by about a third. Should we dismiss this conclusion as "impossible" because it would raise the rate of gross investment to the "unheard of" level of one-third or more of the GNP, we would once again be guilty of "economo-centric bias."

Without placing any undue stock in these purely illustrative magnitudes, it is not unreasonable to anticipate that the main effect of any large-scale disarmament would be to boost the rates of growth of industrial output and of the total national product over what they otherwise might be; or, in other words, to retard their retardation. At the same time presumably the capacity—and perhaps also the willingness—of the USSR to engage in large-scale foreign economic assistance, within its own orbit and elsewhere, may be enhanced.

## Conclusion

This essay has discussed some of the current Soviet economic trends and problems on the supposition that they bear a close, if not always obvious, relation to the behavior of the USSR as a world power. The list is far from complete; some important issues have been touched on only peripherally if at all. For instance, the problem of Soviet agriculture has been only briefly discussed, not because it is unimportant but because it has received its share of attention in the recent American literature on the Soviet Union. On the other hand, such an important development as the renewed eastward movement of the center of gravity of Soviet industry—which may now suffer from the revision of the Sixth Five-Year Plan—has received no attention here because its immediate relevance to Soviet foreign relations is limited, at least in the shorter run.

Nor have we had much to say about Soviet foreign trade, in part because the bulk of it is with the rest of the Soviet orbit, about which little is known; and in part because the remainder, *i.e.* trade with the "free world," about which more is known, is a small element in the total Soviet economic picture. Except in specific instances where political considerations dictate otherwise, such as the penetration of Soviet influence into the "uncommitted" part of the world, it is still reasonable to assume that autarky, not trade, is the watchword of Soviet planners. For this reason it is difficult to subscribe to the view, recently advanced by Khrushchev and not without some currency even in the United States, that western export controls provided the necessary stimulus to the USSR to become self-sufficient in the production of various types of equipment and other articles, which presumably otherwise it would have preferred to import from the West.

If there is a grain of validity to this argument, it is hardly a very large grain. We need only recall with what determination Soviet planners strove for self sufficiency, especially with regard to machinery, during the nineteen-thirties, when there were no export controls on the part of the West.

No one can foretell in what proportion in the next few years the world strategy of the USSR will rely on the country's great military-economic potential on the one hand, and on the extension of trade and economic aid on the other, especially in relation to the underdeveloped countries. The second policy has of course been lately much heralded though the post-Hungary months witnessed at least a temporary *diminuendo* of the theme. It has yet to prove itself both as to the Soviet ability to undertake it on a large scale, and the positive results from the Soviet point of view that it may show. Though we may doubt the last, we would be overhasty to discount the capability of the Soviet Union to carry out a large economic assistance program with credit to itself. Should the regime set its mind on such a program and accord it the necessary priorities, there would be little in the stock of Soviet material and human resources to preclude its success. Furthermore, whatever we know of the economic and technical assistance programs conducted by the Russians within the communist bloc, especially China, does not seem to contradict this impression. Given the willingness on the part of the recipient countries, the main question on the Soviet side would seem to be not the adequacy of economic and technical resources but the readiness of the leadership to commit the necessary resources, to grant the priorities, and to follow through consistently.

Much of what Russia will do depends on what America does. We sometimes forget that, at least since World War II, to a large extent Soviet foreign policy has been a reaction to our role in world affairs, or what they interpreted our role to be, just as much of our foreign policy has been a reaction to Russian behavior. What this means, in positive terms, for American foreign policy of course cannot be summed up in a paragraph. But merely to state the proposition is to dispel an all-too-frequent "illusion of American impotence" with regard to our affecting the external behavior and internal development of the USSR. This seems to be a curious obverse of the "illusion of American omnipotence" in world affairs that has been commented on by D. W. Brogan (in *Harper's*, December 1952).

We have already seen that large-scale disarmament by virtue of an understanding with the United States is likely to have very considerable effects on the evolution of the Soviet economy, not to mention of course the state of international relations in general. It may also have profound effects on the Soviet society and polity. Though these effects may be much less foreseeable than the economic, in the last analysis economic evolution too will be affected by social and political transformations.

Or to take another example. If we should embark on a determined policy to extend personal and intellectual contact between the Russian people and the United States and the rest of the West, might we not expect certain forces to be set in motion or to be reinforced in their operation within the body of the Soviet society? One cannot be certain of cause and effect in such matters, but might it not be that such contact would heighten the pressure on the regime to raise consumption levels, to do more for housing, to grant more intellectual freedom, and to proceed further along the road of economic and social rationality? Might this not even give a push to internal political liberalization? Or, if the regime were unable or unwilling to undertake such steps, would not the onus rest on it and would not the gulf between it and the Russian people spread even wider? Perhaps the effects will not be in these directions at all, but that there will be effects we can hardly doubt.

In short, the answer to our initial question—how strong is the Soviet economy?—is relative not only to Soviet world strategy but also to American foreign policy.

# 3. Competitive coexistence and economic development in Asia

by Edward S. Mason

For the third time since the end of the war the United States is engaged in a wholesale reappraisal of foreign aid programs in particular and our relations with allies and potential allies in general. This reappraisal is taking place against a background of world-shaking events that appear to presage a serious realignment of international relations on both sides of a curtain that—if iron—seems to be rapidly corroding. The Soviet empire built by Stalin with much blood and terror seems in process of partial disintegration, with the end not yet in sight. The series of alliances laboriously constructed by the United States in the interest of collective defense are badly shaken.

Edward S. Mason is Dean of the Graduate School of Public Administration and Professor of Economics at Harvard University. After World War II, in which he served with the Office of Strategic Services, Dean Mason was deputy to the Assistant Secretary of State in charge of economic affairs. He was a member of the President's Committee on Foreign Aid in 1947; deputy to the President's Special Assistant (Gordon Gray) on foreign economic policy in 1950; and a member of the President's Materials Policy Committee in 1951 and 1952. Since 1953, he has served as advisor to the National Planning Board of Pakistan. Among his publications are *Controlling World Trade* and *Promoting Economic Development: The United States and South Asia*.

# Foreign assistance in the postwar period

Since 1947 this country has expended nearly $50 billion in grants and loans in support of foreign aid programs. The Year 1947 is relevant. That was the date of our first great postwar national debate on foreign economic policy. The result was the Marshall Plan and the extension of aid mounting to approximately $16 billion over a four-year period, mainly to the countries of Western Europe. (Not more than $12-13 billion of this was, strictly speaking, Marshall Plan economic aid.) Although our objectives were partly economic and the means almost entirely economic rather than military assistance, it seems safe to say that, in the absence of strong security considerations, grants of this magnitude would not have been voted by Congress. The recovery of Western Europe, it is true, was regarded as essential to world recovery and to the success of our commercial and financial policies. But also of major importance was the fear that, in the absence of Western European recovery, this area, vital to our own safety, would fall a prey to communist subversion.

Although Congress and the Administration were heavily motivated by security conditions, military action was subordinated to economic assistance. The primary threat was judged to be political subversion rather than armed attack. It was hoped that economic recovery would produce stronger and more stable non-communist governments. The emphasis, particularly during the first two years of the Marshall Plan, was entirely on economic means; and until the beginning of the Korean War, military expenditures both in the United States and in Western Europe continued to decline. The estimate that increased economic well-being in Western Europe would promote political stability and a weakening of communist penetration proved to be correct. It remains to be considered whether this relationship is likely to hold true in the underdeveloped areas of the world.

## Effects of the Korean War

The second great postwar debate on foreign assistance programs was introduced by the Korean War. During the year before the war, the pressure for reduction of defense expenditures continued both here and abroad, even though the Soviet Union had shown no signs of reducing its military establishment and Nationalist China had disintegrated on the mainland under communist attack. The mentality of that period is particularly fresh in the mind of the author, who was helping Gordon Gray, Special Assistant to the President on Foreign Economic Policy, prepare a set of recommendations. One of the important unknowns was the prospective level of military expenditures in the United States and in Western Europe. An important document—that many people thought alarmist—pointing out the increasing discrepancy between Soviet and Western armed strength was then before the Security Council. One of its recommendations was an increase in

United States military expenditures by $4 or $5 billion a year. Secretary of Defense Johnson was opposed. He attempted to cut the military budget from $14 to $13 billion and was apparently strongly supported by the Administration and by both parties in Congress.

This episode illustrates a problem we shall continue to have to face. In a democracy it does not require much improvement in the international situation to generate a nearly irresistible demand for reduction in defense expenditures, including expenditures for security abroad.

The Korean War changed all that. The military budget quickly increased from $14 to $60 billion and has never since declined below $35 billion. The Korean War also gave the answer to the debate on foreign aid programs. Foreign assistance was increased rather than diminished as had been expected at the end of the Marshall Plan. The motivation became overtly and almost solely security considerations; and security came to be rather narrowly interpreted in military terms. During the fiscal years 1951-54 inclusive, United States government foreign grants and loans totaled approximately $23 billion.

It is difficult to divide United States foreign assistance expenditures into clear-cut military and economic categories. Probably no useful purpose is served in trying to do so. During the first two years of the Marshall Plan, under the Economic Cooperation Administration, the assistance was given for economic reconstruction and rehabilitation. During the second two years the assistance, although in much the same form as regards commodities, was primarily designed to facilitate rearmament in Western Europe. The changed purpose was indicated by the change in the name of the administering agency to Mutual Security Agency. After the Korean War a substantial part of foreign aid took the form of finished military equipment; most of the so-called economic aid was designed to facilitate military buildup abroad.

## Military and economic assistance since Korea

In 1951 the phrase "defense support" was coined. This was economic aid to countries with whom we were linked by military assistance pacts to permit them to expend their military services beyond their own economic limits. In theory, defense support was the value equivalent of domestic resources diverted to military use; consequently defense support was distinguishable from aid for economic development. Since then most nonmilitary assistance to countries with whom we have military pacts is called defense support. Because we are so linked with all Latin American countries by virtue of the Rio Treaty, much of our economic assistance to them is "defense support." But the military buildup in Latin America probably does not differ by the exact amount of this assistance from what it would have been in the absence of such assistance.

Since 1950 an overwhelming fraction of foreign aid has probably been voted on the Congressional assumption that it would strengthen military establishments. If, however, we look to the results abroad, the

61

fraction actually devoted to this use may be somewhat smaller. But motivation or results apart, the amounts intended and used strictly for assistance to economic development have been small.

Distribution of United States Government Foreign Grants and Credits.
(in $ millions)

| | Postwar Period | Before Korean Invasion | After Korean Invasion | July 1, 1955-June 30, 1956 |
|---|---|---|---|---|
| TOTAL | 56918 | 26347 | 30571 | 5051 |
| Military | 17809 | 1438 | 16371 | 3044 |
| Non-Military | 39108 | 24909 | 14199 | 2077 |
| Europe | 26115 | 18996 | 7119 | 441 |
| Japan | 2588 | 1973 | 615 | -11** |
| Canada | -10** | 1 | -11** | -12** |
| Main Defense Support Countries | 6273 | 2657 | 3616 | 897 |
| China-Taiwan | 1321 | 819 | 502 | 113 |
| Greece | 1362 | 776 | 586 | 66 |
| Indo-China | 563 | --- | 563 | 256 |
| Korea | 1483 | 367 | 1116 | 254 |
| Pakistan | 258 | --- | 258 | 123 |
| Philippines | 846 | 620 | 226 | 26 |
| Turkey | 440 | 75 | 365 | 59 |
| All Other | 4140 | 1281 | 2857 | 669 |
| India | 444 | 12 | 432 | 101 |
| Other Near East, S. E. Asia and Africa | 1137 | -3** | 1140 | 164 |
| Other Far East | 372 | 184 | 187 | 145 |
| American Republics | 1154 | 356 | 798 | 188 |
| International and Unspecified | 1033 | 732 | 300 | 71 |

* Includes sale of agricultural products for local currencies.
** Net repayments.

Prepared by staff of Committee for Economic Development, January 1957.

Rather than attempt further to disentangle military from economic assistance, we will consider these questions:

1. What interests has the United States sought and should it seek in its foreign aid programs?

2. What are the means it has used and should use to advance these interests?

# United States interests in foreign economic assistance

Why has Congress been willing to vote and United States taxpayers to support a program of foreign aid totalling $50 billion since 1947? The answer to this question is usually given in terms of various motivations and interests, chiefly *humanitarian, economic* and *security.*

The overwhelming important explanation lies in United States security interests. It is highly important in the current reassessment of foreign aid to develop fairly explicit notions of what the United States wants to accomplish abroad in order to judge whether the means are adapted to the ends. It is also important for the countries who have been and may be the recipients of assistance to be able to judge the circumstances under which aid is likely to be given and for what purposes.

## *The humanitarian factor*

An attempt to reassess the nature of United States interests is the more important since there appears to be in recent discussion a great deal of confusion concerning the sources of humanitarian contributions and the relative magnitude of our economic and security interests. The chief sources of confusion seem to be the following:

1. A failure to distinguish between, on the one hand, the motivations of American citizens and private institutions concerning foreign assistance and, on the other, the considerations that will lead the government to take actions that, over time, will be supported by American taxpayers and the electorate.
2. A false identification of our security interests with purely military considerations.
3. An exaggerated assessment of our present or future dependence on foreign sources of raw materials or on foreign markets.

The generosity of American citizens and private institutions in the foreign field is legendary. At an earlier period the motivation might have been largely religious; in this century it appears to be almost entirely humanitarian. The results of this generosity are impressive. Roberts College in Istanbul and the American Universities at Beirut and Cairo bear testimony to the magnitude and success of American educational effort in the Middle East. The Ford Foundation contributions in the Middle East and Southern Asia, which currently total about $15 million a year, are larger than the contributions in this area of a number of the Colombo Plan countries. The health and agricultural programs of the Rockefeller Foundation in Latin America and elsewhere have substantially improved living conditions in many countries. These are but a few examples.

There is, moreover, little doubt that the motivations that have led private citizens abroad to assist in promoting the welfare of depressed populations are similar to those that lead many people into the United States government service in technical and other foreign aid programs.

63

Furthermore, it is difficult to explain certain actions of the government in the foreign field—the recent Point Four Program may be an example—except on the basis of humanitarian considerations. This has been an element in a much broader range of foreign aid actions since the war.

Despite all this it is doubtful that humanitarianism (a desire to improve the living conditions and opportunities of people abroad without regard to the security or economic prosperity of the United States) can be considered important either in explaining the actions of this country since 1947 or in laying the basis for a reasonable expectation of future action. Government aid programs are devised and promoted in an administrative and political setting that is not very amenable to humanitarian considerations. The agencies of government responsible for the initiation and administration of these programs have annually to justify them before a Congress concerned with demonstrating to its voting constituencies that their interests are being served. An administration unable to show that taxes for foreign aid programs have some fairly direct relation to the economic interests of important political groups or to the safety of the State will have difficulty in continuing these programs—and, probably, continuing in power.

It seems necessary to labor this point because in many quarters there appear to be expectations that a sizeable international program of assistance, particularly from the United States, can be established without regard to the economic and security interests of the contributing countries. These expectations are set forth most explicitly perhaps by Gunnar Myrdal, Executive Secretary of the United Nations Economic Commission for Europe, in his recent book *An International Economy*. Myrdal's argument simply put is:

> That in the "integrated" societies of the West there has been taking place over the last century, largely because of a revolution in moral ideas, a redistribution of income and an equalization of opportunity. The effect has been that most citizens have acquired a sense of participation in their society that has largely eliminated the significance of earlier class struggles.
>
> That an "integrated" international society requires a similar redistribution of wealth and income and of economic opportunity between the rich and economically developed economies of the West and the so-called underdeveloped areas of the World.
>
> That there is substantial evidence of a spread of the ideas and values necessary to bring this about.

It is no doubt true that in the economically developed societies of the West redistribution of income and equalization of economic opportunity have gone far and have contributed greatly to social cohesion. According to Myrdal

This process has. . . .been determined largely by the ideal—a living force in the minds of these nations—of achieving an ever-greater equality of opportunity for all their citizens. One of the most important of state interventions in the nationally integrated economies has been the increasing application of the principle of sharing burdens. The readiness to share displayed by the various groups comprising the nation state has been an index of the strength of the psychological basis for integration.

Without questioning the change in moral ideas over the last century on what constitutes a "just" distribution of income and economic opportunities, it is pertinent to remark that the redistribution was greatly facilitated by the shift in political power made possible by the spread of democratic practices and institutions. On the international scene there is no political structure within which a shift of power from the "haves" to the "have nots" can take place.

This being so, is it likely that changing attitudes toward burden-sharing and equalization of opportunities will, by their own strength, lead to international channeling of economic assistance from developed to underdeveloped countries?

Myrdal's argument that they will—or at least may—depends partly on what seems to be a misreading of the motives of our postwar aid programs. Of the Marshall Plan he writes, " It does not require any comprehensive or deep study of the American motives for this extraordinary aid to say from first-hand observation of the American people that, in the beginning, the main attitude was much more the positive one of sympathy and solidarity, rather than the negative one of fear of communism."

Myrdal goes on to say

It is true that the Americans tried eagerly to convince themselves at the very inauguration of the Marshall Plan that they were acting solely with their own national interest in view, but this was only a further example of the strange suspicion on the part of the American people of their own generous motives, which I once analyzed as a slightly perverted element of their Puritan tradition.

Flattering as this view of American generosity may be, it does an acute disservice to anyone in the United States or in the underdeveloped areas who is attempting soberly to assess the conditions on which United States economic assistance is likely to be forthcoming.

Professor Jacob Viner, in " The Role of the United States in the World Economy," says

The only factor which could persuade us to undertake a really large program of economic aid to the underdeveloped countries would be the decision that the friendship and alliance of those countries are strategically, politically, and psychologically valuable to us in the cold war, that economic aid on a large scale can be relied upon to assure such friendship and alliance to us, and that the cost to us of a greatly enlarged program of economic aid would not be an excessive price to pay for these strategic gains.

Myrdal objects that " in the United States itself, this hardboiled policy, which is so definitely out of line with the cherished humanitarian traditions of the nation, will not be an inspiring one." And, he goes on, "I personally doubt very much whether a comprehensive and lasting policy of international aid on a strategic basis will ever have a chance of becoming accepted in the United States."

It is here suggested, on the contrary, that the size and duration of a policy of international aid depends much more on the strategic situation than on anything else.

The report of the Commission on Foreign Economic Policy (Randall Report) states that "Underdeveloped areas are claiming a right to economic aid from the United States. .... We recognize no such right." Myrdal characterizes this statement as "harsh." It is indeed harsh— and somewhat inexact. Some part of our postwar aid to underdeveloped areas has undoubtedly been motivated by a recognition of our "obligations" and of their "rights." But as a statement of American unwillingness to recognize any moral imperative to a large and sustained effort toward the economic development of underdeveloped areas, it seems substantially correct.

## The economic factor

We turn now to promotion of the economic interests of the United States as a possible explanation of postwar foreign assistance programs. There can be no doubt that, with respect to the Marshall Plan at least, this was an important motivating force. The United States participated during and immediately after the war in the development of policies and institutions designed to reestablish the network of world trade and international payments on a less discriminatory and freer basis than had existed just before the war. These policies and institutions contributed to the economic interests of the United States—and all trading nations. It became clear, however, early in the postwar period that the "Bretton Woods" policies and institutions were not going to work unless and until the trade and payments positions of Western European countries were brought into better balance than the devastation of the war permitted. One of the important objectives of the Marshall Plan was undoubtedly to bring this about.

Our continued concern with reducing trade barriers, currency convertibility, and nondiscrimination has probably facilitated Congressional acceptance of other foreign aid programs designed primarily for security purposes. Furthermore, the persistence of our foreign aid at the current level of $4 to $5 billion a year has come to be one of the pillars of a world trading system which, despite many barriers, is still much freer than the pre-war system. The contribution to our economic interest in multilateral, nondiscriminatory trade has been, in a sense, an extra dividend from foreign assistance designed primarily to accomplish security objectives.

Assigning full value to these economic considerations, it is, nevertheless, obvious that we would never have put $50 billion into foreign aid programs during the last ten years if our primary objective had simply been the promotion of our own economic welfare. The costs would have been judged too flagrantly disproportionate to the possible benefits. Our dependence on foreign trade is not such as to make even a substantial curtailment of trading relations a serious obstacle to economic growth and prosperity.

If we now consider prospectively the economic case for foreign assistance programs, particularly to underdeveloped areas, the following arguments are frequently pressed:

1. It is said to be impossible for the United States to prosper indefinitely in a world in which half the population continues to be ill-fed and ill-clothed.
2. Our increasing dependence on foreign sources of raw materials will necessitate an increased concern with the economic development of raw-material-producing areas if we expect to continue drawing supplies from these areas.
3. We shall encounter increasing difficulty in maintaining full employment in the United States unless we develop export markets through foreign lending or through foreign aid programs.

None of these arguments can withstand careful analysis. The economic growth of the United States over the last century took place in a world in which more than half the population continued to live at subsistence level. This fact suggests that rising levels of income elsewhere are not a necessary condition to our prosperity. Since the war our total imports have averaged between 3 and 4 per cent of gross national product. Our somewhat higher exports are explained by extraordinary United States aid programs. This small degree of dependence on foreign trade suggests a substantial insulation of American economic welfare from economic conditions outside our borders. It can be admitted that economic conditions in the underdeveloped areas of the world may have political consequences endangering world peace. But then the argument for concerning ourselves with the conditions of others becomes a political-security argument to which we shall turn presently. If one concentrates on economic relationships alone, the facts seem to be that although rising incomes in underdeveloped areas may, on balance, be economically beneficial to the United States, our national income can continue to expand at traditional rates in the absence of such an increase.

*Raw material supplies.* The raw material position of the United States is changing substantially. Before the war we were net exporters of raw materials on a substantial scale. Since the war, while we have consumed roughly 50 per cent of the industrial raw material output of the free world, we have produced only 45 per cent. In 1950, as the Paley Comission observed, we imported net about 9 per cent of our total consumption of industrial raw materials and unprocessed foodstuffs. On the basis of unchanged international trade policies, the Commission estimated that we might be importing 20 per cent of our expected consumption by 1975.

67

Does this projected increase in our dependence on foreign raw material argue for increased support of *general* economic development in underdeveloped areas? It does so only if it can be shown (a) that the availability of raw materials from abroad is closely connected with the rate of over-all economic development in resource countries and (b) that a curtailment of foreign sources of raw material supply would substantially hamper the economic growth of the United States. Neither position can be plausibly defended.

The overwhelmingly important current and prospective sources of our raw material imports are the Western Hemisphere and Africa south of the Equator. In the Western Hemisphere the countries from which we mainly import are already undergoing a process of economic development substantially independent of United States governmental assistance other than largely commercial-type loans from the Export-Import Bank. In Africa south of the Equator United States assistance is probably not a condition of continued access to raw material supplies, though this situation could change. It should be noted in this connection that while the Western Hemisphere and Africa south of the Equator are the important raw material sources, our foreign aid since the war has gone predominantly to Europe, the Far East, and Southern Asia.

In assessing the possible consequences of curtailment of raw material imports, it is important to be aware of some of the magnitudes involved. The value of all industrial raw material and unprocessed food supplies in the American economy is about 10 per cent of gross national product. Our imports of these materials constitute about 1 per cent of G.N.P. A substantial rise, therefore, in the price of these imports would have only a small effect in checking our economic growth. Furthermore, a substantial rise in import prices would lead, in the case of many important materials, to a substitution of domestic for foreign output. The American economy is relatively invulnerable to a curtailment of foreign sources of raw material supply. The same thing cannot be said of our European allies; but if a case is made for aid programs on the ground that otherwise Western European sources of supply will be endangered, this becomes a political or security rather than an economic argument.

One final point: since the war the extraordinary United States governmental expenditures abroad associated with raw materials have been concerned mainly with stock-piling and with the development of sources of supply of strategic materials. While these expenditures have frequently contributed to economic development in resource countries, the objective has clearly been American security.

*Export markets and investment outlets.* There is a view that full employment in the United States requires an excess of exports over imports, financed either by private capital exports or by government foreign aid programs. Since the war this view has been endemic in various underdeveloped areas of the world, particularly Southern

Asia. It leads to the convenient conviction that over the long run the United States will be led by its own economic interests to finance the foreign exchange component of expanding development programs in these areas. If it is replied that, in the event of private savings outrunning private investment opportunities, there are plenty of outlets for public, domestic investment in highways, schools, land reclamation, urban renewal, and the like, it is argued that the volume of public investment required to sustain full employment will be impossible of attainment within the framework of the "capitalist system."

It is a little hard to take this version of the "stagnation thesis" seriously when the combination of public expenditures and private investment and consumption is leading us perilously close to serious inflation. But it is true that an important component of effective demand for labor in the United States since the war has been an annual export surplus of $4-5 billion together with defense expenditures much larger, relative to G.N.P., than before the war. It is at least arguable that, if a change in the world situation permitted a reduction of defense expenditures and of foreign aid programs based on security considerations, we might have an employment problem on our hands. And the American attitude toward exports is somewhat different from that of most industrial countries. In most countries exports are regarded as a means of paying for necessary imports. Here we have sometimes tended to regard them as a sustainer of employment.

Two things may be said about this thesis that our interests in sustaining employment will lead us into foreign aid programs to promote development abroad. First, there are currently no signs that the level of defense expenditures at home and abroad can safely be reduced. Second, if a reduction becomes possible and *if* the employment effects of such a reduction are not offset by increases in private investment and consumption, the opportunities for public investment within the framework of what might be called a "capitalist system" appear limitless. After all, as we have had occasion to see since 1932, the "capitalist system" comprises a fairly flexible set of institutions.

In sum, an appraisal of the "economic interests" thesis concerning our postwar foreign aid programs leads us to the view that we have here at best a very incomplete and partial explanation.

## *The dominant factor—political and security interests*

There remains the overwhelmingly important motivation of our major postwar lending and spending programs and the principal justification for sizeable future assistance—namely, the furtherance of the kind of world in which we can live and prosper under institutions chosen by and not for us. Our security interests, however, comprise a complex set of ends and means. Expressed negatively, the promotion of these interests does not necessarily mean the enhancing of our ability to make war. It does not necessarily involve an increase in military expenditures. And it has no necessary connection with the encouragement of anti-communist sentiments or activities. On the other hand it obviously may and can involve all these things.

Furthermore, the long-run security problem is by no means limited to our relations with the Soviet Union. Conflagrations may break out in the Middle East, Southern and Southeast Asia. Whether or not the communist world is involved, these can be inimical to our interests. And, over time, the world has a way of changing. During the next decade or two the prospect is one of explosive change in Southern and Eastern Asia and in Africa, under the impact of rapid population growth, developing nationalism, and the application of western technologies to unexploited resources. When the power relations in the world a mere half-century ago are contrasted with the situation today, it requires no great imagination to envisage a world fifty years hence in which Africa and Asia, not to mention Latin America, will have assumed quite different dimensions. Since we are presumably going to have to exist in that world, it behooves us to take what steps we can to assure that we live under our own freely developing institutions and at peace with any new constellation.

United States security policy, then, includes measures to assure and perpetuate peace and to insure our defense if peace can not be attained. Obviously there may be conflicts between these ends and their appropriate means. In the search for peace we may be led to pursue measures such that if peace fails we will be ill prepared to defend ourselves. And in the search for increased strength we could be led to act in such a way as to make peace impossible. If, as Myrdal appears to think, something like an integrated international society could be achieved by the voluntary burden-sharing and equalization of opportunities to which he attributes the emergence of integrated national societies; and if this were demonstrably the only road to peace, we might find ourselves embarking on a security program in the exclusive form of large-scale aid to the development of underdeveloped areas. Whether this could be described as a security program or sheer humanitarianism invokes the old utilitarian dilemma of whether a man whose greatest happiness lies in serving others is or is not acting in his own interests.

It is not necessary, however, to solve this dilemma here. We can take the firm position that United States security necessitates military expenditures large enough for an effective defense. But we can still recognize that a purely economic foreign aid program, say in the Middle East, designed to lessen the chance of war in that area, may be an appropriate part of our security policy.

The principal objective of the Marshall Plan was to check communist subversion in Western Europe. To that extent it was a security measure, though the means employed were mainly economic. The predominantly military aid programs of the Korean War and since were no more and no less security measures than the Marshall Plan. The means employed were different because the nature of the security threat was judged to be different.

## *A broad concept of security interests*

Since the Korean War, Congress has been reluctant to support foreign assistance not tied to a military formula. This is an excessively narrow conception of the means appropriate to the advancement of American security interests. Assistance has been denied to countries, like Ceylon, who traded with communist nations even though these nations offered the only feasible outlet for their products. Burma and Indonesia have been led to reject United States aid because of a belief they were being asked to take sides in the Cold War. If aid without strings might plausibly be expected to add to political stability, insistence on such strings has no place in a sensible security policy.

The reaction of those responsible for the conduct of United States foreign policy to recent events in Poland and Hungary is one indication that our interests abroad involve something more than mere anti-communism. Continued support for Tito is another. It may not be to our interests to encourage revolt against communism within the Soviet orbit if the inevitable crushing of these revolts is followed by a reversion to Stalinism in the affected area. On the other hand, an increasing degree of independence among European and Asian satellites, even though they continue to be communist, is to be encouraged.

Security policy, then, is concerned with maintaining peace as well as with assuring defense if peace cannot be maintained. The means appropriate to these ends are in no sense purely military. They do not inevitably involve a merely negative anti-communism. They require a high degree of discrimination in their use as among particular areas. If we recognize all this, we are in a better position to assess the merits of the development programs of underdeveloped areas in relation to a sensible United States security policy.

## The current outlook on the security problem

A sensible security policy is one that correctly diagnoses the nature of prospective threats to peace and safety, and effectively mobilizes the appropriate defense. Among the possible current threats are—

World war with nuclear weapons.

Small-scale "brush" wars with conventional weapons in various parts of the world.

A competitive struggle with the weapons of economic and technical assistance in underdeveloped areas.

Political subversion utilizing the profoundly anti-colonial and passionately nationalistic sentiments ablaze in Africa and Asia.

71

The current reassessment of United States foreign aid programs must be primarily concerned with an evaluation of these possibilities and, in the light of this evaluation, of the appropriateness of various courses of counteraction.

The first great postwar assessment in 1947 diagnosed the threat as primarily one of unrest and subversion arising out of war devastation and dislocation in Western Europe. The response was a large, successful program of economic rehabilitation and recovery.

The second assessment took place under the immediate and striking suppression of the Korean War and the events in China. The diagnosis was that the threat was primarily military. The response was a great increase in our own defense establishment and foreign aid programs of a predominantly military character tied in to attempts to form military alliances in Western Europe, the Middle East, and in Southeast Asia and the Far East.

## Strategic factors predominant but not exclusive

Since 1950 the character of our foreign aid programs has continued under the influence of that diagnosis, even though it has become increasingly clear that in many respects the diagnosis is incomplete and inadequate. For a time it appeared to be our view that the Korean War had, or should have, made the world alignment of forces so abundantly clear that we were entitled to conclude that those who were not for us were against us. In attempting to attach political conditions to proffered aid programs we were rebuffed in Burma and Indonesia. India made it quite plain that an acceptance of economic aid would not affect her position of neutrality. The emphasis we attempted to place on restricting trade with Soviet-bloc countries further weakened our influence in Asia and, to some extent, in Europe. Since to our mind the dominant security consideration was the division between Soviet communism and the rest of the world, we constantly overestimated the unity of the "free world" and paid much too little attention to bitter and continuing sources of friction within it. The Baghdad Pact, regarded by us as a defensive alliance against possible Soviet aggression, was viewed in a different light in most of the Arab states. And the decision to extend military aid to Pakistan may have been taken with too little regard to repercussions in India and Afghanistan.

This over-simple, post-Korean diagnosis of the security threat has to some extent been corrected. We now recognize that neutralism is not necessarily inimical to United States interest and a bar to United States assistance. Certainly, from the point of view of our own security, it is better to support a position of neutrality in an important area than to see that area come under Soviet influence. We have also moderated to some extent our proscription against trading in strategic materials with iron-curtain countries. As one of the results, we now have a technical assistance mission in Ceylon. Nevertheless, as the following figures on foreign aid tend to indicate, the military threat diagnosis is overwhelmingly predominant.

| | Foreign Aid Appropriations F/Y 1957 |
|---|---|
| Direct Military | $2,018,000,000 |
| Defense Support | 1,162,000,000 |
| Economic development, technical aid and all other foreign assistance | 625,000,000 |

Nothing in the current state of affairs would justify a reduction in our present domestic defense expenditures. Nor are there any clear indications that we could safely reduce the size of our military aid programs abroad. The Soviet action in Hungary and threatened intervention in the Middle East are recent enough to make any such reductions questionable. Whatever the outcome of the current debate among the armed services, or between the exponents of exclusive reliance on massive deterrence and those who believe in a more flexible policy, the outlook is for increased rather than decreased defense expenditures. This probability, in itself, may tend to limit sharply the area within which the nonmilitary aspects of a security program can be fruitfully considered.

It means, on the one hand, that our politically feasible taxable capacity will continue largely to be pre-empted by irreducible military commitments. Programs for economic development assistance that might recommend themselves if their financing were made easy by partial disarmament will have to compete in Congress and in the country with military requirements not easily dismissed as superfluous. It means, on the other hand, that such nonmilitary foreign aid programs as can justify themselves in this competition must be considered in relation to our whole security program abroad. Assistance that might in other circumstances contribute to economic development will become in certain countries merely a replacement for domestic resources diverted to military purposes. And, in the distribution among underdeveloped countries of such economic development assistance as may be available, the claims of those whose military preparations are deemed useful to us will tend to be preferred to the claims of those who purport to be neutral.

The limitations imposed by the present military situation on a reassessment of foreign aid programs can hardly be overlooked. Despite this fact there have been changes in the world that make the present security problem look different from that at the time of the Korean War. The first of these is the emergence of a possible shift in Soviet strategy and tactics away from military competition and the threat and practice of armed intervention toward what is commonly called a policy of competitive coexistence. A second is evidenced on both sides of the iron curtain by a certain loosening of ties that in the Soviet orbit had been forged by the policies of Stalin, and in the Free World were the inevitable reaction to the kind of threat that Stalinism represented. The third change is the emergence of China as a rapidly developing Asiatic power with an obvious role to play in any policy of competitive coexistence.

These changes are clearly not independent of each other. And it is equally clear that their main impact, in a security sense, will be in Southern and Southeast Asia and the Middle East. A little more detail on the nature of these changes may be in order. And after that, a discussion of some of the implications of a policy of competitive co-existence in Southern Asia.

## Soviet economic growth

The aspects of competitive coexistence that primarily concern us here are (1) the evidences of a rate of economic growth in the Soviet Union that will permit, while maintaining a high level of military expenditures, an increasing flow of resources to promote the development of underdeveloped areas; and (2) an expressed intention, backed by action in Southern Asia, to use resources in this way. The Sixth Five-Year Plan of the Soviet Union, published in January 1956 boasted that, " The UUSR now has all the necessary conditions for accomplishing, in peaceful economic competition and in an historically brief space of time, its main economic task—to overtake and surpass the most developed capitalist countries as regards per capita production."

Careful studies of Russian economic growth make it clear that this is no idle boast. Furthermore, the reasons for expecting a continued increase of Soviet industrial output are obvious. The fraction of national income devoted to investment is much higher than in the West; the direction of investment into uses that make a maximum contribution to economic growth occurs to an extent not possible in democratic societies; and the same thing is true of technical and professional skills.

The following table[1] presents figures on gross and net fixed investment as a per cent of gross and net national product in 1955 in the United States, the United Kingdom and the Soviet Union.

| Country | Gross Fixed Investment as % of G.N.P. | Net Fixed Investment as % of G.N.P. |
|---------|--------------------------------------|-------------------------------------|
| U.S.A. | 17 | 8-12 |
| U.K. | 17 | 6-8.5 |
| U.S.S.R. | 26 | 13-18 |

[1] These and the following figures and comments are taken from an unpublished mss. by Bruce Cheek. "Some Industrial Implications of Peaceful Co-existence."

The high rate in the Soviet Union is possible only because of a strict control of consumption. The current Five-Year Plan contemplates an increase of national income of 60 per cent and of productivity by 50 per cent, but real wages are to rise only 30 per cent. The relationships among these magnitudes are likely to be observed whether or not the figures themselves are attained. In the West, of course, there is a strong tendency for wages and consumption to rise in proportion to national income.

In the Soviet Union, 1953-55, 50-60 per cent of gross fixed investment was allocated to manufacture, mining and public utilities. The corresponding figure for the United States was 34 per cent and for the United Kingdom 42 per cent. Housing, on the other hand, absorbed about 12 per cent of gross fixed investment during the same period in the USSR, while the figures for the United States and the United Kingdom were 24 and 25 per cent respectively. While investment in housing may have some long-run effect on productivity, the impact of investment in manufactures is direct and immediate.

Finally, as Cheek observes:

Once a high rate of investment has been attained, and labor is fully employed, increases in industrial capacity depend largely on technical progress and managerial efficiency. The Soviet allocates considerable resources to education and research institutions. Wage differentials and working conditions are designed to attract Soviet youth to trained posts. Recent visitors to the Soviet Union are almost unanimous that Soviet science is on a par (at least) with the best Western endeavors. Moreover, the Soviet now turns out more scientists and technicians than the United States. Such concentration on research could give the Soviet a lead in innovations for industrial and military purposes.

Such observations, of course, must be qualified by considerations much less favorable to the Soviet Union. In any case the attained rate of growth cannot be projected with assurance far into the future. The USSR has been notably unsuccessful in raising agricultural output; and it is by no means certain that curtailment of consumption, on which their high rate of savings and investment depends, can continue indefinitely. Nevertheless, for the time now under consideration it will be prudent to forecast a rate of growth in the Soviet Union substantially higher than in the United States.

This is likely to have two consequences for our security situation in Southern Asia. In the first place, this rate of growth attained by a communist society greatly impresses political leadership in countries in which economic development has become the major objective. In the second place, it permits the Soviet Union, while maintaining a high level of military expenditures, to divert voluminous resources to the promotion of development elsewhere if it thinks such diversion will pay off. In the United States, foreign assistance programs must compete on decidedly unfavorable terms with military expenditures for the limited supply of tax revenue. In the Soviet Union this competition takes place under quite different auspices.

## Loosening of the bipolar power blocs

At present it is foolhardy to speak with assurance of the second change that might affect the current reassessment of foreign aid programs—a loosening of ties among countries on both sides of the iron curtain. Within the Soviet orbit since the death of Stalin there has appeared to be a progressive relaxation of totalitarian controls, accompanied by a growing area of independence for at least certain of the satellite states. This developement was harshly interrupted by the Soviet repression in Hungary. It is too early to say whether this heralds a partial return to Stalinism and, if so, what the repercussions may be both inside the Soviet orbit and out.

On this side of the iron curtain the relaxation of Soviet controls was obviously encouraging a movement away from the system of alliances built up after the Korean War. It also led to questioning the assumptions on which these alliances in particular and United States security policy in general were based. Pressure for reduction of defense expenditures has been growing in Western Europe. Nehru, the chief spokesman of the Asian neutrals, has repeatedly argued that developments in the Soviet bloc demonstrate the futility, or worse, of anticommunist alliances. And in the face of Soviet developments our continued emphasis on military aid is coming to be viewed in many parts of the world as evidence of incorrigible warmongering.

Along with these consequences—and in part encouraged by them— cleavages among the countries of the Free World have widened rapidly. No doubt Nasser's version of Pan Arabism would have developed regardless of events in Russia, but it is questionable whether he would have gone as far as he has toward dependence on Soviet support if Stalinism had continued unabated. And it is difficult to believe that France and Britain would have undertaken their Suez adventure if the danger of Russian aggression had not seemed to them to be substantially abated. French difficulties in North Africa, the continued tension between Pakistan and India and Afghanistan, the reaction of the Baghdad Pact countries to events in Egypt, and persistent opposition in Africa and Asia to present and former European colonial powers—all provide further evidence of growing divergence of interest.

Following the impact on world opinion of the Korean War, it might have been possible for the United States to conceive of a security policy to unite most of the countries of the Free World into a system of collective defense. It no longer seems possible. The Soviet reaction to events in Hungary and elsewhere may be sufficiently threatening to recement the NATO alliance, but elsewhere in the Free World other interests and considerations seem likely to motivate national actions. At the very least these changes promise to make the adaptation of foreign aid programs to our security interest a much more complex problem than it has hitherto seemed.

## The emergence of Communist China

The emergence of China as a great Asiatic power and a possible new competitor in the struggle for coexistence is a third development that is changing substantially the character of our security problem. Since Korea, the Chinese threat has been viewed by the United States as almost exclusively military. This view has heavily colored our attitude toward diplomatic recognition and the admission of China to the United Nations. This threat, no doubt, continues to exist and may continue to justify our extensive programs of military aid and defense support in Korea, Formosa, Japan, the Philippines, Vietnam and Thailand. But the economic development of China also poses another threat that impinges to some extent on these countries and to an even greater extent on the uncommitted countries of Southern Asia.

China is the first Asiatic nation to embrace communism and apply totalitarian methods to the promotion of economic development under conditions similar to those existing elsewhere on the continent. The example of China will inevitably have an enormous impact in Southern Asia. Although most of the countries there are currently led by men imbued with Western ideals of liberty and democracy, aversion to the totalitarian methods of communism is substantially less intense in peoples recently emerged from colonial and earlier feudal auspices than in the democratically conditioned West. If China can accomplish a sharp rise in per capita income, the harshness of the methods may be overlooked. The unfavorable ratio of population to resources and the extremely low level of per capita income from which China starts make the problem of economic development very difficult, but the indications are that substantial progress is in the making.

# Economic development in underdeveloped areas as a United States security objective

It has been the contention of the preceding sections that United States foreign aid programs since the war have in the main been supported by the government and people because of a conviction that these programs have contributed to American security. The character and amounts of future aid programs will also be mainly determined by these considerations. But it is a disastrous mistake to identify security with military preparedness. This is particularly true in a period in which, in addition to the threat of war, there is emerging the possibility of a silent, but no less intense struggle by political, economic and ideological means, for the allegiance of people everywhere.

## The relation of security interests to economic development

Our security interests properly include not only the maintenance of peace but the promotion of a world order in which if countries are not aligned with us they at least will not be aligned with our potential enemies. Despite the fact that our trade with South and Southeast Asia is small and the opportunities for mutually beneficial investment seem limited, what happens there concerns us deeply. The economies of South Asia may not be complementary with our own, but they are complementary with the economies of our Western European allies and, increasingly, with the economy of the Soviet Union. Currently the exchange of European manufactures for the raw materials of South and Southeast Asia is a part of world trade on which our allies heavily depend. A large-scale shift in the economic relations of South and Southeast Asia from western Europe to the Soviet Union could have profound economic and political consequences.

From the purely strategic point of view the importance of Asian space presumably does not need to be argued. These are relatively short-run interests. But South and Southeast Asia now contain a quarter of the population of the world and may, with economic development, embrace a much larger share of the world's economic resources than now. In the longer run, therefore, our relations with that area could well become a matter of vital concern. Today we are primarily interested in the effects of developments in South and Southeast Asia on our relations with the Soviet powers. Tomorrow we may be confronted with a different alignment.

## Economic development and the new nationalisms

Most of the uncommitted countries are in areas usually called underdeveloped. Having shaken off the bonds of colonial dependence, many have turned the fire of their recently acquired nationalism to the promotion of economic development. Mistakenly or not, they are inclined to attribute their present lamentably low standards of living to colonialism. They tend to view with a jaundiced eye any strings attached to foreign assistance that may suggest a period of continued tutelage.

In qualification of these statements it should be said that not all underdeveloped countries are passionately devoted to economic development and not all political interests in areas in which there are popular demands for development are willing to yield to these demands. In the Middle East, Arab nationalism puts victory over Israel and successful opposition to Western influence several notches above economic development in its scale of values. It may well be that nothing within the realm of foreign economic assistance would change these attitudes. In other countries political power in the hands of feudal rulers may frustrate for a long time to come pressure for economic development building up from below.

Nevertheless, the pressures are there, and in many countries political power is in the hands of governments willing to give economic development top priority. The problem is of vast dimensions, because some 65 per cent of the Free World's people live in underdeveloped areas stretching over most of Asia, the Near East, Africa and Latin America. Perhaps these economic "aspirations of the peoples of the underdeveloped world are a new imperative of world politics, a force that cannot be ignored in considering the security and leadership of the United States in world affairs."[1]

There are mounting popular aspirations for economic development in the underdeveloped areas of the world, and in certain countries these aspirations have found expression in governments dedicated to the promotion of economic growth. Admitting this is so, how does this fact relate to American security interests and what do we do about it? A familiar reply is that if means cannot be found within the framework of popular government to bring about a substantial increase in per capita incomes and the prospects of continued economic growth, these countries will turn to communism. If, on the other hand—so the argument runs—sustained economic growth can be brought about with assistance from the United States and the West, there is every prospect of political power remaining in the hands of popular governments that, if not oriented toward the West, will at least be neutral.

The problem is not so simple. In certain underdeveloped countries the prospects for economic development in the sense of increasing per capita income, under present political regimes, are highly dubious— with or without foreign assistance. In these countries one of the possibilities is the growth of communist influence. Other possibilities are continued political instability and the emergence of political dictatorship of a noncommunist type. In some countries prospects for economic growth are favorable. It does not necessarily follow that democratic government will thereby be strengthened and communist influence will decline.

The complexity of the problem may be illustrated by looking briefly at the current situation in those countries in Southern Asia that have recently attained independence: Indonesia, Burma, Ceylon, India, and Pakistan.

## Indonesia

Per capita incomes in Indonesia are still substantially below pre- war. Even so, the country will be fortunate if over the next few years these incomes can be sustained at present levels. Since the war Indo- nesia has received some $300 million in economic and technical as- sistance from foreign governments. A substantial part of this, includ- ing nearly the whole $130 million from the United States, has been used for rehabilitation rather than development. Although some foreign private investment continues, mainly in oil properties, this is partially offset by the capital disinvestment occurring on other foreign prop- erties, mainly Dutch. Domestic investment is assumed to be less than

---

[1]Quotation from draft statement of the International Sub-Committee of the Committee for Economic Development, " A Program for Economic Development Assistance."

5 per cent of national income; and of this, public investment accounts for about half. The almost complete lack of an entrepreneurial class and the gross inexperience of the Civil Service (the Dutch did not follow the British practice of training the local population in the exercise of administrative responsibilities) handicap the effective investment of even this small volume of domestic savings. The Indonesian government has been deeply divided on the direction of the development program and on the question of reliance on foreign assistance. Moreover its attention has been largely engrossed by the maintenance of order. That the economic situation is not worse is due primarily to the fact that a very high percentage of economic activity is in agriculture and cottage industry. The peasants and local artisans keep going in traditional ways regardless of what happens in Djakarta.

The wealth of Indonesian natural resources makes it probable that a sensible development program, heavily financed from abroad, could bring about a substantial and a sustained growth in per capita incomes. This, however, presupposes political stability and, in view of administrative inexperience, considerable foreign assistance both in shaping and in executing a development program. But political stability is lacking, and the Indonesian government has shown itself unusually sensitive to anything that suggests strings or conditions attached to aid from the West. In 1952 a watered-down Mutual Security Administration agreement negotiated with the Indonesian government led to the fall of that government. Although the International Bank has extended a credit of $100 million to Indonesia for development purposes, the use of the credit has been handicapped by the opposition of the Indonesian government to technical surveys deemed by the Bank essential to a sensible investment program.

The United States Technical Cooperation Mission is spending about $7 to $8 million a year in Indonesia, and a capital assistance arrangement is currently being negotiated by the International Cooperation Administration. At the same time the Indonesian government has exchanged letters with the Soviets looking toward a $100 million Soviet credit; and the trade agreement with Red China, which to date has been dormant, seems to be in process of implementation. Regardless of the amount and source of foreign assistance, however, a substantial increase in per capita incomes in Indonesia awaits political stability, a development program which the Indonesian government can and will support,[1] and a larger reservoir of private and public managerial competence. It is unlikely that the government would accept either from the Soviets or the United States the technical and administrative assistance necessary to the effective use of a large foreign aid program. The natural-resource base for sustained economic growth is present, but the political and administrative requirements are lacking. Meanwhile com-

---

[1] A development program has now been approved by the Cabinet and will shortly be placed before the Indonesian legislative assembly.

munist strength is growing somewhat. But an alternative to communism may well be a prolongation of the current instability.

## Burma

The situation in Burma in some respects resembles that in Indonesia. Burma has a very favorable ratio of natural resources to population and on the eve of independence had a large export potential in several commodities in world demand, including rice, oil, teak, tin and tungsten. However, she has not been able to restore per capita incomes to much more than 85 per cent of the pre-war level. The following factors appear to be mainly responsible for the continued unsatisfactory levels of consumption: (1) the necessity of diverting large resources to putting down revolt and maintaining order; (2) the almost complete lack, as in Indonesia, of an entrepreneurial class and experienced public administrators; (3) the premature nationalization of certain economic activities, in particular the international rice trade; (4) a substantial withdrawal of foreign capital and know-how; and (5) the undue emphasis in Burma's development program on a few spectacular industrial installations rather than on expansion of food, textiles and other necessities.

Currently the Burmese national income appears to be increasing at the very satisfactory rate of about 5 per cent a year, but this must be interpreted in the light of recovery from the very low level of some 50 per cent of pre-war to which national income had been reduced in 1949 and 1950. In all respects save managerial experience and competence the conditions for economic development in Burma are good. The natural resource base per capita is large, and the population is increasing at a rate of only 1.3 per cent per annum—substantially less than the 2 per cent rate in Indonesia and the 2.5 per cent rate in Ceylon. Domestic savings in Burma have been estimated at 15 per cent of national income, which, as the highest rate in Asia, compares favorably with savings rates in the West. Burma's export potential is large enough to permit foreign exchange earnings adequate to support a very sizeable development program. But, perhaps even more than in Indonesia, *the* limiting factor to economic development is lack of entrepreneurial and managerial competence.

Until recently, Burma has shown an almost pathological resistance to foreign assistance. Neither capital nor technical assistance from the United States government has been acceptable, although American engineers and economists have been employed by the Burmese government to assist in development planning. This attitude, however, seems in process of change. Burma has recently received a technical mission from the Soviet Union and has been carrying through a trade agreement exchanging rice and other raw materials for imports of Russian development goods. This trade agreement has apparently worked very much to the disadvantage of Burma, and the Burmese are somewhat disillusioned by such barter agreements. Last year the United States government purchased $1 million of Burmese rice for delivery to

India and Pakistan in order, in part, to relieve the pressure for further sales to the Soviet Union. Currently ICA is negotiating a $20 million program of capital assistance to Burma. Foreign assistance to Burmese development from all sources, however, has been small; and despite some evidence of change, Burma is unlikely to accept the kind of managerial and technical assistance that would make a really effective development program feasible. The 1956 elections produced a substantial gain in communist representation, but whether this has any long-run significance is by no means clear.

## Ceylon

Per capita incomes in Ceylon have been, except for Malaya, higher than elsewhere in Southern Asia. The main reason for this has been the development, by foreign enterprise and capital, of a plantation agriculture oriented principally to the export of tea and rubber. The course of political events since Ceylon acquired independence has jeopardized this investment. Capital is not being replaced and it is doubtful, if full account is taken of foreign withdrawals, whether there is currently any net investment in process. At the same time, owing to the phenomenal success of the anti-malarial campaign, the rate of population growth is among the highest in the world. The United States has a small technical assistance program in Ceylon, with expenditures currently running at about $5 million a year. Ceylon has marketed substantial quantities of one of her two main exports, rubber, in China, but to date has received no Soviet capital or technical assistance. The country badly needs technical assistance in formulating, executing and probably, because of private capital withdrawal, in financing a development program; but the anti-western orientation of the present government suggests that such assistance might not be acceptable, on practicable terms, from the United States or from anywhere else.

## Pakistan

The basic difficulty in Pakistan is continued political instability and the fact that no government has emerged as yet willing to look for popular support on the basis of an effective development program. The current economic situation is well summarized in a recent statement by the able Chairman of the National Planning Board, Zahid Hussain:

Population is growing fast while food production is stationary if not deteriorating. A poor or even a medium harvest tends to create famine or near famine conditions in large areas. The country's foreign exchange earnings are barely sufficient for importing essential consumer goods, raw materials, fuels, and replacement parts. For development goods we are dependent on foreign loans and aid. This dependence becomes complete and hurtful to national self-respect in periods of poor harvests. The incomes per capita are very low and leave small margins for expenditure on improvement and development of productive capacity. The defense services consume a disproportionately large proportion of national resources. This situation will not improve unless the Government and the people dedicate themselves to development.

The natural resource base in Pakistan is substantially less favorable than in Indonesia and Burma. The rate of domestic savings is low— probably about 5 per cent of national income. And with her heavy dependence on exports of jute and cotton, Pakistan's foreign exchange prospects are poor. On the other hand, the governmental services, inherited from the British, are substantially better than the average in Southern Asia; and there is a growing reservoir of private managerial competence. Given substantial capital, foreign exchange and technical assistance, Pakistan has the capacity for economic growth. The United States has a military aid program in Pakistan; and economic assistance, mainly under the heading of defense support, amounts to about $100 million a year. The country is probably somewhat less allergic to foreign advice and technical assistance than most others in Asia. With adequate government backing of the development program, and continued United States assistance of about the current magnitude, a substantial growth in per capita incomes is possible.

## India

Among those countries in South Asia who have won independence since the war, India is the only one to achieve anything like success in economic development. National income increased 18 per cent during the First Five-Year Plan; and while some part of this increase is attributable to better than normal harvests, the record is still good. The Second Five-Year Plan proposes a further increase of 25 per cent. The achievement of these targets may require somewhat more than five years, but there is every indication that there will be a substantial increase in national and per capita income. The primary reason for this success is a stable government enjoying the support of the people in a single-minded devotion to the process of economic development.

The United States contribution to India's economic development has been small. Our Technical Cooperation Mission operates at the level of about $70 million a year. We have made ''wheat loans'' to India and are currently negotiating a sizeable program ($340 million) of surplus crop disposal. This effort is currently matched in magnitude and probably overshadowed in its political impact by Soviet credits and technical assistance, discussed in the next section. The Soviet program of technical assistance in Southern Asia concentrates heavily in India. The International Bank has made loans to India totalling $214 million, and a small flow of private investment continues from the West. The foreign exchange requirements of the Indian Second Five-Year Plan, over and above expected foreign exchange earnings, are large—of the order of $3-$400 million a year. India can probably use these amounts effectively, and it is quite possible that they will be obtained from one source or another.

## Southern Asia in summary

In summary it can probably be said that while there are strong popular sentiments for improved standards of living in all, India is the only country that to date has shown itself capable of producing a sustained increase in per capita incomes. Pakistan has a feasible development program and an ally willing and able to pour in large amounts of capital and technical assistance but has not yet found a government capable of getting this program off the ground. Indonesia and Burma have rich natural resources. However they lack the private and public managerial competence to devise and administer a development program and thus far are apparently unwilling to accept assistance from abroad on the only terms that would make it feasible to extend a large amount of assistance. Because of governmental attitudes to foreign capital and enterprise and because it is confronting a nearly unmanageable rate of population increase, Ceylon seems to be in process of losing the advantage in per capita incomes it has hitherto held over most of Southern Asia.

Despite the somewhat pessimistic current outlook for economic development in Southern Asia, the area could use substantially larger amounts of foreign technical and capital assistance than it is now receiving. Furthermore, if the United States administers its foreign aid programs in underdeveloped countries with less regard for immediate political advantages than it has sometimes shown since the Korean War and with greater concern for our longer-run interests, there is a reason to believe that resistances to the technical and managerial advice necessary to the effective use of foreign aid may, in time, be overcome.

If the economies of Southern Asia are to develop rapidly, increased amounts of foreign capital and technical assistance are necessary. Dependence on foreign investment was characteristic of most of the areas of economic growth in the nineteenth century, including the United States. There are strong reasons for believing that the dependence of Southern Asia economies is substantially greater. The foreign exchange component of development expenditures is probably very much higher in all Southern Asian countries than it was in United States investment early in the nineteenth century. Furthermore the difference in technological knowledge and competence between, say, Britain and the United States in the early nineteenth century was very much less than the current difference between even India and the United States.

## The role of private investment

The foreign investment in the United States and in the Western Hemisphere during the nineteenth century was private investment. This flow of investment funds frequently carried with it indispensable technical competence and knowledge. A dollar of foreign private investment in Southern Asia is worth two or three dollars of foreign government assistance to the general economic development of the area. Nevertheless, apart from investment in exportable raw materials—predominantly oil—the foreign private contribution to general economic development in Southern Asia is going to be small. Southern Asian markets for many of the products that foreign enterprises might produce locally are undeveloped; various governmental policies in Asia are inimical to private enterprise both domestic and foreign; yields on investment in the United States and Western Europe are currently high and consequently the incentive to invest abroad is small; and, finally, a very large fraction of the investment now required in Southern Asian development programs is in public utilities, transport and public services, which lie outside the normal channels of private investment. Although time and space to develop these points are lacking, their import leads one to the view that, if foreign capital and technical assistance is to be made available to assist economic development in Southern Asia, a substantial fraction must be in the form of governmental loans or grants.

## *The need for effective internal institutions*

Enough has been said to make it clear that foreign capital and technical assistance is only one of the conditions necessary to economic growth. Furthermore it is a condition that cannot be effectively satisfied without a concomitant evolution of internal institutions. William Lockwood's comments on the process of economic development in Japan are pertinent throughout Asia: "No nation can simply import the Industrial Revolution from abroad, uncrate it like a piece of machinery and set it in motion. . . . In the traditional East, as formerly in the West, the Industrial Revolution requires a revolution in social and political arrangements no less than in production technology."

Nevertheless, foreign capital and technical assistance *is* one of the indispensable conditions of economic growth in Asia, and the necessary social and political adaptations required for its effective use are, though falteringly, underway.

If it is true that " the aspirations of the people of the underdeveloped world are a new imperative of world politics," it is not clear how this imperative, as expressed in the aspirations of the 600 million people of Southern Asia, is going to be met. Should we undertake a much larger program of economic development assistance and, if so, what could we expect to gain from it? Before attempting an answer to this question it may be useful to consider briefly the Soviet trade and investment programs in this area.

## Soviet economic penetration in Southern Asia

Earlier in this paper it was pointed out that the Soviet Union and, to a lesser extent certain of the European satellites and China, are in a

85

position to undertake substantial programs of capital investment and technical assistance in the underdeveloped areas of the world. National income in the Soviet Union is increasing at a rate of $8-10 billion a year, and the increase is largely in the form of the industrial equipment and manufactured products required in the development programs of these areas. Furthermore, the failure of Russian agricultural output to expand creates a demand for the imports that raw-material producing countries can supply. Finally the extent of training facilities in the Soviet Union, the current output of technicians, and the ability of a totalitarian society to direct their employment make the provision of competent technical assistance a relatively simple matter.

## The volume of Soviet activity

The increasing size of Soviet capital and technical assistance programs in the Middle East and in Southern Asia is making it clear that the Soviet Union not only has the capacity but now considers it to be in her interests to undertake such programs. In India, Russia has financed a steel mill, oil drilling operations, and pharmaceutical plants. India has recently announced a new Soviet credit of $126 million for other development projects. Substantial numbers of Soviet technicians and a training program for Indians in Moscow have accompanied these credits. A loan of $100 million, partly for arms but mainly for public utility and transportation development, has been made to Afghanistan. Indonesia is in process of negotiating a Soviet credit of $100 million, and Burma has accepted substantial technical assistance. A very large credit has been extended to Egypt for rearmament; lesser credits have gone to other Arab countries.

Altogether the Soviet Union and its satellites may have advanced during the last three years approximately $1 billion to the countries of the Middle East and Southern Asia.[1] In addition to credits and technical assistance, trade agreements between Russia and China and various of the Southern Asian countries have provided for the exchange

[1] There are no very firm figures on the amount of Soviet-bloc credits extended since 1954 to the countries of the Middle East and Southern Asia, and the figure of $1 billion indicates merely a general order of magnitude.

The Staff Study of the Senate Committee on Foreign Relations, "Soviet Technical Assistance," (1956) reports, "An incomplete compilation by the Department of Commerce of Soviet credits to non-Soviet bloc countries shows specific items totaling $436.6 million." Secretary of State Dulles testifying before the Senate Foreign Affairs Committee on the Mutual Security Act of 1956, estimated "Soviet economic and technical assistance projects to free countries at approximately $600 million."

Since the date of these reports reliable sources have indicated additional credits of several hundred millions. As far as is known, no one has attempted to break this total down into estimated annual rates of expenditure.

of development goods against exports of food and agricultural raw materials.

## Possible Soviet motivations

These developments represent a rather startling change from former Soviet policy. They can only be explained on the assumption of a rather drastic reversal of Soviet views on how best to promote their interests in underdeveloped areas. In Stalin's day the predominant pattern of foreign relations was, on the one hand, the securing of military control of countries within the Soviet orbit and, on the other, the subversion of governments outside the Soviet orbit through the activities of local Communist parties. Currently we are witnessing the development of some degree of independence among the satellites and in Southern Asia. In the short run this may well strengthen rather than weaken the existing noncommunist governments. How is this shift in attitude to be explained?

In the first place, it should be recognized that these arrangements do not cost the Soviet countries very much. The trade agreements are straight barter deals, and the available evidence suggests that the terms of exchange are highly favorable to these countries. The capital assistance is in the form of loans, rather than grants. These are payable in goods or in local currencies, which are acceptable to the Soviets because they need the materials Asia can export. Nevertheless these are something other than straight business transactions. The length of payment, the interest charges, and the quantities involved suggest a noneconomic motivation; and the political interest is confirmed by the geograhical direction of these investments.

It is widely supposed that a primary explanation of Soviet economic penetration in Southern Asia is the facilitation of subversive activities, perhaps in cooperation with local Communist parties. This is almost certainly not so. The governments of Southern Asia, by and large, are severe with their local Communist parties and show little hesitation in using force to suppress subversive activities. Soviet trade, investment and technical assistance programs, like our own, operate through the machinery of the governments involved. Any evidence that governmental activities were being sabotaged with or without the cooperation of local Communist parties would quickly lead to the termination of these programs. As a matter of fact, the available evidence suggests that Soviet technicians in Southern Asia behave with scrupulous rectitude and eschew contacts with local communists as they would the plague. On balance it appears that Soviet development programs will hamper rather than help the activities of domestic communism in its struggle for power. Insofar as these programs promote development, they tend to increase the stability of existing governments, and an obvious failure would certainly not enchance communist prestige in Southern Asia.

87

## The dangers involved

There is some danger that large and continuing Soviet trade and investment activities may make the recipient countries so dependent that the dependence can, at some stage, be used for political purposes. This may have happened already in Afghanistan. It seems to have happened in Egypt, Syria and Jordan; but here the dependence is not on assistance for economic development but on a flow of arms to promote political ambitions in the Middle East. In the countries of Southern Asia, Soviet trade and investment programs might over time create such a reliance on the iron curtain countries for markets, sources of capital, spare parts and technical assistance that political leverage could be exerted. But this seems unlikely. The trade relations of these countries are still overwhelmingly with the West, and the West will probably continue to remain a highly important if not the principal source of capital and technical assistance.

The chief threat posed by the current Soviet economic policy in Southern Asia would appear to be the strong stimulus it may give to a predisposition to look to the Soviet Union and China as the prime exponents of economic development in underdeveloped areas. The governments of most of these countries are in the hands of elitists who, though mainly educated in the West, are too far removed in their attitudes and experiences from the mass of their fellow countrymen to be much influenced by the sentiments of a popular, grass roots democracy. In general they have tended to date to be rather pragmatic in their approach to problems of economic development, rejecting with equal firmness doctrinaire free enterprise and partisan communism. A rather ill-defined brand of democratic socialism tends to be put forward as the official doctrine in Southern Asian countries. However the problem of bringing about a rapid rate of development through a thoroughly democratic political process encounters difficulties in largely illiterate peasant societies wedded to traditional practices and attitudes inimical to the changes inevitable in a developing economy. In these circumstances there is always the possibility that totalitarian methods could move people about expeditiously and extract from the population the public funds needed for an accelerated development program. The Soviet Union and China have shown how it can be done; and the existence of large trade, investment and technical assistance missions in Southern Asia may not only facilitate the learning process but promote the desire. The possibility of totalitarianism from above seems in many ways to be a greater threat than communism from below.

While admitting this possibility, it should be observed that the Soviet view of the political consequences of their economic intervention in Southern Asia must be about as obscure as our own. This intervention may promote a turn toward communism either from above or from below. On the other hand, if economic development is greatly assisted by Russian capital and technical assistance, it may well lead to a perpetuation of the present political situation and strengthen the hands of those who want to achieve economic development by democratic means. There may be reason to believe that "reassessments" of foreign aid programs will become as familiar a feature of the political landscape in Soviet Russia as in the United States.

One final word needs to be said about Soviet economic penetration in Southern Asia. The Soviet program seems in many respects better designed than our own to accomplish a favorable impact and to avoid unfavorable political repercussions. The Soviet loans provide for long periods of amortization, bear an extremely low interest rate—usually 2 or 2 1/2 per cent—and are repayable in goods or local currency. In extending both loans and technical assistance there seems to be little disposition to question the use to which they will be put. The assumption seems to be that the receiving country knows best what it wants and needs. No doubt this procedure leads, in countries without a carefully prepared development program, to a misuse of resources. But it avoids any taint of "strings," intervention, or dictation. On its face it is a straight business proposition, and the attendant propaganda plausibly describes it as mutually beneficial. Furthermore, loans and technical assistance contracts are invariably negotiated by high-level Russian officials with a maximum of fanfare. If the objective of current Russian economic policy in Southern Asia is to promote the view that the Soviet Union and China not only hold the secret to rapid economic development but are anxious to share their know-how, the means seem well adapted to the ends.

## United States assistance to economic development

American government loans and grants to the countries of the Middle East and Southern Asia for technical and economic development assistance are currently small: $200 - $300 million a year. Is it in our interest that the level of this assistance be increased? If so, under what conditions? As we have seen, the answer must take into account a number of considerations.

United States military expenditures are on the increase, and a proposed expansion of economic development assistance will have to compete with these expenditures for the taxpayer's dollar. How does economic assistance to underdeveloped areas stack up against, say, a needed expansion in military air transport in a security program designed to meet the threats that confront us? Should we attempt both?

The prospects for economic development in a number of countries in the area are currently not very good, with or without foreign assistance. Continued political disorder and the failure of certain governments to devise a sensible development program or to take the steps necessary to execute such a program make a substantial increase in per capita incomes improbable. Should we withhold technical and economic assistance, at least until these governments "put their house in order," on the ground that some substantial prospect of economic growth is a necessary condition to those political developments that alone justify our concern?

The relationship between economic growth and political trends is obscure, even in those countries in which growth prospects are good. Are we to assume that economic development assisted by our government grants and loans will eventually promote political stability and strengthen democratic institutions? Should we therefore continue to extend assistance regardless of what appears to be the course of political development in the interval? If we are not to do this, what kind of political development would justify a discontinuance of an assistance program?

## Some key questions

The impact of current Soviet investment, technical assistance and trade programs in various countries in Southern Asia, particularly India, is large. Does this argue for an increase or decrease in the magnitude of our programs or for any change in the form or terms of these programs?

The United States has military pacts with Turkey in the Middle East, and with Pakistan and Thailand in Southern Asia. If the security threat is held to justify a continuation of these arrangements, how does this affect a program of economic development assistance in the area? Can we afford to be more generous to "neutralist" countries than to our own allies?

The foreign policies of various countries, notably Egypt, Syria and Jordan, are definitely inimical to United States interests and those of our closest allies. Are we to extend economic development assistance to these countries in the hope that we may encourage a change in political attitudes? If not on these grounds, then what considerations might lead us to extend assistance?

The list of questions could no doubt be extended. It is sufficiently long to indicate that we are confronted with a complex problem of many facets. Currently the extreme views of appropriate United States policy with respect to economic development assistance are represented on the one hand by Professors Millikan and Rostow's *A Proposal: Key to an Effective Foreign Policy*, and on the other by a paper of Professor Z. Brzezinski, "The Politics of Underdevelopment" (*World Politics*, October, 1956). Both papers approach the problem essentially from a security point of view and ask what course of action is in the American interest. Millikan and Rostow argue the primacy of economic development and support a large new program of private and public capital and technical assistance. The United States and other capital exporting countries would participate up to the limit of the underdeveloped areas' capacity to absorb this assistance. While recognizing that economic development is not a sufficient condition for political stability and the growth of democratic institutions, they do feel that is is a necessary condition. They are vastly more optimistic than Brzezinski that a proper economic foreign policy as they define it could advance the political and security interests of the United States in the non-Soviet world.

Brzezinski argues the primacy of political development and holds that there is little or nothing the United States can do through foreign aid programs to change the course of political developments in Southern Asia, which, he thinks, is running strongly in the direction of communism. The gist of his argument is that political leadership in Southern Asia is in the hands of "elitist" groups resentful of the West because of their recent colonial past and ambitious to emulate western power and economic strength; that in communism they will tend to find the political instruments best suited to their task; and that the social "distance" of the leaders from the masses together with the embryonic character of local democratic institutions, will make the use of totalitarian methods more acceptable to Asian than to Western European governments. Thus, "The moment may have arrived for a radical shift from the position of an active external 'doer' (so characteristic of United States policy since the great success of the Marshall Plan) to that of a sympathetic observer, willing to engage in such activities as will benefit both us and the Asian without exacerbating the presently unfavorable trends."

These contrasting points of view neatly bracket the problem. It may well be that the "solution" is somewhere in between.

## The Millikan-Rostow proposal

The Millikan-Rostow proposal is based on an imaginative and persuasive analysis of the state of economic development, the aspirations of the underdeveloped areas, and of American interests in these areas, with which this writer largely agrees. However the relationship between economic development and political behavior is not by any means as close as is tacitly assumed. Consequently it is doubtful that a long-range commitment to economic development regardless of political behavior would be or should be acceptable either to Congress or to the American people.

The essence of the proposal is a long-term (initially five years) commitment by Congress to supply from $10 - $12 billion in additional capital and technical assistance to economic development, with no political or military strings attached. It would be expected that other capital exporting countries—mainly in Western Europe—might add $2 - $3 billion to this amount. A maximum coordinated use of world agricultural surpluses would be made to promote development without disturbing normal commercial channels. And it is thought that, with concerted effort, an increase of $2 - $2.5 billion in private investment in the underdeveloped areas might be undertaken during this period.

The conditions necessary to the effective pursuit of this program are envisaged by Millikan and Rostow as follows:

91

1. The additional sums envisaged must be large enough to remove lack of capital as a bottleneck to growth, while maintaining the tough criteria of productivity envisaged.
2. There must be no tie between economic aid and military pacts and no explicit political conditions within the Free World beyond the requirement that national development goals be democratically established. An aid program with strings yields satellites, not partners.
3. The plan must look to a long future and envisage a sustained United States effort.
4. There must be a real measure of international contribution and international administration.

Millikan and Rostow want to make maximum use of foreign private investment, agricultural surpluses and the resources of existing agencies such as the Export-Import Bank and the International Bank. But, after the potential of their resources is fully utilized, there will remain a gap of from $1 to $1-1/2 billion a year to be supplied by additional government loans and grants if the "absorptive capacity" of the underdeveloped areas is to be satisfied. The United States would be expected to supply about three-quarters of this.

There is no fault to find with these magnitudes nor with the proposal for a long-term commitment. The magnitude of United States interests in the underdeveloped areas may well be such as to justify a development program of this size; a long-term commitment would greatly increase the effectiveness of United States aid. The quarrel is with the implied direction of development assistance, the conditions under which it is to be extended, and the proposed administrative machinery.

## The concept of absorptive capacity

The direction of aid under this proposal is presumably determined by strict economic considerations—that is, by the ability of various countries to use capital and technical assistance effectively to promote economic development. Although "absorptive capacity" is nowhere precisely defined it presumably means the capacity of investments to produce a persistent increase in national income that, after covering all operating costs, is sufficient to replace the capital and to yield some positive return. This notion of "absorptive capacity" is certainly a great advance over early United Nations proposals to supply to underdeveloped areas whatever capital assistance is needed to raise per capita income by 2 per cent or at some other arbitrary rate. In most of these areas important limitations are imposed by political instability and serious lacks in both private managerial and public administration competence. Factors of this type greatly curtail the ability to use capital assistance effectively.

Nevertheless the standard of "absorptive capacity" for determining the quantity of development assistance presents certain ticklish problems. What is involved is not an estimate of the profitability of investment in a particular project producing goods or services for sale in the market. It is the more difficult problem of establishing a relationship between a development program of some proposed dollar magnitude and the persistent increase in national income expected to result from that program. A large subjective element in such an estimate is unavoidable, and differences of opinion between granting and recipient countries are likely to present serious problems to an international agency charged with establishing a country's "absorptive capacity." The slide rule that might objectively determine this result has not yet been invented.

Furthermore, assuming absorptive capacity to be determined, from what sources is it to be satisfied? Among the contenders will be foreign private investment, dollar loans from the Export-Import Bank and the International Bank, governmental local currency, or "fuzzy" loans, and grants. Under these circumstances it may be difficult to preserve that degree of "hardness" in the provision of capital that the stage of development of a particular country justifies.

Although a precise determination of the absorptive capacity of various countries is difficult, enough is known to guess the probable distribution of assistance were this criterion to be used. In Southern Asia the lion's share would go to India, which has an effective development program well under way. Pakistan, beset by political instability, is currently experiencing difficulty in using the aid now being made available by the United States. In Burma and Indonesia the shortage of administrative capacity indicates a rather long period of low "absorptive capacity." In the Middle East, on the basis of the proposed criterion, Egypt together with Turkey would be the principal claimants for assistance.

If economic development is an end in itself regardless of its effect on the redistribution of power and on political developments, there are good reasons for assisting those who can make best use of the assistance. To countries now floundering on the edge of development, the availability of aid on the basis of performance would be a powerful stimulant to put their houses in order and to qualify for external assistance. On the other hand, political considerations will not and should not be neglected.

## Political considerations and political strings

Are we to furnish economic assistance to Egypt, Syria and Jordan to the limit of their absorptive capacity on the assumption that economic development in these countries will promote the growth of democratic institutions and contribute to peace in the Middle East? On present prospects it would appear that the opposite result would be more likely. There may well be a case for a large program of development assistance in the Middle East but, if so, only as a part of an over-all political settlement. Far from eschewing political "strings," the political settlement is the core of the matter; economic development assistance can, at best, only be an inducement that may facilitate such a settlement.

It also seems that, in a number of countries in the Middle East and Southern Asia, political developments have a dynamic of their own that may be influenced, but not determined, by economic development or foreign assistance to economic development. It is inevitable that these political events be taken into account in any aid program based fundamentally on security considerations. Needless to say a sensible aid program should be well content in most of these countries with a political evolution of a "neutralist" character. In no country can the United States be expected to emerge as a winner in an international popularity contest. But in certain Asian countries there may well be a political evolution that will justify a termination or a drastic change in the direction of economic development assistance.

As a matter of fact the administrative aspects of the Millikan-Rostow proposal would leave the United States free to take these political considerations into account despite their intention to eliminate political "strings" from economic development assistance. Under their proposal the quantity of aid to underdeveloped areas would be determined by international negotiation, with the United States assuming three-quarters of the burden. The claims of the recipients would be determined by an expert staff, presumably attached to the International Bank, on the basis of an assessment of absorptive capacity. But the decision of who is to receive what would be left to the individual donor countries. After arguing the merits of a new international agency to distribute the proposed increased assistance, the authors conclude, "Is it realistic to hope that any United States Congress, even if it accepted the principles advocated in this book, would turn over nearly a billion dollars annually for administration and allocation by a new and untested international organization free of any United States control or accountability? It may be worth testing the realism of this hope; but we are skeptical."

This skepticism seems fully justified. It follows that whatever statement of faith in the primacy of economic development Congress might be willing to make in authorizing a large and long-term development assistance program, the actual administration of funds would inevitably be influenced by political events in the recipient countries. It should be. Although Millikan and Rostow have set forth in effective and persuasive fashion the nature of American interests in the economic development of underdeveloped areas and although they have justified a substantial increase in the amount of United States assistance, the assistance must be provided on a much more selective basis than they are willing to support. This inevitably argues for an aid program substantially more bilateral and less international than they would wish. This conclusion is strengthened when one considers the number of underdeveloped countries in which the United States already has military and defense support programs. Any additional assistance to these countries could sensibly be administered only in conjunction with our existing bilateral arrangements.

## *What development assistance can accomplish*

On the other hand to say with Brzezinski that American assistance to economic development in Southern Asia and elsewhere can have little or no effect on the course of political events almost certainly goes too far in the direction of the primacy of political causation. It is a fact that in most parts of the underdeveloped world popular pressure for economic growth is strong and that democratic or quasi-democratic governments have come to power committed to the promotion of economic development. It is also a fact that most of the prosperous countries in the world that developed during the nineteenth century were heavily dependent on the inflow of foreign capital and technical know-how. Economic development in Southern Asia is at least as dependent on foreign capital and technical assistance, and changes in the climate of private investment have been such as to make it clear that to achieve sizeable totals will require substantial participation by government.

If this assistance is to come from the West, the United States must inevitably be the largest contributor. In countries ripe for economic development, having popularly based governments committed to economic development, there are certainly strong reasons for believing that American assistance could make a substantial contribution to economic growth. Failure to provide such assistance or to abdicate in favor of exclusive Soviet participation, could produce political consequences decidedly unfavorable to our interests.

The answer is neither a large economic program operating without political considerations, nor a program of masterful inactivity, while "waiting for the dust to settle." It is something in between.

## Conclusion

The conclusions of this paper may be summarized in a number of propositions.

1. The Congress of the United States and the American people are unlikely to accept a sizeable, continuing foreign aid program unless convinced that such a program will contribute to our own security.

2. Our security, however, may be endangered not merely by military action or threats of action but by political disturbances in various parts of the world and by realignments favorable to the Soviet bloc in the hitherto uncommited areas of the world.

3. Since the end of the Korean War, and increasingly since the death of Stalin, the security threat has changed. Without minimizing the military danger we must now take account of the Soviet attempt to

extend its influence in these underdeveloped and uncommitted areas by political, economic and ideological means.

4. Relevant to this threat, certain changes since 1950 must be considered in devising a sensible security policy. Among these are: (a) the rate and direction of Soviet economic growth, which has provided the incentive and means for large trade and foreign lending operations; (b) a highly significant change in Soviet foreign policy that has led to the initiation of these operations on a large scale; (c) the emergence of China as a developing Asian economy; and (d) a substantial loosening of ties on both sides of the curtain. The present fluidity of relationships holds dangers of and opportunities for a serious realignment of countries.

5. The Soviet rate of growth and the size and direction of Soviet-bloc trade and lending programs have created "competitive co-existence" in Southern Asia and in the Middle East. The aspirations of Southern Asia run strongly toward economic development. If a satisfactory rate of this development is to be brought about, substantial foreign capital and technical assistance will be required. On the other hand the current prospects for economic development vary widely among these countries, and there is no very certain relationship between economic growth and a specified set of political consequences.

6. The total United States contribution to what can properly be called economic development assistance has, to date, been small. Total American foreign aid expenditures from April 1948 to June 1956 in countries with which we do not have military or assistance programs have been slightly over $1 billion. In the fiscal 1956 we spent $280 million in these countries. If we add to this that part of our economic assistance to military pact countries falling outside the rubric of defense support, no more than 5 per cent of the $60 billion we have expended on foreign aid programs since the war can correctly be called economic development assistance. The relationship between our foreign military and economic development assistance spending reflects an inadequate assessment of the current nature of the security problem.

7. It does not follow, however, that we should now embark on a large program of economic assistance to the underdeveloped areas of the Free World regardless of their location, foreign policies, or prospects of political development.

a). The competition in Congress between military and economic assistance programs for the security dollar suggests that economic development assistance should largely be directed to areas where an effective contribution can be made by such assistance to the security problem, always bearing in mind the need for an up-to-date and appropriately broad concept of our long-term security interests.

b). In certain areas economic development assistance can be justified on security grounds only as a contribution to a basically political settlement. In the absence of such a settlement there should be no aid.

c). The relationship between economic and political development is sufficiently obscure to suggest that it is unwise to commit ourselves to economic development in any country without consideration of political events.

8. What we need is a substantially enlarged but selective program of economic development assistance. In the Middle East very sizeable programs may be justified if they can be made a condition of a satisfactory long-run political arrangement. In Southern Asia effective use can be made of larger assistance than we now supply in all countries except, possibly, Pakistan. The political prospects in all these countries are sufficiently promising to justify such an increase. It seems unnecessary to say that in countries that do not have, or wish to have, military pacts with the United States, any suggestion of political strings in the sense of seeking to buy alliances is stupid. It also seems unnecessary to say that political developments may, at any stage, make it unwise to continue the economic development program.

# 4. The policy background
# for military assistance

by Paul H. Nitze

It will be the purpose of this paper to lay a background for the discussion of certain questions raised by the continued military assistance of the United States to a large number of other countries in the world. Is the magnitude of our effort too big or too small? Is it directed to the right countries? Are the methods of providing military assistance appropriate? What are the purposes of the assistance? Is it proving to be an effective tool to accomplish its purpose? What are the major grand

Paul H. Nitze, president of the Foreign Service Educational Foundation, an affiliate of the School of Advanced International Studies of The Johns Hopkins University, was director of the Policy Planning Staff of the Department of State from 1949 to 1953. His previous positions in the Department of State include those of Deputy Director, Office of International Trade Policy; Deputy to the Assistant Secretary of State for European Recovery Program Coordination; Deputy to the Assistant Secretary of State for Economic Affairs, and Deputy Director of the Policy Planning Staff. During World War II Mr. Nitze was financial director of the Office of the Coordinator of Inter-American Affairs, chief of the minerals and metals branch of the Board of Economic Warfare and the Foreign Economic Administration, and vice chairman of the United States Strategic Bombing Survey. He received a Medal of Merit for his service with the Bombing Survey.

strategy alternatives in which military assistance can play a part? From the political point of view are we overemphasizing or under-emphasizing military assistance?

In recent months we have seen a number of important events which bear on the problems suggested. We have seen the uprising in Hungary and related symptoms of developing unrest behind the iron curtain which may have an important bearing on the nature of the military problems of Europe. We have seen the British-French intervention in Suez following the Israeli attack, and have yet to digest fully the lessons to be learned therefrom. Below the surface are the continuing and still unresolved influences of the further development of new weapons and of military technology.

The philosophy of military assistance has never been very fully debated by the American public. This has in part been due to the classified nature of much of the underlying factual and policy material. But even those who have worked on the policy in the government and have had access to the classified material have not always been able wholly to resolve their policy problems. Involving as they do the interrelation of basic political and military considerations, this is no easy task.

For some time an outside examination of the foundations of our military assistance program has appeared warranted. With recent historic developments such a re-examination seens doubly appropriate.

The focus of this paper will be primarily upon the strategic policy alternatives within which military assistance can be considered as being a potentially effective or ineffective tool of United States foreign policy. The attention given to the tactical details of amounts and methods will be secondary. If one is not clear as to the validity and importance of the purposes of a program, it is difficult to find criteria on which to base judgments as to amounts or methods.

The paper will first summarize the history of our military assistance effort to date. It will then discuss the broad strategic alternatives within which the continuing problem may be viewed, and it will conclude with the application of these considerations to Europe, to the Middle East and to the Far East.

## Historical background

Peacetime military assistance, as a regular and accepted tool of United States foreign policy, can be considered as having begun with the Truman Doctrine and the initiation of the Greek-Turkish aid program in the spring of 1947.

On March 12, 1947, President Truman appeared before the Congress to request a program of large-scale economic and military aid to Greece and Turkey. In his speech the President discussed the broader implications inherent in his request and stated his belief that " it must be the policy of the United States to support free peoples who are resisting attempted subjugation by armed minorities or by outside pressure." Congress responded with the Greek-Turkish aid program, which authorized the expenditure of $400 million dollars up to June 30, 1948.

The Truman Doctrine with the related Greek-Turkish aid program was not an isolated decision. It was the first of a series of decisions in the spring and summer of 1947 which in total represented a major shift in the general orientation of United States foreign policy. Prior to that spring the United States had been reluctant to face up to the responsibilities which the course of history had thrust upon it and which, it was becoming increasingly clear, could be ignored only to our very great peril. During the preceding year it had been demonstrated beyond doubt that we could not expect even that limited collaboration from the USSR which we had obtained during the war, and that we must, on the contrary, count on unmitigated Soviet hostility and unlimited Soviet ambitions for the indefinite future. It had also been demonstrated that the United Nations, in the face of Soviet hostility, had only as much strength and influence as we and other independent nations were prepared to put behind its recommendations. And finally it had been demonstrated that the United Kingdom no longer had the resources and will to take primary responsibility for maintaining the peace against all the widespread and diverse types of mischief of which the Soviet Union was capable. There was no escape from the United States itself tackling the job of building free-world strength, will, and cohesion, burdensome as that job might be.

There followed in rapid succession, after the Truman Doctrine, the Marshall Plan, the new policy toward Germany which led to the formation of the Bonn government, the initiation of our world-wide system of alliances, the Point Four program and military assistance on a world-wide scale.

## The 1949 military assistance program

After the basic decision had been made, in the spring of 1947, to face up to United States responsibilities as the principal world power on whose shoulders the central defense against the Soviet threat must rest, not everything could be tackled at once. It was felt that the most immediate task of policy was in the economic sphere. Europe was on the brink of economic collapse, and without some sort of functioning economic system there would be no foundation upon which to build progress in the political and military spheres. It was decided in the first instance to concentrate on Europe. In Europe the remaining devastation from the war was greatest; the stakes involved seemed to be most important, and the opportunity for getting something done most favorable. The Marshall Plan, with its economic focus and its focus on Europe, was therefore initially given central attention.

The Czechoslovakian coup in February 1948, which owed its success in part to the threatening presence of powerful Russian military forces on the Czech borders, and the Berlin blockade in the summer of 1948 emphasized that economic recovery, if not backed by military capabil-

101

ities, might be insufficient for continuing security. And full economic recovery itself required a degree of confidence in continuing security.

The initial response was the North Atlantic Treaty, which committed United States power, reinforced by our then atomic monopoly, to the defense of Europe. This was essentially a political commitment, not a military program. It was believed, however, that this political deterrent, though of the greatest importance, was not in itself enough. From the standpoint of the Europeans, the prospect of an invasion by the Russians followed by an atomic attack on Russia and an eventual liberation of Europe was not good enough. From the United States point of view there were also serious doubts as to whether an atomic attack, with weapons of the limited power and number then available, could by itself be decisive, and whether liberation of Europe occupied by Russia in the early days of a war would in fact be a feasible operation. As one looked further forward to the time when Russia could be expected to have atomic weapons, the prospects for a successful liberation of an occupied Europe looked dim indeed. With these thoughts in mind it was decided to make a start in assisting Europe to contribute to its own defense and to move toward a position where there might eventually be a prospect of containing a possible Soviet attack before it overran all of Europe.

In the spring of 1949 a Military Assistance Program proposing the authorization of $1.45 billion was presented to the Congress. Of this amount approximately $1.1 billion was allocated to Europe and the balance to other countries, including Greece and Turkey and Korea, the Philippines and Iran.

The strategic implications of the program were not, and perhaps could not be, clearly and precisely thought through. United States military planning officers had made a preliminary estimate of what it would cost to create and equip enough forces to give Europe some prospect of not being overrun in the event of a full-scale Russian attack. These rough and preliminary estimates were of the general order of magnitude of $30 billion just for the equipment and facilities involved and excluding continuing troop pay and maintenance. This was about double the entire Marshall Plan. Even if spread out over a number of years there was no prospect that the European countries could by themselves finance any such effort. It was also unlikely that Congress would appropriate for military assistance sums which would bear any reasonable relationship to the necessary United States component of assistance to such a program. It was finally decided within the State and Defense Departments that approximately $1 billion of United States assistance was the maximum to be asked of Congress for military assistance to Europe during the initial year of the program. The hope was that this assistance, coupled with as great an effort as could be made by the European countries, allowing a clear priority for the targets of the economic recovery program, would at least make a worthwhile beginning in the military field.

The equipment originally made available was largely World War II surplus. Its value was charged against the military assistance program, and the equivalent funds allocated to the Defense establishment for new and more modern equipment for United States forces. A small portion of the original funds requested was for the purpose of assisting the European countries involved to develop their own military equipment production industry. It was hoped that eventually Europe would itself produce the bulk of the equipment needed for its own forces.

It should be repeated that when the original military assistance program was presented to Congress, no one was wholly clear as to its strategic implications. Some in the military establishment thought that the transferring of old equipment and its replacement with new and modern equipment was in any case a good thing in that it strengthened our inadequate United States military position. Some thought that any improvement in Europe's then almost totally defenseless military condition would add to the deterrents against Russian military adventures. Some thought that an improvement in Europe's over-all political tone would come from a shift from complete defenselessness to an inadequate but at least more respectable military posture. A few looked forward to the day when Europe's military forces might really have substantive utility in the event of a Russian attack. And one or two even then foresaw the need to build toward the day when the heavy reliance we were then putting on our atomic monopoly might have to be reduced, either because the Russians had developed an atomic capability of their own or because the international control and regulation of atomic weapons, which it was our policy to promote, had come to pass.

The amounts made available for areas outside of Europe under this initial program were obviously too small to have much impact except as against internal subversion and guerrilla type attack, as in Greece, or against the threat thereof, as in Iran, the Philippines and Korea. They could carry little weight in the over-all stretegic military situation versus either Russia or Communist China.

## Military assistance in subsequent years

The actual amount appropriated by the Congress for fiscal year 1950 was $1.3 billion, and expenditures during that year came to a mere $100 million as against appropriations of $3.9 billion and expenditures of $3.4 billion for nonmilitary assistance programs.

Following the Korean attack in June 1950 the scope and magnitude of the entire program were revised. During the next four years appropriations for military assistance averaged $4.5 billion per year while appropriations for economic, nonmilitary assistance declined to an average of less than $2 billion per year.

Even prior to the surprise attack against the Republic of Korea, the Executive Branch of the United States government had concluded that a substantially increased program of rebuilding the military strength of

103

the United States at home and increasing the defensive strength of our allies was needed. The consolidation of Chinese Communist control over the mainland of China and the explosion by the Russians of an atomic device in the fall of 1949 had been coupled with signs of greatly increased belligerence on the part of the communist leaders. Very great dangers for the security of the entire world, and particularly of the United States, were foreseen for the intermediate-range future if the growing military imbalance between the communist bloc and the rest of the world were permitted to continue unchecked.

It is doubtful whether this conclusion could have been translated into any very important shift in magnitude of effort if the attack against South Korea had not been launched with every evidence of Russian preparation and control. Up to that time few had really believed that the communist leaders would order organized military forces into aggression across a recognized border with complete deception and surprise and in the absence of any substantial provocation. Many had believed that not to maintain a respectable military posture was to run a certain degree of risk. But few believed that Stalin and his henchmen would really put the issue to the test with full ruthlessness and brutality.

The attack against Korea transformed what had been a theory among competing theories into a concrete actuality and may have resulted in a reaction of overcompensation. In any case from the summer of 1950 on, the emphasis on assistance programs which had been primarily economic switched progressively to military. Furthermore, the geographic focus of interest gradually tended to shift from Europe to Asia and, in part, to the Middle East.

## The military assistance program to date

By the end of fiscal 1957 the United States will have expended $18.3 billion in military assistance over an eight-year period. During the first six of these years United States deliveries to its partners included:

|           |                                                    |
|----------:|----------------------------------------------------|
| 40,000    | tanks and combat vehicles                          |
| 1,200     | naval vessels of all types                         |
| 44,000    | artillery pieces                                   |
| 7,000     | aircraft (50% jets)                                |
| 2,000,000 | small arms and machine guns, and billions of rounds of ammunition |

These expenditures and deliveries are not tremendous in relation to expenditures for, and deliveries of, equipment to our own forces. Military assistance expenditures constitute some 7 or 8 per cent of our domestic defense expenditures. But they still represent a substantial investment. What are we getting for this investment? How does what we are getting fit into our military strategy? And how does that military stretegy fit into our over-all policy, what some would call our "grand strategy"?

# The defense of Europe

Something more than half of our military assistance has gone toward strengthening the defense of the European members of NATO. Over 85 per cent of the over-all cost of the European NATO defense build-up has been borne by the European countries themselves. In 1949 their defense expenditures were running at the rate of about $6 billion per annum. By 1955 the rate had risen to approximately $12 billion per annum. A higher proportion, perhaps one third, of the cost of equipment and of common base facilities has been borne by United States military assistance.

In comparison with 1949 there has undoubtedly been a substantial increase in the NATO defense potential. The Mutual Security Program presentation for fiscal 1957 talks of 90 to 100 divisions in varying stages of readiness in 1955, as against 12 divisions in 1949. It refers to 6,000 planes being available as against 400 in the earlier year.

A sober and realistic evaluation of the present NATO European defense capability is difficult to obtain. There is an American Army of approximately 150,000 men in $5\frac{1}{2}$ divisions stationed in Europe; there is a British Army of 80,000 men in 4 divisions; the Belgians have 3 understrength divisions of 32,000 men; the Dutch have one division of 10,000 men; the Canadians and the Danes amount to another. The French division is reported to be nothing more than a series of training cadres. Almost the entire French strength is currently committed to Algeria. The British are proposing some reduction in the forces currently committed to the continent. We know that the German target of a contribution of a 500,000-man force has been cut to 300,000 men and that this force is still in the early stages of recruitment and training.

The American forces are backed up by tactical air forces and by units with atomic cannons and various types of missiles. There has undoubtedly been a very great improvement in the infra-structure and air base back-up for European defense.

But in sum total European defense still rests upon the deterrent power of our Strategic Air Command for the major component of its potential effectiveness. General Gruenther and General Norstad have given us no assurance that the present NATO forces, or those now planned for the future, would be able, even with the support of tactical atomic weapons, to hold a determined Russian attack—not unless Russia itself is very rapidly beaten in the initial phase of a strategic air war in which SAC would be the primary instrument on our side.

Many Europeans question the importance of the military contribution they are now making. Is not the main deterrent provided by SAC? Is it really worthwhile to make what they deem to be heavy sacrifices for forces which may be inadequate to provide a forward defense? If such forward defense as is possible is to be provided by tactical atomic weapons will much be left in Europe if their use has to be invoked? Questions of this kind complicate the political task of European governments in securing the appropriations and manpower necessary for a more certain and flexible defense.

## Defense in the Far East

The next largest component of our military assistance has been directed toward Korea, Taiwan, Vietnam, Cambodia, Thailand, and Laos. Except for Thailand these countries have all suffered from the effects of the communist use of armed force, and all feel themselves to be threatened by the presence of large communist forces on or near their borders.

The Republic of Korea is attempting to maintain a force of twenty divisions, which is far beyond its capacity without outside assistance. Even with our assistance the economic strain has been difficult to manage, and very serious inflation has taken place.

On Taiwan and the offshore islands the Chinese Nationalists maintain a force of some 600,000 men (of which some 400,000 may be effective), which again is far beyond the capacity of Taiwan itself to support.

The new states of Vietnam, Cambodia, and Laos, after the withdrawal of French forces, could not have maintained even the most meager military defense forces without assistance from the United States.

As we reduce the number and effectiveness of United States forces stationed in Japan, an increasing defense burden falls on the Japanese forces now being trained and equipped there. The equipment for those forces has had to come almost entirely from United States inventories.

## Military assistance in other areas

In the Middle East all the nations of the northern tier—Turkey, Iraq, Iran, and Pakistan—are receiving military assistance from the United States. In this area there is at present no communist satellite such as North Korea ready to be used as an instrument for aggression. The principal threat is from Russia herself. It is doubtful that military forces of a magnitude to count significantly in the event of an attack by the USSR can be developed in the Middle East except by Turkey. But even minor elements of local strength add their bit to the general deterrents to Russian ambition and adventurism.

The question of military assistance to the countries of the Middle East not directly adjacent to the USSR is more difficult. It can be argued that the competition in armaments between Israel and the surrounding Arab States leads more to instability than to stability. British, French, and American coordinated control of the arms traffic to this area has seemed desirable in the past and perhaps should again be an objective of policy once the current crisis is surmounted. The Russians have suggested a total embargo on arms shipments to the Middle East but have coupled it with conditions which would leave the area as a whole defenseless.

It is impossible to ignore either the internal or the external political importance of military assistance in this area. Partly because of the breakdown of traditional cultural patterns and a lack of depth of commitment to the new and differing political standards offered by contact with the West, there is a tendency in all these countries for internal political power to gravitate into military hands. In some countries the military act as the strong binding cement of the cummunity and a principal channel through which the transition to the modern world is being made. In other countries internal political power, though in other hands, depends on support of a strong military group. In either case these military men want modern arms and want a military establishment which is regarded with respect by the other countries of the area.

Egypt has demonstrated what can happen if Russia is willing to supply military equipment to these men and we are not. It does not necessarily follow that the politics of a country are long influenced by the source of military equipment. Both Ataturk in Turkey and the Israelis got their initial supplies of military equipment from the Russians and then turned against them politically. It is to be expected, however, that Russia will be prepared to make all the political capital she can out of the desire of the Middle Eastern countries for arms. This is a problem we cannot ignore. By the same token, if intelligently handled, military assistance can make a very considerable contribution to internal political strength and stability. In much of the Middle East and North Africa a principal source of United States presence and influence is through the military.

We also supply military equipment in small quantities to many other countries even though the military threat facing them is extremely remote. These include twelve of the Latin American countries and Ethiopia. The great bulk of military aid to Latin America has been on a reimbursable basis. We procure the equipment for them through our procurement facilities but are subsequently reimbursed by the receiving country. Consideration of obligations flowing from mutual defense treaties and of the political importance of the military in each of these countries make it advisable to give them small amounts of additional grant assistance. The over-all potential military contribution of these countries, though individually small, is not negligible in the aggregate.

## Alternate strategies

A judgment as to whether our current, or future, military assistance programs should be expanded or contracted, or should be changed in emphasis or manner of implementation, can hardly be made apart from a judgment as to the over-all national strategy we should be following. If one believes that United States strategy should be one of unilateral disengagement, of reducing our external commitments, of withdrawal to this hemisphere or to this country, then a number of possible conclusions for the redesign of our military assistance programs become obvious. If one believes that our primary reliance for security should

107

be placed upon our strategic air forces, certain conclusions flow. If one believes that both big and little wars are now impossible and that only nonmilitary techniques of power really count, then other, but perhaps similar, conclusions flow. If one believes, however, that there is both the responsibility and the opportunity to secure a considerable improvement in the international climate within which the United States will have the chance to work out its future, but that this can be done only if we substantially improve the general strength and cohesion of the non-communist world, then still different conclusions as to military assistance become logically necessary.

It is not the purpose of this paper to discuss all the possible issues of our national and foreign policy. It may be useful, in narrowing the field to be covered by the subsequent discussion, to be explicit about certain points on which it is assumed there is general agreement and which are therefore not further debated.

The *first assumption* is that, even though most Americans would prefer to see the external responsibilities of the United States less rather than greater, this cannot be safely accomplished merely by unilateral disengagement and withdrawal. In other words it is assumed that the Russian and communist threat will not go away just because we try to be as nice as possible. Related to this point is the assumption that the obvious difficulties the Russians are having with their satellites is caused, not only by the great extent of their empire and the particular methods by which they run it, but also by the continuing presence and pressure of a vigorous external world which is keeping alive the example and hope of freedom. Indigestion in the Soviet world is therefore not to be obtained by merely turning additional countries and peoples over to the Soviet will.

Further related assumptions are that the military capabilities of the Soviet and of the communist bloc will remain large and varied; that communist intentions toward us will continue hostile for the foreseeable future; and that a comprehensive settlement with the Soviets, involving both outstanding political issues and a workable system for the control and regulation of armaments, is impossible of negotiation or, for one reason or another, is not negotiated. If such an agreement were negotiated and really became effective, an entirely new look at the military assistance problem would obviously be necessary.

The *second assumption* is that nuclear war has not become impossible merely because Russia and the United States both possess large numbers of such weapons. In other words, it is assumed that continuing effort is necessary to provide an effective deterrent to the use of nuclear weapons. The requirements and nature of this effort will be discussed later on.

The *third assumption* is that even if an effective deterrent to nuclear weapons is maintained, there remains a continuing threat that nonnuclear military forces will be used by others to affect the international political world to the disadvantage of our interests. It can be argued that the more thorough mutual deterrence of the use of nuclear weapons becomes, the more probable becomes the resort to lesser weapons.

The *fourth assumption* is that even in the absence of overt military aggression, military capabilities will have an important indirect impact upon international political developments.

Even if one accepts these assumptions and thus narrows the area of possible debate, a considerable range remains of possible alternative strategies for fostering our security. The differences between them are of emphasis or of degree; but such differences may be of vital importance both in determining the nature of the military assistance program which it is wise to adopt and to the effectiveness with which we assure an international climate in which the United States can survive and prosper.

## Primary reliance upon nuclear weapons launched from United States bases

Virtually no voice is raised today in favor of placing no reliance upon nuclear weapons in support of our national security. Few voices are raised in support of scrapping all nonnuclear supports and concentrating solely upon nuclear weapons. The debated issue on which strong and differing views are held is the issue of the relative weight to be placed on nuclear weapons and in what specific contingencies and for what specific purposes we should contemplate their use.

The extreme position, which has wide support in the Air Force and at high levels in the Administration, is that primary reliance for our security should be placed on the availability of the largest and most powerful nuclear weapons. These would be delivered primarily from bases or launching sites in the United States and would be used, if must be, against the enemy in a manner which would destroy not only his forces and installations but also his major centers of industry and population. The supporters of this view acknowledge that not every minor threat to the world's, or even our own, immediate interests would warrant the use or threatened use of such weapons in this manner. They argue, however, that we cannot count on overseas bases, that we cannot afford both to develop an adequate deterrent force from United States bases and also provide forces capable of handling lesser threats to our security. They further say that the main point is to deter the Soviets from launching a major attack which would truly jeopardize our vital interests and which would, if launched, justify our using the most decisive weapons in our arsenal. The lesser threats, they say, are by definition lesser threats and we must absorb the minor losses which may result from not having the capability of meeting them.

On this theory military assistance becomes an operation separated from the hard core of our defense strategy. The advocates of this strategic alternative consider military assistance to be somewhat of a toy which diplomats and the less serious branches of the military

109

services can be permitted to play with in their interesting but not very essential cold war games. But they would tolerate this diversion only to the degree that no real bite is put on our capability to fight the all-out nuclear war from United States bases which they consider to be the only serious element of our military security.

## Primary reliance on nuclear weapons and a world-wide base system

There are those who believe that an adequate nuclear deterrent cannot be maintained by utilizing merely United States bases. They stress the interrelation between defense and offense in nuclear war, the importance of sheer geographic space in organizing an effective defense, and the dispersed and varied base structure necessary to absorb an initial blow and still have an effective retaliatory capability. As long as manned aircraft or missiles of intermediate range are important factors in delivery systems, overseas bases would appear to be essential components of an effective nuclear deterrent.

Some opponents, however, argue that five or ten years from now intercontinental missiles will be available in quantity with the effect of reducing the importance of range and of geographic dispersal. Others argue that missiles launchable from submarines can be developed and this weapons system will be less vulnerable to surprise attack and to political uncertainties than are overseas bases.

The issues raised by this debate involve two considerations which bear on the military assistance program. The first consideration is that of what is to be done to bridge the period until intercontinental or submarine based missiles become available with adequate performance and in adequate numbers. Until such time—and the time itself cannot be precisely estimated—overseas bases remain essential components of a nuclear deterrent adequate to discourage an enemy from gambling on a surprise attack on the United States. The more important question, however, is whether the capability to deter a surprise nuclear attack is all we are seeking from our military establishment.

## The strategy of graduated deterrence

For those who believe that the objects of our foreign policy and of our national defense policy are deeper and more complex than merely deterring a surprise nuclear attack, more complicated strategies come to mind. To them it is important that we have the means, and the will to use those means, to deter, to defeat, or to manage all the various threats to our interests, and the interests of those associated with us, which it seems likely that the enemy may attempt to exploit. To them it also seems self-evident that an all-out nuclear war is something we should attempt to avoid at almost any cost short of dishonor, and that a deterrent is apt to be effective only if one is in fact prepared to use it and the enemy believes that this is so. Starting from these premises they logically conclude that for lesser military threats it is important for us, alone or with allies, to have adequate military capabilities in addition to the nuclear deterrent, without having to invoke the ultimate sanction of full-scale nuclear war.

The principal argument of this strategic concept revolves about the reliance to be placed upon what are called tactical atomic weapons as against nonatomic weapons in handling these lesser threats.

One school is impressed with (a) the potential manpower superiority of the enemy, (b) the greater effectiveness of tactical atomic weapons than their nonatomic counterpart, (c) the great cost of providing protection both against the use of atomic weapons by the enemy and also providing a nonatomic capability, and (d) the political difficulty of getting either our own citizens or those of our allies to support the sacrifices necessary to make the effort involved. Impressed with the great danger of relying solely on strategic nuclear weapons systems, they therefore place heavy emphasis on having precision tactical weapons and mobile ground units to fill the gap.

The other school is impressed with the thought that where military action less than all-out war is conceivable there appear to be strong arguments against the use of atomic weapons of any kind. In most of these situations the primary objectives are political and not solely military. Neither the Russians in Hungary nor the British and French in Suez could possibly have furthered their interests by using atomic weapons, no matter what tactical atomic capabilities they might have had available. It is also dubious that the United States, fighting far from its home bases and dependent on ports and relatively small numbers of airfields for the logistic support of such operations, would have anything to gain from the use of tactical atomic weapons if the enemy also must be presumed to have such weapons.

In summary this school believes (1) that in situations where it can be presumed our side can use tactical atomic weapons without risk that the enemy will use them, political considerations will make their use unwise; and (2) that in situations where it must be presumed that the other side will retaliate with atomic weapons if we use them, nothing is to be gained militarily from their use.

It may very well be that under current conditions the first school has the better of the argument in the concrete case of a presumed communist aggression in Asia backed by mass Chinese Communist forces but only indirectly by the USSR, or in the very unlikely case of a mass attack on Western Europe by the communist Eastern European satellites, only indirectly backed by the USSR. Where the USSR is directly involved it is difficult to see how general nuclear war can be avoided, at least until such time as there has been a considerable increase in the free world's nonnuclear military capabilities. Where neither the USSR nor Communist China is involved, it is difficult to see how the use of tactical atomic weapons would be militarily necessary or politically wise.

111

Under conditions which might be foreseen or created for the future, different conclusions might flow. In the past it has always been presumed that Russia and the Eastern satellites must have a manpower superiority in Europe which can be overcome only by superior weapons technology. Recent symptoms of the depth of satellite unrest in Eastern Europe raise doubts as to whether this must always be so. Russia has a population of some 200 million people, not all of whom are efficient and not all of whom are loyal. The satellite divisions are today certainly unreliable. They may even constitute a net liability to the Russians. Western Europe and North America have a population of some 450 million. It seems absurd to posit that effective manpower superiority must always be on the Russian side. In spite of recent Chinese Communist support for Soviet policy in central Europe, it is not certain that the Chinese Communists must always be counted as an effective ally of the Russians on issues other than Asian.

It is conceivable that the primary reliance on the Strategic Air Command for the essential defense of Europe could be reduced in the future. A considerable reorientation of our military planning with respect to Europe and a substantial increase in nonnuclear defenses, and in military assistance to Europe, would be necessary preconditions.

It is quite possible that developments of modern technology will make it possible to provide an adequate deterrent against surprise nuclear attack at much lower cost than now seems to be necessary. The fall-out effect of two or three hundred large-size nuclear weapons exploded almost at random in the populated sections of the USSR could be expected to produce casualties of over 50 per cent of the total population. It now appears probable that missile systems capable of achieving such a result from widely dispersed launching sites and at speeds that would make a complete defense almost impossible can be provided at relatively small cost. If an effective long-range missile could be secured for $4 million per unit—and this does not seem out of the question—a thousand could be provided for $4 billion. It would be unwise to rely solely on any one delivery system. But it is conceivable that three or four overlapping delivery systems, each theoretically capable of doing three or four times the destruction necessary for deterrence, could be provided at a fraction of current expenditures aimed at providing a deterrent against all-out surprise nuclear attack.

In that event substantial resources might be released to provide military capabilities for a more adequate and flexible defense against the lesser, but perhaps more likely, threats to the security of our allies and of ourselves.

## Primary reliance upon economic, diplomatic, and political defenses

Some believe that ever since the Korean attack there has been an excessive militarization of United States policy. They argue that the major threat is not Russian nuclear attack or even limited military aggression on the Korean pattern. They see in Russia a rapidly growing economic base. Even though the rate of expansion of Russian heavy industry may now be slowing down, they see the prospect that a somewhat slower development in that sector will be accompanied by a more balanced development of the economy as a whole. Russian economic development may well in future years be followed by China. From this platform ever growing economic and political pressures and attractions can be mounted against the presently uncommitted peoples and even against those whom today we consider to be our allies. They acknowledge the necessity for some form of military defensive shield but believe the main drive of our policy should be to win the economic and political battle for the allegiance of the preponderant body of mankind.

From this point of view military strategy in general and military assistance policy in particular take their place as subsidiary arms of political policy. The more extreme advocates of the economic branch of this point of view would favor the complete elimination of our military assistance programs and the substitution therefore of a greatly expanded program of economic assistance addressed to assisting the non-communist portions of the world to equal the rate of economic development which the USSR and Communist China are likely to achieve. The more politically oriented branch of this point of view would continue military assistance where it is strongly desired by all important segments of political opinion in the recipient country but would be very chary of pressing other countries to build up military forces beyond those which they can support themselves or which are desired by local military leaders and not by the broad base of the population.

In support of their position this school advances the argument that only if countries have the necessary political and economic base and the prospect of achieving some progress and dignity in their lives are they apt to have the will and the determination to fight for their continued independence if and when that independence is threatened. The counter argument, however, also deserves weight. That argument is that political health will require confidence that successful defense against military attack is possible and that the prospect for successful defense requires prior preparation and collective military planning.

## Primary reliance upon moral suasion

A more extreme possible strategy would put primary reliance upon moral suasion and relegate to a secondary category not only military capabilities but also the more obvious forms of direct economic and political pressure or assistance. The proponents of this thesis argue that of the two components of prestige—sympathy with the purposes one is pursuing and respect for one's capacity and will to accomplish those purposes—the first component is not only prior but all important. They argue that the bravery and resistance of the Hungarian people, against the overwhelming military capabilities and the demonstrated will of the Russians to use those capabilities, proves once for all that the rightness of the cause is in itself in the long run invincible.

Those who question this point of view may agree that the rightness of the purpose being pursued is prior but still insist that the means and will to accomplish that purpose cannot just be ignored. They also raise a question as to whether a two-thirds majority vote in the General Assembly of the United Nations can always be counted on to back the right view and ask what is to be done in the event it is impossible to get such overwhelming backing for any view at all. What happens if there is no general consensus of moral force or if that consensus proves to be continuously ineffective?

To those who believe in the absolute primacy and adequacy of moral suasion, military assistance in any form is to be deplored and discouraged irrespective of the desires of the recipient country or the particular military threats to which that country may be exposed. There is a certain tendency for the absolutist view about normal suasion to be associated with a military strategy of primary reliance upon nuclear weapons based in the United States.

## Summary and conclusion as to strategic alternatives

Even though many people do in fact hold to one or another of the five basic alternative strategic approaches outlined above, or variations and combinations thereof, it can be argued that an enlightened view would take all five approaches into account while eliminating the primacy of any one of them.

The argument might run as follows: It is important that we support the right purpose and that if possible a consensus of the views of mankind be behind those purposes. If these purposes are to be brought to realization, moral suasion must be buttressed by other action. The tools of diplomacy and economic action are the preferred tools for this purpose. But occasions may very well arise where military capabilities are also necessary. If we must engage in military action, it is to be hoped that that action can be limited in scope and in the weapons used. If conventional weapons cannot by themselves restore the situation, certain types of situations may require tactical atomic weapons as well. In order to deter the Russians from any nuclear attack upon us or our allies it is essential that we have an adequate nuclear deterrent. Such a deterrent is surer and more easily developed if we have access to a world-wide system of bases. If such bases are denied to us, we must attempt to maintain such a deterrent from United States bases alone.

United States policy emphasizing first one element of defense strategy and then another has not followed any straight line of development or had any very clear and articulate formulation. It has grown like Topsy, with pressures first from this side and then from that. Viewed as a whole, it may very well be said to have followed the lines here

114

summarized, although in recent years there has been a tendency to concentrate on the nuclear deterrent and on the force of moral suasion.

## Applicability to the military assistance program

Even if the above line of reasoning is accepted, the question still arises as to how this strategic view can be applied to the questions of scope, magnitude and method of future military assistance programs. Those programs must be developed within certain budgetary and resource limits. They must take account of the particular problems that individual countries or areas have or believe they have. They must build upon what has in fact been done in the past. They must reflect a judgment as to the developing nature of the main thrust of the Russian and communist threat.

Before dealing with concrete suggestions area by area, it may be useful to clear away some general points which have more to do with the manner of our presentation of the military assistance program than with its substantive content.

The first of these is the question as to whether it is wise to emphasize the defense element of those portions of our assistance program which, from the foreign affairs viewpoint, could as properly be viewed either as economic assistance or as defense assistance. This applies particularly to Defense Support for which in Fiscal Year 1957 the Administration requested appropriations of $1,131 million, while all other forms of nonmilitary assistance requested amounted to only $730 million. But even beyond this point there remains the question as to whether we would not better support our foreign policy if we chose to assist countries needing help by earmarking United States funds against economic projects having particular local appeal while the resulting fiscal relief to the local government enabled that government to finance an increased share of its military program from its own resources.

Similarly there is a question as to whether it is wise to finance the modernization of United States forces through foreign military assistance budgets. There appears to have been some modification in pricing policies in recent years, but for many years money voted by Congress for foreign assistance was spent, in substantial measure, to relieve our domestic United States defense budget.

On these issues past practice has been influenced by domestic budgetary and political considerations. It was easier for the military to get budgetary allocations by adding modernization through foreign assistance to the foreign assistance bill than to do it directly through the defense budget. It was also considered easier by the Administration and by the Congress to defend appropriations for military assistance and defense support than to defend appropriations for economic assistance programs.

But irrespective of the description given a program of assistance,

115

real costs are involved in the development of military forces; and in so far as the United States is giving assistance of any kind to a particular country, it has an interest in the nature and magnitude of the military forces maintained or developed and the allocation of resources between military and other types of programs. The suggestions which follow are therefore addressed to the type of military programs we might be encouraging in various parts of the world apart from the issue as to whether that United States assistance, which, added to the efforts of the recipient country is necessary to make those programs possible, is presented as being primarily an economic program or primarily a military assistance program.

## The military problem of Europe

Europe understandably has no particular stomach for an all-out nuclear war. It is almost impossible to conceive of a realistic air defense against modern manned bombers in the limited geographic area available. Defense is even more difficult against missiles of a range reportedly being tested by the Russians. Six large hydrogen weapons on target would presumably make England uninhabitable except for those who could find deep shelter and stay in it for a number of weeks.

On the continent there is also understandably little popular enthusiasm for a defense which depends upon the use of large numbers of tactical atomic weapons. The reported results of exercise Carte Blanche, indicating 1,700,000 German civilians would have been killed and 3,500,000 wounded if tactical atomic weapons had been employed as in the exercise, had a very chilling effect on German enthusiasm for NATO's defense strategy.

Until such time as conventional forces can be developed to give Europe a reasonable prospect of holding a Russian attack, it is necessary to rely on both tactical atomic weapons and upon strategic nuclear attack, not merely to deter the Russians from using such weapons but to deter them from using conventional weapons. We must recognize, however, that from the political point of view this situation is not sound. In the long run it would be politically desirable if nuclear and atomic weapons in European defense policy could be restricted to the role of assuring that such weapons are not used by the enemy.

If this point of view were accepted as a basis for United States policy, then the planning for United States military assistance would be an exercise in gearing our own and available European resources into a common military program to build ourselves, as rapidly as technological, economic, and political factors will permit, out of an excessive reliance upon weapons which it would be disastrous to use.

One of the considerations which inhibit both the Europeans and the United States from facing up to a decision on this matter is the hope that through negotiations it may be possible to reduce the military threat to Europe. It is not the purpose of this paper to discuss the prospects of a negotiation which would have as one of its objects the withdrawal of Russian forces from Central Europe into Russia itself. The point is pertinent, however, that the prospect for provident and successful negotiation presupposes the availability of some satisfactory alternative in the event the negotiation fails.

If the Russians cannot be negotiated back to the Bug, what happens next? The present military posture in Europe is hardly satisfactory to any of the NATO participants. It is hard to believe that the present line of strategy represents a stable position. It would seem likely that if we do not move toward building greater and more flexible strength in Europe, even that partial strength which has been built up in the past may be eroded or withdrawn. We will then be left with a "trip wire" situation where we will have forfeited power of decision and the capacity to manage our fate and must rely on the hope that a professed willingness on our part to play Russian roulette will be balanced by rationality and restraint on the part of the Russians. The greater the degree of our commitment to use nuclear weapons and the greater the automaticity of the chain of developments that could trigger off that commitment, the more important it is to us that the USSR does not get itself into similarly automatic commitments. If it were to do so, we would both face a very real danger that unforeseen developments in central Europe will start off an interacting chain of developments which will bring on an all-out nuclear war against the interests of both sides. We will also run the very real risk that the Germans, the French, and even the British will come to doubt either the seriousness of our commitment to the "trip wire" concept or the wisdom of such a defense concept and will be tempted individually to make the best peace they can with the Russians.

At the present time, much interest is developing on both sides of the Atlantic in the proposition that we make atomic weapons available to our European allies. The Europeans naturally would prefer to have such instruments under their own control. They also welcome the increase in political prestige which would accompany possession of atomic weapons. Those on our side who believe that weapons are weapons and who deplore the political distinction often made between atomic weapons and conventional weapons believe the possession by our NATO partners of atomic weapons will cause them also to play down political objection to their use.

Others, however, are concerned that a wider spread in the ownership of atomic weapons increases the risk of a process getting under way and beyond our control which could increase the risk of our involvement in a general nuclear war. The British, of course, are in a position to manufacture weapons of their own. In the longer-range future the French, the Germans, and others will be in a position to do so too. The real question then is not so much whether we choose to accelerate the process but whether we are able to think through, and convince our allied partners of the soundness of a military posture, strategy, and program in the best interests of all.

117

## The defense of the Middle East

The defense of the Middle East against overt military aggression by Russia itself is primarily a function of our global strategy rather than of Middle East strategy. The military potential of the Baghdad Pact powers can conceivably be expanded to a point where they could expect to contribute at least delay and harrassment to a Russian drive. It is hard to see how they could contribute more than delay and harrassment.

Military assistance to the Middle Eastern countries other than Turkey and Greece, which are also NATO powers, must therefore be viewed primarily from the point of view of its contribution to cold war politics. But the primary risk to the Middle East is in the political realm and not from the threat of direct Soviet attack.

In the political realm the risks are obviously very great indeed, and the role which military assistance can play, for good or ill, is large.

The Russians have recognized the uses to which military equipment (obsolete in comparison with the newer equipment they are supplying to their own forces, but completely modern and serviceable by Middle East standards) can be put in upsetting the power equilibrium of the Middle East. We have seen the far-reaching effects of the Russian arms deal with Nasser. In what the Russians are now saying there is every indication that they propose fully to exploit the possibilities of this technique. If Nuri es Said is upset in Iraq it will not be because of the inadequacy of Iraq's program of economic development. It will be because Iraqi army officers envy the superior military equipment which the Syrian army is receiving from the Russians.

It is much more difficult to use the technique of freely supplying military equipment for constructive purposes in a confused situation than to use it for disruptive purposes. The specific decisions as to amounts, conditions, and methods of supplying such assistance can probably best be judged by those in the Executive Branch who have responsibility for conducting our policy there. Those outside the Executive Branch can recognize that in the Middle East military assistance is a political tool which cannot be ignored and do what they can to support an appropriate degree of flexibility of decision for the Executive Branch to take necessary and timely action.

## The defense of the Far East

In the Far East, defense against a coordinated Russian and Chinese Communist aggression must similarly be a function primarily of our global strategy. But the offshore island chain can potentially play a larger role in that strategy than can the Middle East. In so far as the island chain is seriously weakened, the potential pressure on the other flank, the European flank, is increased. Furthermore Communist China, acting with only indirect Russian support, presents the possibility of lesser military threats which may well not merit the use of the all-out nuclear sanction.

Military assistance to the Republic of Korea, to Japan, to Taiwan, and to the Philippines is therefore not just a matter of cold war politics. It is probably true nevertheless that political considerations with respect to these countries are potentially more important and certainly more immediate than purely military considerations. What are the dangers of subversion at the lower levels in the Chinese Nationalist government and army? What are the prospects of Japan requesting that we withdraw United States forces from Japan? What are the political effects of continuing overstrain of the Korean economy? Why have United States-Philippine relations deteriorated over the last two years to a point where the base negotiations have had to be terminated?

In the Far East it seems clear that military assistance is a technique which must be continued both for defense reasons and for political reasons. It is suggested, however, that a greater subordination of military considerations to the developing political issues of the area would be appropriate.

## Conclusion

Perhaps the main thing which the United States can do is to demonstrate to the rest of the world—friend and foe alike—our serious purpose to resist a Soviet take-over. It is important that what we do makes sense, that it increase the flexibility of our possible responses, that it meet the political as well as the more narrowly military requirements of the situation. But it may be even more important that we clearly demonstrate our purpose to use such economic, military, psychological or other means as may be necessary. The presence of the United States in the disputed areas is of the essence. Military assistance would appear to be an essential tool in that over-all endeavor.

# 5. American aid and economic development: some critical issues

by Thomas C. Schelling

Nineteen fifty-seven was to be a pivotal year for American foreign assistance. A year earlier—long ago when our preoccupation in Egypt was with what to do about the Aswan Dam—there was widespread recognition that a profound change had occurred in the international scene since the last serious reexamination of the foreign aid programs. The Far Eastern wars had been terminated. Europe's economic recovery was virtually complete, and the NATO military expansion had reached a plateau of expenditure. Technical assistance activities under the Point Four Program were expanding and achieving important results

Thomas C. Schelling is Associate Professor of Economics at Yale University. He joined the staff of the Economic Cooperation Administration during the first months of the Marshall Plan, and served in Washington, the Mission to Denmark, and the Office of the Special Representative in Paris, returning to Washington at the end of 1950 to join the staff of the Special Assistant to the President (Foreign Affairs). With the establishment of the Office of the Director for Mutual Security, at the end of 1951, Mr. Schelling served as Officer-in-Charge, European Program Affairs in that Office and in the subsequent Foreign Operations Administration. Since joining the faculty of Yale in 1953, Mr. Schelling has been consultant from time to time for the Foreign Operations Administration, the International Development Advisory Board, and several private organizations, on matters of foreign economic policy.

but were evidently not by themselves going to revolutionize productivity and living standards around the world through the inexpensive provision of knowledge alone. Most important of all, the increasing bargaining power of underdeveloped countries in world affairs had brought American policy to the point where it was about ready to settle in some cases for neutrality as second best. Constructive ways were being considered of insuring against worse than second best and of helping to create something more positive and dynamic than the term "neutrality" suggests. Finally, there was an annoying feeling that the inflexible Russians had been flexible enough to catch us napping in Asia, Africa, even Latin America. A competing bidder having suddenly appeared at the auction, we looked with renewed interest at the item on the block.

## Studies of foreign aid

Foreign assistance programs involve an enormous amount of detailed budgetary analysis and prior negotiations. They cannot easily be given new direction in the midst of Congressional consideration of an annual program. The need for reexamination therefore took expression last year in the idea of study aimed at the 1957 Congressional cycle. The fiscal-year 1957 program was permitted to proceed on its original premises. After several months of what may have been tactical maneuver behind the scenes, but may have been just inaction, a three-cornered program of official study emerged.

The President appointed a group of "Citizen Advisers" on the Mutual Security Program: "If the results of your deliberations are to be recorded in legislation which I may submit to the next Congress, it is important that I receive a progress report by December 1, 1956, and your final report by March 1, 1957."

The House Committee on Foreign Affairs undertook a study of the "objectives, methods, and results" of the foreign aid programs, and heard testimony in October and November.

Third, the Senate created a Special Committee to Study the Foreign Aid Program which, in turn, commissioned eleven studies by outside organizations on various aspects of the programs and ten survey teams to visit foreign countries.[1] Simultaneously, the International Development Advisory Board, originally established as a group of official consultants in connection with the Point Four Program, conducted a study of aid programs in relation to economic development abroad.

Outside the government there was an increase in the tempo of activity. The Committee for Economic Development and other organizations issued policy statements; newspaper columnists devoted increased attention to the subject; articles by Paul G. Hoffman, Barbara Ward, and many others, received wide attention. Several books helped to crystallize issues; a paper by Professors Max Millikan and Walt

[1]The research projects and country-survey missions are listed at the end of this paper.

Rostow of the Center for International Studies at M.I.T. was first circulated informally and then published as *A Proposal: Key to an Effective Foreign Policy*. Dr. Gunnar Myrdal of the Economic Commission for Europe (author of *An American Dilemma*) published *An International Economy*, a book that raised sharply many of the issues involved in our aid programs.

## Timing of the studies

As the 1957 legislative and budgetary cycle got under way there was no official evidence that these studies would have an effect on the following year's foreign aid. Studies like those of the House and Senate Committees, and the Citizen Advisers to the President, have a deceptive chronology. It seems plausible to start planning a year ahead of time. To set up a study group in July to influence the Congressional decisions of the following April and May for the fiscal year beginning the following July seems reasonable. But it usually is not. Even before a study group has begun its work, after the usual delays, the Executive Branch will have begun the budgetary process for the following July. Major decisions will be taken in December, and more detailed legislative proposals will be completed by sometime in March. A study that will be available on the first of March can at most serve the purpose of influencing consideration of the Executive Branch's program (if it has been designed for that purpose). It is months too late to influence the detailed planning of the Executive Branch.

## The Administration's proposals

On April 8, 1957, Secretary of State Dulles presented to Congress the Administration's views. In broad outline he proposed some fundamental changes in the content and administration of the program and in the philosophy behind it. The most salient feature was an economic development fund to provide loans "on terms more favorable than are possible through existing institutions." The fund would need "continuing authority and a capital authorization sufficient for several years, to be renewed when needed." Such a fund should be able "to make loans which, not for the fiscal year 1958 but over the future, might come to reach $750,000,000 a year . . . . . On the other hand, the needs may become more compelling." (While the proportion of present programs to be incorporated in the proposed loan fund is not yet clear, it may be estimated at perhaps $250-$400 million dollars.)

Additionally, the Secretary proposed a deeper cleavage than formerly existed between assistance in support of foreign military efforts and assistance for other purposes. Aid in the form of military equipment and training, together with economic ("defense support") assistance needed to meet "so much of the economic burden of military defense as the country cannot itself afford," would be put on a continuing basis and handled as part of the appropriation to the Defense Department.

123

The philosophy behind the development fund was epitomized in the Secretary's statement that military defense alone cannot assure that the free world will be maintained intact. "There is also a threat to future independence and freedom where moderate leaders despair of being able to lift their nation out of hopeless poverty and stagnation."

He quoted the President's second inaugural address:

In too much of the earth there is want, discord, danger. New forces and new nations stir and strive across the earth, with power to bring, by their fate, great good or great evil to the free world's future. From the deserts of North Africa to the islands of the South Pacific one-third of all mankind has entered upon an historic struggle for a new freedom: Freedom from grinding poverty. Across all continents, nearly a billion people seek, sometimes almost in desperation, for the skills and knowledge and assistance by which they may satisfy from their own resources, the material wants common to all mankind.

The Secretary added, "It is in our direct self-interest that these new nations should succeed in the historic struggle of which the President spoke." The philosophy was not new; but punctuated with a request for money, it seemed for the first time to have become Administration policy.

The Administration's statement did not, however, settle the issues, even those that it raised specifically. What it did was to make certain that most of the issues would be faced, and to provide a specific focus for many of them. If the several studies reviewed in this essay provided an essential "background" of information and argument, the Administration's recommendations had at last provided what is even more essential, a "foreground."

## Status of the studies

Before turning to the contents of these studies and the questions they raise, it may be worth while to indicate the status of them at the time the Administration made its views known. The reports of the Citizen Advisers and of the International Development Advisory Board were finished; they had been formally submitted to the President and made public. The House Foreign Affairs Committee had published in December a document containing some 350 pages of hearings and an 84-page draft report. The report was done by the staff of the committee for Congressman Richards, who was then chairman but is no longer in Congress. The latter submitted it to the Committee. There had been no formal action.

The Senate Foreign Relations Committee had published most of the eleven research papers that were done under contract for it, and many of the reports of the survey groups that visited foreign countries. The procedure was to publish one or two reports per week and hold hearings on the published subjects. There had not yet been a Committee report; the published materials had the status simply of studies submitted to the Committee.

## Points of general agreement

This essay will not review systematically the several studies and reports. It is more useful, for the purpose of the American Assembly, to orient this paper toward the issues that are raised. Before taking up the issues it is worth while to ask whether a consensus seems to be emerging. But we should keep in mind that the studies do not represent the House or the Senate, and that the Executive Branch has endorsed no views on these issues beyond those specifically expressed by the President or the Secretary of State. The outside organizations and individuals, including those that prepared materials for the Senate Committee, are not a random sample of the population, or of influential interest groups. To find a consensus in these materials does not therefore imply that a broader consensus necessarily exists. Nevertheless, these materials will be a dominant part of the background against which further study and discussion will take place. They will compel attention, partly just because they exist and partly because some of them are invaluable as sources of information or provocative discussion.

On one point there is a consensus. It is that *the area of greatest urgency, of widest choice, of least settled policy, in connection with foreign assistance, is the newly independent countries of Asia and Africa.*

A second point that seems at last to be taken for granted is that our interest in these countries cannot be comprehended by such a simple-minded distinction as whether they elect our side or the other side in the cold war or a neutral position in the middle. Most of the studies expect that many of the countries will elect the attitude that used to be referred to as "neutralist"; but they recognize that there remains a wide range of possible outcomes, within these countries and between these countries and the rest of the world, depending in part on whether successful economic development can be initiated.

A third point recognized is that technical assistance alone will not solve the problem of economic development.

*There is no consensus on what should be done.* The International Development Advisory Board believes "that the size of the present development program—both capital and technical assistance—should be substantially increased." The Citizen Advisers on the Mutual Security Program only "recognize the necessity for some economic development expenditures" and envisage no increase. The draft report of the House Committee recommended "that the annual expenditure by the United States for foreign aid shall be reduced rather than increased," and by implication included aid to economic development in this recommendation.

George Kennan "would like to see a discriminatory approach to economic aid." Howard Petersen of the CED believes that "we should move ahead with parts of our program for economic development abroad as soon as those parts can be decisively formed, rather than to await formulation of a complete program," and that "our approach to

125

the problem of a program for economic development abroad needs to be pragmatic, evolutionary, and adaptable.''

On the other hand, Norman Buchanan of the Rockefeller Foundation believes ''that a country-by-country approach to the problem of the development of the underdeveloped areas is not the best one. An international approach, or, at the very least, a regional approach seems to me to be required... This is the Marshall Plan approach, and, of course, stresses the cooperative, collaborative nature of development.''

Max Millikan and Walt Rostow believe that the United States, together with other developed countries, ''should give assurance to every underdeveloped free world country that it can secure as much capital as it can use productively.'' They furthermore believe that ''a politically neutral program of economic aid will provide a setting in which the other instruments of foreign policy can operate more effectively.... Our economic aid program should operate according to impartial economic standards.''

In contrast, the draft report of the House Committee believes that it is ''important for the United States to develop favorable bilateral relationships with as many nations as possible and that such relations include as many tangible elements as possible.''

Thus there are important differences on whether the program should be enlarged or not, on whether it should be divorced from the rest of foreign policy, and on whether there should be a world-wide and integral program or a pragmatic country-by-country approach. On many other issues differences appear. There is one point on which there is virtually unanimous agreement—that a way should be found to separate the military assistance programs from those in support of economic development.

## The program and its context

The idea of assistance to the economic development of other countries originated in the Point Four Program in 1949. That program was originally confined to *technical assistance*. As the Secretary of State explained in 1949, ''by its very nature, this is not and never will be a big-money enterprise.... It involves salaries and expenses of people —not vast purchases of machinery and raw materials. Its objective is to show other people how to meet their own needs, not to attempt to meet those needs ourselves.''

Since that time the cost of technical assistance programs has grown from less than $50 million a year to about $150 million, partly through expansion of the number of people involved, and partly through enlargement of the concept to include more in the way of ancillary equipment and supplies. But, for a program spread over three continents with more than a billion of population, it is of very modest cost compared with the other programs. Its annual cost is no more than 3 per cent of the Marshall Plan in 1949. It is, for the whole world, barely half of our present "defense support" economic assistance program for South Korea alone.

During the last several years there has grown up alongside technical assistance a variety of programs listed under the heading of *assistance to economic development.* These are distinguished from technical assistance in that they finance commodity imports into the country, either imports in general to offset the inflationary consequences of enlarged investment, or specific imports in connection with investment projects. They are distinguished from "defense support" assistance in that the latter is extended to countries primarily in consideration of military costs that they incur in agreement with the United States. A good example of "economic development" assistance, and one of the earliest, was for the Middle East in 1953. It was hoped that by financing the development of the Jordan Valley and similar areas in the Middle East, attention could be diverted from the Palestine dispute into more constructive channels. It has been characteristic of this type of assistance that it arose in response to crises and emergencies, that there has been no explicit philosophy or set of criteria, and that even in the countries that receive it the assistance has generally not been related to any long-term program of development. Development assistance for Guatemala, for example, was a consequence of the disturbances in that country a few years ago; it is not at all clear that it bears any profound relation to economic development.

The total amount of development assistance appropriated for 1957 was $250 million. In 1956 it was about the same, although only $200 million was actually programmed during the year. We are dealing again with amounts that are small by comparison with, say, the Marshall Plan. The countries receiving development assistance have a total population of over half a billion; per capita the amount is therefore not quite fifty cents, which is unlikely to have a major impact on the growth of capital in those areas.

There is, however, some component of assistance within the *defense support* category that contributes to economic development. In Turkey, Iran, Pakistan, South Korea, Philippines, Thailand, Viet Nam, Formosa, Laos and Cambodia, a total of $1 billion is being provided in forms other than military equipment and training. Much of this serves to offset the use of the country's own resources for defense; but in several of these countries, economic development has proceeded at a faster rate than if the defense programs and defense support assistance were not there. There have been efforts to estimate the "development assistance" portion of the "defense support" total. Estimates range from $200 or $300 million to $500 or $600 million, or from about one-third to one-half the total.

In judging the total American assistance that contributes to economic development, it would make a great deal of difference whether the correct figure is $300 or $600 million. If one wants to know how much of the total annual aid program, of nearly $4 billion, is devoted to economic development, the calculation is significant. The correct calculation is extremely important in judging the results of the particular countries affected—Korea, Pakistan, etc. Here are countries with a combined population of about 200 million that may be receiving outside assistance to economic development of the same order of magnitude as the total of such assistance to the rest of the underdeveloped world.

On the other hand, the importance of the "correct" figure for this development portion of defense support aid can be exaggerated. Whatever the correct figure—whether it is zero or $1 billion per year—it has nothing to do with the adequacy or inadequacy of present programs for any but those particular countries receiving defense support. And they account for a minor fraction of the area and population under discussion. India will not develop the faster, nor will Ghana or Ecuador, if we double the amount of assistance to development in South Korea, the Philippines, or Turkey.

In the last two years a new source of assistance has arisen—*agricultural surpluses* sold to foreign countries for their own currency, with the proceeds lent to the countries for their economic development. An agreement with India, for example, will provide over $300 million worth of agricultural surpluses over a three-year period, with the major part of the sales proceeds available to finance investment in India. Similar agreements with Brazil and Indonesia bring the total to over half a billion dollars. The total for underdeveloped countries may be in the neighborhood of three-quarters of a billion dollars so far. (The definition is somewhat ambiguous depending on how the local-currency sales proceeds are allocated; furthermore the rate at which the amounts are to be utilized is in many cases unclear.) It is fair to conclude that this type of assistance is of the order or magnitude of the "assistance to economic development" contained in the Mutual Security Program, and is available to serve similar purposes.

In judging the size of these various programs it has been common to compare economic with military assistance, or development assistance with the sum of military equipment and defense support. The question is often raised whether the '"*balance" between the military and the economic programs* is a proper one. Stress has been put on the proportions or percentages of the different types of aid. For one purpose it is important to stress the proportions. An uninformed public may interpret a $4 billion aid program as being largely economic assistance. In the face of this misapprehension it may be worth while to point out that aside from "defense support" to a limited and special group of countries, all types of economic aid (including a number of small, miscellaneous items) probably amount to no more than one-seventh of the total Mutual Security appropriation; and with a reasonable allowance for the "economic" portion under the heading of defense support they would probably amount to no more than one-quarter.

It would, however, be an unfortunate mistake to view the problem as one of proportions, or of "balance." To focus on the percentage composition is unnecessarily to force development assistance and military assistance into competition with each other. Properly, *each should be judged on its merits.* The wisdom of assisting economic development in India or Indonesia is only remotely related to the wisdom of contributing to the NATO defense build-up or the equipping of troops on Formosa, or to providing economic aid to Spain in return for air and naval bases. It would be unfortunate if the argument in favor of economic development had to be an argument against military assistance, especially when the military assistance is for different countries and frequently for different areas of the globe.

There is, to be sure, a budgetary restriction that makes all programs compete with each other; but the various parts of our assistance programs should more properly be viewed as competing within the 70-odd billion dollar total budget rather than within the $4 billion aid program. The comparison of the two parts of the aid program also suffers from the fact that costs are not a good indication of the emphasis that one attaches to objectives. (Furthermore an increase in military assistance may in some cases reduce the defense burden on the country itself; if that occurs the apparent increase in military emphasis may be an actual release of resources within the country for economic development).

American aid under the Mutual Security Program is not the only source of capital for underdeveloped countries. The *Export-Import Bank* has made substantial loans; in Latin America they have exceeded the Mutual Security Program for that area. In addition, there are *International Bank* loans, and there is of course private overseas investment. Total disbursements of the IBRD since its establishment have reached $2 billion. In recent years, its annual rate of lending has averaged nearly $400 million. But the portion of these totals that has gone to Asia, the Middle East, and Africa, has been small. By June 30, 1956, only $320 million altogether had been disbursed there. New loans to those areas jumped from an average of less than $100 million per year to about $180 million in 1956. If the higher rate of lending continues, disbursements will eventually average nearly as much per year as they have reached in total up to the present. But they would still amount to but 25 cents per capita per year in the whole area. In Latin America, IBRD loans have been more substantial; the absolute amount of disbursements has been about double those for Asia, Africa, and the Middle East, and of course per capita the difference is much greater.

American *private investment* abroad has averaged about $1.5 billion a year since the end of World War II, and something over $2 billion per year for the last two years or so. Most of this has been "direct" investment, rather than purchase of securities. From the point of view of world development this amount is quite significant. For underdeveloped countries the figure has to be substantially reduced by the amounts going to Canada, Europe, and other developed areas. Of the remainder a sizeable part—nearly $400 million per year on the average—has gone to Latin America. Asia, Africa, and the Middle East have averaged barely $200 million per year; and the bulk of this has

129

gone to the Middle Eastern countries that produce oil. (In judging the significance for economic development of American investment abroad, we should keep in mind that there is an important "technical assistance" component to it as well as the supply of capital.)

A comprehensive survey should take into account both the aid and the overseas investment that originate in countries other than the United States. But the general picture would not be greatly changed. There are important parts of the underdeveloped world to which the flow of outside capital is extremely small. If we ask ourselves why all of our aid for the last many years has failed to make much impact on countries like India, Indonesia, and Burma, the answer is a simple one. Although technical assistance can make a contribution out of proportion to its cost; and token amounts of aid may occasionally have political effects out of proportion to their costs, the total amounts of aid have been too small to make much difference. For underdeveloped countries (other than "defense support" countries) in Asia and Africa with about three-quarters of a billion people, the inflow of American capital and technical assistance in all forms—grants, loans, and direct investments, public and private, plus World Bank and United Nations programs—is probably at an annual rate at the present time of between $1 and $2 per capita.

## The prior questions

The remainder of this essay will consist of questions raised, and not settled, by an examination of the recent literature on foreign assistance. These questions necessarily fit into a wider context of foreign policy. The specific objectives of aid programs, the conduct and administration of them, the achievement of the programs measured against their costs, raise issues that can only be answered against a background of prior questions. For some of these, answers can be taken for granted; for others answers have to be found. One in particular stands out as needing answer or, at least, confirmation. It concerns our relation to the underdeveloped countries, particularly those that have not chosen sides firmly between east and west.

Do we wish to force them to choose sides? What is our attitude toward those that do not? Do we wish to strengthen existing governmental institutions in them? How badly—in terms of the costs we might be prepared to meet—do we want them to develop into stable, civilized, and independent countries even if they remain outside our main orbit of influence?

As remarked earlier, some consensus on these questions emerges from the recent literature; but as also remarked, a consensus there does not by any means indicate that policy is, or is about to be settled. The discussion that follows presumes a rudimentary agreement on these fundamentals; but it is not clear that such agreement actually exists. If the process of debate and re-examination that is under way, and that has been stimulated by the Suez crisis, accomplished no more than to straighten out our attitude toward these uncommitted countries (including those whose "commitments" are weak) we shall have made real progress. Though there would remain all the "unsettled" issues specifically relating to foreign aid, we could attack them with confidence that they could be settled.

## Major issues

### 1 The aid-giving relationship

Is the aid-giving relationship a healthy one? Is the aid-giving program merely an instrument for transferring resources to other countries; or is it also a desirable and influential relationship between us and the recipient countries? It has been argued that to receive aid causes embarrassment, resentment, and suspicion of the grantor, and that this reaction accounted for much of the "anti-Americanism" reported from Western Europe during the early 1950's. On the opposite side it has been argued that in some countries, like Greece, which lacked administrative competence and the unity to take necessary measures, the guiding hand of an aid-granting country may at times have been as important for its influence on decisions as for the aid that it provided. The World Bank has certainly had a healthful influence in forcing careful economic programming and analysis on loan recipients. Furthermore, some of the friction that develops between the giving and the receiving country may be the necessary overhead cost of a close relationship. The intimacy between the United States and the countries of Western Europe that resulted from the Marshall Plan and subsequent programs has been an important asset in Western unity and cooperation, in spite of the frictions. Some of the frictions, too, may have been the avoidable result of unwise legislative conditions, inadequate personnel, and other weaknesses of administration.

There are strong statements on both sides. Gunnar Myrdal (*An International Economy*) has expressed an overpowering distaste of unilateral aid, which is "akin to the charitable contributions by the lord of the manor." He would "warn off any country from giving, or receiving, unilateral aid except where there are not other means available.... As experience shows, bringing politics into international aid carries the danger that the moral and economic foundations may crumble."

The opposite position is taken by the draft report of the House Foreign Affairs Committee, which emphasizes "the importance to the United States during the next few years of building up bilateral relationships with as many nations as possible.... One of the best means available.... is the provision of assistance.... It would not be desirable in the situation likely to prevail in the world for the next several years for the United States to deny itself the advantages to its foreign policy which should be derived from working directly with individual nations in carrying out assistance programs."

131

There cannot be many who make this issue central in the question of *whether* to extend assistance. Milliken and Rostow do say that " a program adopted for the wrong reasons may well be worse than useless," and the Myrdal quotation seems to warn us away from any unilateral program; but these may be extremes of emphasis only. The issue is more pertinent to the question of *how to conduct a program*: what conditions to attach, what organizational arrangements to utilize, how to program a country's needs, and how to administer aid. It arises not only in the choice between unilateral and multilateral channels. It concerns whether we prefer a program with a minimum of discretion and judgement, one that works through criteria and procedures that are as objective and non-discriminatory as possible, or whether we prefer a more flexible, discretionary program either for the influence that it gives us or because effectiveness in the use of aid would outweigh the costs in resentment and illwill. The same issue arises specifically in our next question.

## 2  Insulation of aid from foreign policies

To what extent can we insulate economic development assistance from the rest of our foreign policy, if we wish to? If we should decide in response to the first question that we wish a means of extending aid that is as "neutral" as possible, we must still consider how neutral that can be. Can we in fact isolate from the rest of our foreign policy an activity that for many countries would be (especially if the program were expanded as proposed in many of these studies) our single most important relationship to them? Can we convincingly divorce the program from other diplomatic or military activities? The problem is most difficult in countries where we have very tangible other objectives. It would be necessary to separate economic development assistance from negotiations over air-base rights in such countries as Morocco, Libya, Saudi Arabia, and Iran, and from assistance in support of military programs in Pakistan, Turkey, and Vietnam, to say nothing of South Korea and Formosa.

Can we persuade countries that our future decisions to enlarge or curtail development assistance programs will be independent of their diplomatic and military behavior in the years to come? One thing seems clear: if we wish to convince countries that the aid program is independent of our other interests in them, we must find unambiguous criteria for deciding on assistance—what the M.I.T. authors call " an explicit code of ground rules for an assistance program"—and make these criteria perfectly evident and comprehensible to all countries concerned. The Marshall Plan demonstrated how difficult it is to make either a pretense or a serious try at leaving future programs "unaffected" by future events, when those future programs have not yet been determined and when the method of determining them depends on judgment rather than mechanical formulae. We shall look at this problem of criteria, and of separating development aid from other programs,

132

below. But an interesting aspect of the separation problem arises in the following question.

## 3 Insulation—the recipients' views

Do recipient countries want development assistance insulated from the rest of our foreign policy and, if not, can they prevent insulation? Spokesmen for several countries have from time to time voiced objection to the intermingling of United States aid and other aspects of American diplomatic policy during recent years. Several of the witnesses before the House Committee emphasized the desire of foreign countries to receive aid without "strings" and outside the context of our immediate diplomacy. But we should keep in mind that there is no spokesman for all aid-receiving countries as a group, that some countries will prefer any alternative system of aid that yields them relatively more, and that some of the ostensible demands for "pure," nonpolitical aid without conditions attached, like that reported from Jordan in the heat of the Suez crisis, are directly inspired by the possibility of a political bargain. We should not take for granted that recipients invariably prefer an antiseptic relationship.

Some countries fare well under a system that is discriminatory. Many are in a position to make American aid a condition for their own actions. George Kennan has given a blunt answer to one such type of situation. "I do not think we should ever give economic aid when there is any tinge of pressure or blackmail. When anybody says to you, 'Give us this or we will go communist,' the chances are they will not do it; and if they are so crazy as to do it, they are not worth aiding."

Such out-and-out cases of blackmail may not often be the problem, however (outside a limited portion of the Middle East, anyway). More likely are cases in which a country has to incur a risk and needs a little inducement; or in which there is division of opinion within the country, and aid may be hoped to strengthen those who favor the better choice. But even these cases may be rare. The "bargain" is not likely to be explicit. And if it were, there can often be construed a basis for compensation that seems moral to the other country. It may or may not be true that a country incurs an enhanced risk of destruction if it admits United States troops or joins an anti-communist pact; but it is not logically ridiculous for a country to argue so. A country may also argue that desperate internal measures would be required for economic development if it had no relief in the form of foreign assistance. Is this "blackmail" or the communication of an honest dilemma?

To complicate further this matter of impersonal aid administration, we should keep in mind that countries often take an interest—not entirely impartial and friendly—in other countries' aid receipts: India in aid to Pakistan or Formosa, Pakistan in aid to India, the Arab countries and Israel in each other's aid, Greece and Turkey in each other's, and so forth. Sometimes the interest is only envious, sometimes antagonistic. Furthermore, we may not always be in a position

133

to decide the relationship ourselves if there are other countries extending aid to the same recipient—Commonwealth countries under the Columbo Plan, "European Common Market" countries to North Africa, and hopefully additional instances of aid by the advanced countries. It has occasionally been proposed that Japan, poor as it is, might assist in granting aid to the much poorer countries of South and Southeast Asia. It is hard to imagine that Japan would wish to "insulate" its interests completely from the aid it extended.

These thoughts certainly do not prove the futility of trying to insulate development aid from the rest of our foreign relations; and for the most part they emphasize the desirability. But they do suggest that the difficulties deserve serious attention before a program is devised in such fashion that it depends for its success on its complete freedom from the exigencies of current diplomacy.

## 4 "Strings" on assistance

Should aid to economic development be without "strings"? With respect to "political" strings, this question is an aspect of the preceding ones. Millikan and Rostow have argued that "it may be a condition for the success of a development program that it be made unmistakably clear that our assistance is not contingent on narrow political concessions and does not carry political "strings." One of the Senate studies, by Hoselitz at the University of Chicago, refers to "an open or thinly disguised suspicion in many countries that American aid is often used as a bribe," and argues that "the more impartially economic aid is extended the less basis will there be in the long run to such a charge."

But another aspect of the question was raised by Howard Petersen, representing the CED in testimony before the House Committee. "Our assistance should not be encumbered with unrelated, improper conditions, although there are circumstances in which some conditions are proper and necessary for efficient execution of economic-development programs.... Most of the conditions would relate to the utilization of funds in matters wholly related to the economic aspect of the aid program."

Does the aversion to "strings"—which is nearly unanimous among the studies reviewed—arise from a feeling that they do damage in themselves, or from the belief that *unsuccessful* conditions might be attached to an offer of aid. An explicit "string" caused Indonesia to abstain from receiving assistance; the foreign-policy assurances demanded by Congress were not acceptable. At a later date Burma discontinued receipt of assistance, ostensibly because there were *implicit* strings. These were *unsuccessful* strings; the United States wished to extend the aid, and it ended with neither the conditions nor the aid program. It is interesting, incidentally, that the Burmese conditions were not explicit. It takes more than abstention to prevent the supposed existence of strings.

Perhaps the main objection to strings is suggested by the Citizen Advisers. By implication they do not envisage the insulation of aid programs from the rest of foreign policy. "It is not logical for the State Department to avoid direct responsibility for these functions if by their use it seeks to promote the foreign policy objectives of the United States." At the same time, they urged that the administrators of the program "resist undue emphasis upon the short-run political advantages to the detriment of achieving the longer-run economic development objectives." In other words, it is short-run strings that are a nuisance, a dispersion of bargaining power, and at best an objective the value of which is eclipsed by the longer-run purposes of the program.

Even if it is decided to keep "first things first" and not to clutter up a program with minor and short-run conditions, there is still a serious problem of "strings." Emilio Collado, treasurer of Standard Oil of New Jersey, adverted to one such difficulty in his testimony before the House Committee. He said that the government should "make clear to all countries that the record of their treatment of private capital, domestic and foreign, will be an important factor in any decision on foreign aid." The point itself is an important one, and we shall refer to it later under another heading. But aside from whether we should try to impose our own ideology on governments receiving assistance, there is an inescapable connection between the amount of aid that we might have to extend to a country for its development, and the way the country treats the foreign private capital that might do the job as well or better. This problem worried the Randall Commission three years ago, when it said that we should "make clear that primary reliance must be placed on private investment to undertake the job of assisting in economic development abroad." The Commission stressed that American aid should not compensate countries for the foreign private capital that they turned away.

But as soon as we insist that a country welcome private foreign capital we are not only protecting against the abuse of our aid, we can be accused of attempting to force our own private-enterprise ideology on the country concerned. Here is a "string" that is natural and logical and, in the words of the CED witness, "wholly related to the economic aspect of the aid program," yet it can be construed as interference.

The same difficulty arises if we oppose autarkic development of a country. We may believe that high cost, inefficient industrial projects embarked on for the sake of prestige or self-sufficiency are an uneconomic use of the resources we provide. Perhaps if we only refuse to finance such projects directly with our funds we can avoid the accusation of "strings." If we insist that we will not meet the country's requirements for "sound" projects while they simultaneously divert their own resources to "unsound" ones, we are only being logical. But we are unavoidably involved in an argument over self-sufficiency, industrialization for its own sake, and the theory of economic development.

135

Another such problem was adverted to by Chester Bowles before the House Committee. In discussing India, he said that " the one criticism we would be likely to make of their efforts involves speeding up their land reform." Land reform, changes in legal systems, improvements in the civil service, etc., are essentially involved in the improved use of resources for economic development; yet they can be highly controversial. So can taxation, either the general level or the income-distributive aspects of it. Yet taxation is a central feature of a country's own development program and can hardly be considered an improper topic for an aid program to take into account.

In sum, an aversion to "strings" and conditions faces a dilemma. The " purely economic" conditions that would seem not only appropriate but essential, from the point of view of the country extending aid, may be construed by the recipient as intervention or, at least, as subject to abuse. Awareness of this problem should forestall any hasty confidence that we need only avoid " improper strings" in order to make the problem disappear altogether.

At the same time there is a danger of exaggerating the resistance to conditions that we genuinely believe to be legitimate. It has been a common occurrence for aid-receiving governments, or at least parts of governments, to resist vocally while silently appreciating the moral support for what they knew was right and necessary. Economic burdens are not the only burdens that governments may wish to share with an aid grantor. If we can be a scapegoat for painful decisions from time to time, we may help to share a burden of unpopularity (hopefully only temporary) that would otherwise exceed the capacity of the recipient government. Following the Bell Mission to the Philippines our aid to that country was made subject to quite rigorous conditions of economic reform and fiscal rectitude, of a severity that evoked many outcries and that had been successfully resisted before. There is little doubt that American firmness at the time earned eventual respect and appreciation, and there is evidence that some of the appreciation within the Philippine government was immediate.

## 5 Criteria for allocating assistance

What should be the criteria for the allocation of aid among countries? If one decides that more aid should be given, and that it should be given to a wide range of underdeveloped countries whether or not they participate with us in the cold war, it is still necessary to decide *which countries* should be eligible for assistance, and *how much aid* each should get.

There is one case in which the criteria can be greatly simplified and the problem of establishing priorities among countries can be virtually avoided altogether. That is the case in which the resources available are adequate to meet all reasonable needs. The proposal of Millikan and Rostow escapes by this means from the need to " divide" aid among countries. They propose that the program be based "solely on economic criteria." Safeguarded by their estimate that "relatively small amounts of capital ($2.5 billion to $3.5 billion more per year from all sources) would amply suffice even if every underdeveloped country of the free world were to avail itself fully of this opportunity," and that "in practice it is unlikely that more than 50 to 60 per cent of this amount would be taken up," they propose a program based on the "banking principle." That principle is that no good loan prospect is turned down: a banker, they argue, judges projects on their economic merits, not in terms of which customers he likes best. The criterion they would use is "absorptive capacity"—the ability of a country to make good use of additional capital for internal investment.

They do attach two limits to the use of absorptive capacity as sole criterion. One is that countries with a comparatively high level of income per capita should not be allowed to exploit the principle fully. The other is that countries should not be permitted to absorb "huge individual projects that are feasible only because they can be operated by outside management and outside technicians."

Even Millikan and Rostow have the problem of deciding how high a level of income disqualifies a country, and whether the formula can be made uniform over the world. But aside from that, they do solve, or evade, the problem of criteria if two conditions are met. First, their estimate of the total that might have to be made available must not be too far wrong. Second, "absorptive capacity" must prove to be a fairly objective, unambiguous concept, capable of straightforward estimate. It must be visibly fair, nondiscriminatory, and "objective" to the recipient countries. Otherwise the advantages claimed for a nondiscriminatory, politically neutral, "bankers" attitude, with reduced suspicion and resentment on the part of recipient countries, would be lost. If we cut the Indonesian request by two-thirds on the grounds that they are incapable of using the money properly, and even incapable of realizing that they cannot use it properly, for lack of experience, analytical ability, and sophisticated government, their belief that we have discriminated unfairly against them may be as strong as if we had actually done so.

Suppose our resources are not up to the total envisaged by Millikan and Rostow, or that their estimate is seriously on the low side. They have referred to their proposal as an "all-or-none" proposal, many of whose virtues would be lost if a less ambitious program replaced it because of the resulting need to find inherently discriminatory criteria. If we are faced with the need for criteria, where can we find them?

There is nothing but intellectual laziness to favor the criterion of maximum economic impact. If we put all of the aid money into the countries that can most effectively use it, in the sense that they can achieve the greatest increase in production levels per dollar of aid received, we have not necessarily maximized our achievement of any important objective. There is no reason to suppose that the countries that happen to have the resources for a rapid rise in income are those where economic development is most urgently needed from the point of view of world peace or United States foreign policy. Nor is it true that the result would be a "fair and equitable" distribution of the resulting rise in aggregate income.

It is equally impossible to justify giving the aid to the poorest countries. This too would be only accidentally related to the objectives of peace, stability, etc., and it furthermore pays too little attention to how well countries can use aid. The poorest countries could often, at least in the early years, make so little use of assistance that it would only serve to raise consumption levels for as long as the aid lasted, without generating the kind of indigenous, self-sustaining growth that must eventually be the main source of their development.

Where else can we find criteria? Distributing the aid in equal amounts per capita would bear no necessary correlation with the achievement of fundamental objectives. It may not even strike most countries as being "fair" except in a purely arithmetical way. We may be left taking refuge in the principle of distributing aid in accordance with the maximization of United States policy objectives, defining those objectives in an enlightened way. Even this suffers two disadvantages. One, which is serious or not depending on how much we agree with the view of Millikan and Rostow, is that such a criterion will appear discriminatory, discretionary, and politically motivated, and would be difficult to accompany with convincing professions that there were no "strings" attached. The second difficulty is that the "maximization of United States foreign policy objectives" is no answer to our question; it *is* the question. Under what criteria will our objectives be maximized?

There probably are no criteria that can be stated in advance, written down objectively, or expressed in a formula. This is not to say that the application of intelligence and judgment would fail to work out a reasonable distribution of the aid—only that the resulting distribution could not readily be rationalized in terms of criteria that could be simply expressed. (It is interesting that the same conclusion is reached by the Senate Committee's Civilian-Military Review Panel in connection with military assistance. "It is a fallacy to believe that any given set of criteria can have universal applicability." Their reasoning is strikingly parallel to that presented here in connection with economic-development assistance.)

The problem is especially difficult in view of the necessity for judging assistance in the light of the country's own saving, including its tax program. We cannot talk about the need for aid without talking about the level of consumption and the level of taxes. Worse still, in countries that have sizeable military programs—whether the programs are of interest to the United States or not—the use of resources for military purposes directly competes with economic development. To judge a country's request for assistance reasonable is to judge that it is making reasonable use of its own resources, which means that the diversion of resources to military use is acceptable. This implicit military judgment could be avoided if we could take military programs as fixed; but in this connection, as with taxes, they probably cannot be taken as fixed in a long-range program in the course of which both government revenues and national income are expected to increase substantially. We should not be too confident that we can predict the attitudes of governments toward military forces for the next half-dozen years, judging by some of the surprises of the last half-dozen.

The latter point can be made in reverse too, further complicating the problem of separating military and economic development assistance discussed in a later section. The Institute of War and Peace Studies stated in its paper for the Senate Committee that "by increasing the quality, mobility, and firepower of local forces, it should be possible to get the same degree of military effectiveness with fewer men under arms." In other words, increased military assistance can to some extent be used to reduce the economic burden on the recipient. To that extent it is capable of substituting for "economic" assistance.

In establishing priorities among countries for the receipt of our aid, one special question arises.

## 6 Priority for countries allied with us

Should we give deliberate preference to countries allied with us or cooperating with us in our strategic plans? The Citizen Advisers appointed by the President gave a straightforward answer to this question:

In foreign assistance programs a higher priority should be given to those countries which have joined in the collective security system. We recognize that some nations apparently do not entertain either the same apprehension as we of the threat of the Communist conspiracy or the same judgment as to the measures necessary to defend against it. We fully respect their right, indeed their obligation, to take whatever course they believe to be in their own national interest. Our Government is obligated to do likewise, and we should marshal our resources to that end.

The last three sentences are a terse and powerful statement of our moral right to follow the course recommended in the first sentence if that course is the right one; they do not establish that it is the right one. It may be useful to divide the question into two parts.

First, are we obligated to follow a *nondiscriminatory* policy, as proposed by several of the studies, and abstain from showing favoritism to allies even when favoritism seems to be in line with our security interest? Second, are we obliged to follow a *discriminatory* policy, and show favoritism to our allies even when it seems not to be the wisest allocation of resources or the soundest diplomacy, from the point of view of our own security? The Survey of Southeast Asia done for the Senate Committee referred to the "embarrassing subject: how to explain the fact that 'neutral' countries seem to be getting priority attention in United States consideration of dollar assistance and economic development." It reports that the American-aid team in Thailand "therefore feels fully justified in recommending a broader program for Thai operations." (The quotation reminds us, incidentally, that the embarrassing nature of the "fact" is somewhat independent of whether the fact is true—also that it may depend, for each allied country, on which particular neutrals it is most sensitive about.) This is the same problem, it will be recalled, that trapped the Eisenhower Administration when it first attempted to withdraw its moral condemnation from neutrality. The outcome was, perhaps necessarily, a little like the Orwell principle that "all countries are equal but some are more equal than others."

The dilemma is a real one; and it is not confined to the paternalistic question of rewards. It involves also how strong a reciprocal obligation the United States will recognize to countries that have taken commitments, sometimes quite irrevocably, often in the face of Soviet threats and at the risk of some domestic unpopularity. On the other hand, it must be recognized that mutual obligations are sometimes quite opportunistic on one side, or even on both. In "bargains of mutual convenience," especially where there is not even a pretense at the sharing of fundamental values between the parties, it is the letter rather than the spirit of the bargain that counts, and loyalty to partners is involved only slightly if at all. Certainly it is not difficult to find at least some "neutrals" that are more reliable as potential allies than some of the countries on "our side." Thus systematic discrimination, even if accepted in principle, is far from simple to apply.

There may be a fallacy in thinking of this "priority" problem in purely quantitative terms. If criteria for determining the proper size of country programs are as complicated as has already been suggested above, it may be no easy task to tell whether discrimination has favored one country or another. The amount of aid is surely no measure; nor is the amount per capita, especially among countries with very different income levels to begin with. If the International Development Advisory Board cannot ascertain (and nobody else can either) whether the "economic-development" component of defense support for Asian countries is closer to $250 million or $700 million, it will be most difficult to decide whether Thailand (with income per capita of an estimated $100 per year) is receiving better treatment than Indonesia (income per capita estimated at about $125) or India ($80) or—since there must be degrees of alliance and priority—South Korea or Viet Nam. And how much do we value the "invisible aid," if any, contained in a United States guarantee to help defend a country?

The practical policy issue—it appears from these considerations—is therefore not whether we *should* discriminate in favor of allies and collaborators but whether we *may*. A policy of indiscriminate discrimination, aside from being dubious policy, is incapable of being translated into programs.

140

# 7 Separation of military and economic assistance

Should military and economic assistance programs be separated in concept, in administration, and in the budget and appropriations? There is virtually unanimous agreement on the desirability of such a separation. The reasons are strong, if not altogether clear. Most frequently stated is the "public relations" effect on the other countries, both recipient countries and others. It is argued that our economic aid programs suffer in the shadow of the much larger military programs.

It is also argued that Congress and public could comprehend the programs better if military assistance were merged with the defense budget. The draft report of the House Committee, for example, stated that "foreign military aid is part and parcel of our own defense program. Funds for military assistance to our allies should be placed in our defense budget and presented to Congress on that basis." The House Committee found no witness, whether from the Defense Department, the State Department, or private life, who objected to such a separation. There is probably no single point on which there is such unanimity. All of the studies that touched on this question argued for the separation.

One of the difficulties with this point, as with almost every other point we are touching on, is that they have usually been discussed in the abstract. In no case has any study, or any witness, used a check list of the world's countries to see precisely where the proposal was intended to apply and where exceptions would have to be made. In the present instance, it has often not been clear whether military and economic aid are to be segregated for impact on the particular countries that receive both kinds, or for the more general propaganda effect on the whole world, aid recipients and others.

It is in the countries that receive both kinds of assistance that complete segregation is most difficult and, with an exception or two, probably least worth while. It has been argued that Pakistan, perhaps Iran, and conceivably Turkey, are countries in which military and economic aid should be more clearly separated; it has seldom been argued that the same is as true of Formosa. Proponents of separation apparently have in mind the effect on India, which does not receive military aid, as much as the effect on Pakistan, which does. (It should be noted that the Dulles statement proposed, for countries like South Korea and Turkey that receive economic aid in support of defense costs, to separate such aid from any economic aid intended to support the economic development of these countries, and to include the former along with military end-item assistance in the Defense Department's own appropriation.)

Arguments in favor of segregation are apparently so persuasive that it may be worth while to raise a few questions about it. First, would the propaganda problem be as important as it is now, if the economic-development assistance program were not really as subordinate in size as it presently is? If the CED proposal for an expansion of economic-development aid by $1 billion or so per year were adopted, would the problem of emphasis between military and economic be a serious one still?

Second, what kind of treatment would be accorded the countries that continued to receive military assistance? Could they simultaneously receive "pure" economic-development assistance unrelated to the military program? Much of this question depends on what we mean by "unrelated." Certainly there is no insoluble technical problem of distinguishing military end-items from other commodities (even though there are borderline cases like vehicle tires that can only be allocated arbitrarily.) And certainly a portion of a country's economic assistance can be called "defense support" and appropriated in a different Act of Congress, and put through administrative formalities that accentuate the military orientation of the program. This is done to some extent already, and could be done more. On the other hand, if "separation" of the programs refers to the determination of each without regard to the other, or of negotiating each part with the recipient country in complete isolation from the other, and in general of treating each as though the other did not affect it, then there are serious logical difficulties.

Everything that was said in justification of the Marshall Plan, about shipping consumer goods to facilitate investment in Europe, everything that has been said in justification of "defense support" in NATO or the Far East, and everything that flows from the simple arithmetic that is used in deriving a country's requirements for economic development assistance—all of it argues that the military and the development claims on resources are competing and interdependent, that military-force levels cannot be determined without regard to the inflow of financial resources, and that the countries own resources available for development will depend on how much is going into military strength. (This is aside from the borderline problems of roads, railroads, harbor facilities, and technical assistance, that serve both objectives simultaneously and in indeterminable proportions.) The decision on how much of a country's defense burden the United States will assume is perforce a decision on how much of the country's own resources will be free for economic development, and vice versa.

There are two choices here. One is to count such countries out of the economic development program and treat them as a special category of military aid recipients. This would be no problem for some but seriously difficult for others, particularly those that have no desire to appear to be satellites of the United States as well as those that might feel that they would do better under a development assistance program. It would improve our propaganda with respect to the "clean" economic development countries, but probably worsen it with respect to border-line cases like Pakistan, Iran, Philippines, and Viet Nam. (It would also seriously complicate any effort to organize assistance of any kind of "regional" basis. India and Pakistan, or Burma and Thailand, or

Indonesia and the Philippines, would be incompatible with each other under this kind of segregation, if one had concluded on other grounds that regional arrangements were desirable.)

The other option is to pretend that military and economic aid can be separated in logic, while knowing that they cannot be. The arrangements and the formalities could be devised with this in mind. The result would not be wholly satisfactory, but it might be workable. We should be careful, however, not to forget that it is only a pretense, since the need for coordinating military and economic programs in a country like South Korea can be extremely important. Of course, if military programs could be taken as fixed for the next many years, leaving only economic-development as a variable to be considered, the logical relation between the two could be ignored. But there is no reason to suppose that military plans are immutable for the length of an economic development program—nor even for supposing that new military programs may not arise where there are none now.

*Foreign policy supervision of military aid.* There is another aspect of the military-economic separation that may deserve mention. It is an attitude that can occasionally be sensed but can not easily be documented. With the growing interest in economic development, and some growing disillusion with the value of military alliances, there may be a tendency to slough off military assistance onto the military services. It has lost the glamour of NATO or of Indochina. There is perhaps even some regret that the programs ever reached their present size outside the NATO area, and a belief that they should now be demoted, perhaps even starved by having to compete directly with service needs in the Defense budget. It may deserve to be stressed that badly conducted military assistance can do extraordinary harm; that the past will not be conveniently undone by wishing some things had been done differently; and that the military services have a primary responsibility to their own forces, not to those of other countries and not to American diplomacy. If military assistance is being let go by default, the trend may be a bad omen.

A vivid statement of the need for close foreign-policy supervision of military-aid programs is contained in the following quotation from the Columbia University Institute of War and Peace Studies, on "the kind of relationship into which the United States has entered" in some of its military-aid arrangements:

A nation politically and economically underdeveloped, without hope of independently sustaining a significant military effort, has been given outside support sufficient to build up its armed forces. In the process of lining up openly with the United States, it relinquishes the uncommitted role that at least several Asian nations have found rather comfortable, and identifies itself before Soviet or Chinese power as a growing point of potential opposition. Thus, if the United States had a sufficient security interest in the independence and integrity of the particular country to begin an aid program in the first place, there would be a strong presumption against the termination of assistance so long as the Soviet threat persisted and the aided country remained a loyal ally. For military, and

143

especially psychological reasons, to interrupt the program for any length of time would probably be to leave the country more 'exposed' to the adversary than if military assistance had never been begun. It would also, one may presume, do severe damage to the prestige and national reputation of the United States in Asia.

The problem is not, of course, peculiar to underdeveloped countries; Norway might also be an excellent example. Another problem is special to the underdeveloped countries, however. It concerns citizens who have done their military tours and have been released. To quote the Columbia study again:

These men receive a sort of dual conditioning: on the one hand, to appreciate a standard of living frequently higher than they enjoyed before (however low the standards in the local armed forces might appear by our criteria); and, on the other, to handle small arms with facility. Turning loose on the country substantial numbers of men conditioned in this way may provide numerous potential recruits for armed guerilla and bandit gangs. This problem would arise to some degree under any system of rotating service. But it would become critical in a situation where it was necessary to reduce, suddenly and materially, the level of military aid to an underdeveloped country where extremely large forces were being supported by American foreign assistance.

Whatever the applicability of these (and other, similar) considerations to particular countries, they should give pause to any cavalier proposal to treat military assistance as a purely "technical" problem for the armed services or to demote them from a major component of foreign policy to a minor component of the defense budget. The Senate's Civilian-Military Review Board also strongly emphasized the need to coordinate and evaluate these programs from a military, political, and economic point of view. At the present time, according to the Board, that need is for more coordination of military assistance with the rest of American foreign policy, not less.

*Fiscal arrangements and foreign policy coordination.* But is not the need for coordination and for careful foreign policy supervision quite a separate question from the formalities of budgeting and appropriations? Secretary Dulles has said that "all aspects of our Mutual Security Program should be under the effective foreign policy guidance of the President and the Secretary of State." But he went on, "This can be done by the exercise by the President of his inherent power to direct the Executive Branch of government. To achieve this result does not require throwing into the Department of State heavy operating responsibilities." Accordingly he has proposed, as mentioned earlier, that military assistance (including "defense support" strictly defined) be budgeted as part of the Defense budget.

The Brookings Institution, in a study of *Administrative Aspects of United States Foreign Assistance Programs* for the Senate Committee, was skeptical where Dulles is confident. It considers the "veto power" of the Secretary of State to be essential to the proper coordination of military assistance with American foreign policy. But it does not believe that the exercise of this power can be easily divorced from the funding process. Referring to the coordinating responsibility of the Secretary of State, Brookings says that "much of the integrating effect of these responsibilities would be lost if the authority to determine the value of military country programs were to be withdrawn." "Moreover," continues the Brookings Institution, "there is a direct relationship between the continuation of that authority and the continued consolidation of funds for military and other forms of foreign assistance in a single appropriation—on which a unified presentation of appropriation requests depends."

The deciding factor—in whether the Department of State (or some other agency) can coordinate and supervise these programs without any control of the funds—is probably the degree of complexity of the problems that arise. If only basic issues are involved, of the kind that can be settled at the highest level and embodied in unambiguous directives, then clearly the President and Secretary of State do not need to rely on fiscal procedures to enforce their determinations.

If, on the contrary, the problems are continual and complex, involving the exercise of day-to-day judgment and recourse to specialized talent, and involving matters on which different agencies may disagree, then the administrative problem is of a different character. In this case participation in the funding process is one of the few tested means whereby an agency can exercise any effective authority on problems other than those that are worth the provocation of a cabinet-level dispute. Brookings apparently believes, and the Institute of War and Peace Studies amply documents, that the problems are of the latter character.

## 8 Separation of development from other economic aid

Can we separate economic development assistance from other kinds of financial assistance, including "crisis" aid and the aid in consideration of a *quid pro quo*? John J. McCloy, speaking to the House Committee, said, "Apart from any sums which should be set aside for emergency conditions, such as existed in Guatemala or Bolivia, or whatever particular brush fire might appear—and there certainly will be some—there should be authorized a pure development program classified and labelled as such." Others expressed similar views, and presumably had in mind programs such as our aid to Yugoslavia or Spain, perhaps to Morocco.

The study for the Senate Committee on *Foreign Assistance Activities of the Communist Bloc and their Implications for the United States*, however, concluded that a policy of economic assistance should be broader than the promotion of development. "At times the United States may find it expedient to purchase foreign products (e.g. Icelandic fish) to head off a Soviet move; or at times special assistance may be required to avoid a balance of payments problem which otherwise would be exploited by the bloc." Others have referred to the need for occasional flexibility to meet crises. Those who have concerned themselves with this problem have usually forecast that such crises will continue to occur.

The question is not, then, whether there needs to be another kind of assistance, aside from purely military and purely development, but whether such assistance can and should be kept conceptually and administratively separate from the assistance to development.

Here the problem is in two parts. Can it be kept separate *within* a country in which both kinds of assistance are given? Can it be kept separate *between* those countries that receive one kind and those that receive the other? Within a country that receives both kinds, the logical problem is much like that in the attempted separation of military and economic aid. If a country has a sudden foreign-exchange or budgetary crisis, or a natural disaster, it is not easy to identify what part of its requirement for assistance is due to the sudden emergency. This is especially true if there is any choice of how far to meet the crisis. In that case, the less special assistance provided the more it may be met at the expense of development assistance, and vice versa, so that the two are interconnected.

On the other hand, in cases of this sort there may be an especially strong reason for trying to keep the two separate, in appearance if not in logic. The one may be a temporary program while the other may be much longer range. It is always embarrassing to reduce or eliminate an economic aid program, especially if the population has come to expect its continuance. If it is difficult to disentangle the separate *objectives* of a single program, it may be important to put one part of the aid through a special set of formalities, if only to dramatize the extraordinary and non-continuing nature of it.

The greatest difficulty arises in a country in which we have a continuing interest in a *quid pro quo*, or an objective that is not too easy to identify and make public. In Morocco, Libya, Iran, or Iceland, an aid program is influenced by a fairly direct interest in base rights or something similar. For the integrity of a development assistance program it may seem desirable to label as such the aid that is really for base rights. But the negotiating process that leads to the total may not be one that neatly divides the total in two parts. The recipient country may object to overt payment, and prefer its aid construed as economic development for its own sake. Most countries would rather exchange favors than sell privileges; and most would like it on the record that they warranted development assistance in the full amount, irrespective of what specialized concessions it behooved them to make to the United States.

This does not imply that the United States has to give them their way, nor that in every case this will be their wish. But we should keep in mind that where important bilateral negotiations are involved, it takes two to make a bargain; and the other party may have a very different interest from ours—or from third countries—in whether to distinguish between the "clean" and the "messy," or the "economic" and the "political," portions of their aid.

Spain may be a good example. It is anybody's guess what the United States might have paid outright for the base rights that it acquired through the aid program. One thing was clear; it was of the highest concern to the Spanish government after a long period of ostracism, to be welcomed into the community of aid-receiving nations and to join the United States in a treaty of "mutual defense" rather than a unilateral sale of defense facilities. Under the original agreement there was every expectation that most of the counterpart funds under the economic aid program would be available for the construction of American air bases, so that the result would be almost as if the United States used economic aid money to buy Spanish currency with which to carry out its own construction expenditures. But the formality of "economic aid" was important to the Spanish government, and it is doubtful whether an outright "rental" of Spanish soil could have accomplished the purpose except at a greatly elevated cost. The same delicacy may attach to our relations with Morocco, where the original status of our air bases was negotiated when the French, not the Moroccans, were making the concessions.

The proposal mentioned above about Iceland is another example, and not entirely hypothetical if viewed as a counterpart to the earlier question of base rights. The authors of the quoted study were concerned about the dependence of Iceland on the Soviet market for their fish. One can imagine an aid program according to which the United States gave dollars, say, to Iceland, took the fish off their hands and delivered them elsewhere under an aid program, to avoid the question of what to do with the fish at home. If this were labelled as a deliberate program to destroy trade with the Soviet bloc, it is by no means clear that Iceland would be as willing to participate as if it were referred to as "triangular development assistance."

In earlier years, when Iceland received defense support at a time when American bases were important in that country, our aid was not independent of the fact that we needed bases there. But to have identified the aid as an outright bargain for air bases would probably have aggravated the political problems that arose a few years later.

(The "purity" of economic development aid would also suffer from the obvious mixture of motives evidenced in agricultural-surplus disposal.)

*Parellel with military assistance.* There is again a close parallel with the conclusion reached by the Institute of War and Peace Studies on the "value of having a variety of kinds of assistance programs at the service of American diplomacy." The Institute says:

It is entirely possible that under an economic or technical assistance program, measures of considerable military defense significance (public works like bridge and road construction, and the building of factories which are convertible from 'plowshares to swords') could be accomplished. If the country is

147

really neutral and not 'neutralist' it presumably wishes to be able to protect itself and would welcome assistance to improve its ability to do so. It is often the name, connotations, and accompanying conditions of military aid, not the substance of what is accomplished, that present the obstacle.

It points out that military assistance has provided leverage in negotiations for base rights with other countries. "It was reported from Lisbon in June 1956, that 'problems of aerial defense,' which presumably could be solved by the supply of certain military end items, were beclouding Portuguese-American relations temporarily. By a coincidence, negotiations were at that moment under way for renewal of base rights in the Azores."

The Civilian-Military Review Board also referred to diplomatic and other gains that would from time to time justify "giving countries weapons and equipment which are not best suited to their individual needs or to United States military objectives. The United States sometimes accedes to these requests because of its need for bases or other concessions, or for other political and economic considerations which have validity." Thus the need—or temptation, anyway—to violate the purity of the program appears to arise as forcefully with the military portion as with the economic.

## 9 Soviet aid activities

What attitude should we take toward the "aid" activities of the Soviet bloc? According to the study done for the Senate Committee, the Soviet bloc had by August 1956 extended credit to the underdeveloped countries amounting to $1.4 billion in the last two years, and another $200 million was known to be under negotiation. As the study revealed, "Credit offers in 1954 and 1955 were often regarded as mere propaganda—but the fact is that $1.4 billion is now committed and accepted. The Soviets are quite capable of extending considerably more; and all countries approached need credit from some source."

Though it has been customary to belittle these credits for not being grants, the fact is that the terms on the loans are usually quite easy: interest from 2 to $2\frac{1}{2}$ per cent, amortization running from 10 years up to 30, with repayment frequently in kind or in choice of currencies. If these credits are utilized within five years or less, they will finance more than a quarter of a billion dollars a year in capital goods and arms, plus whatever is provided under new loan agreements still to be negotiated. The importance of these credits is enhanced by the fact that they mainly involve capital goods, which carry with them technical assistance and technicians and a degree of dependence on Soviet technology and spare parts. We must also recall that large numbers of technicians from the underdeveloped countries, especially the Asian countries, are currently being educated in the Soviet Union.

There are three possible attitudes toward this activity. One is to ignore it. That would be a mistake, especially if we ignore it because we think it is a fake or because we think it has been a one-shot operation and will disappear. Rather than ignore it we should take it as a lesson: in imputing to Russian policy a rigidity that made such credits unthinkable, we were ourselves inflexible in our thinking about the Soviet bloc. We should remind ourselves that the bloc values these areas of the world, has in many ways fewer inhibitions than we in embarking on a bold and discriminatory program, and can spend billions of dollars to bring a major Asian country into its orbit and still profit. We should not impute to the Soviet bloc too much of our own inhibitions about foreign policy.

A second possibility is to recognize the Soviet activity as an enhancement of the general threat, increasing the urgency of our problem in the underdeveloped areas, but not necessarily one that is to be combatted in any direct, specific way through competition in kind or an effort to induce countries to refuse Soviet trade and aid.

The third possibility is to organize our aid program so as to embarrass the Soviet bloc, to compete more directly with it, or to force countries to choose between us. On the latter point the draft report of the House Committee states its view with eloquent simplicity. "It is important that we avoid making the so-called uncommitted nations formally choose sides under the conditions that exist in the world today."

Recent events in the Middle East illuminate these issues more than adequately. Here it may be sufficient to indicate the recommendations of the Council for Economic and Industry Research, Inc., which did the study for the Senate Committee. The authors are skeptical of challenging the USSR to match United States aid. They are afraid that we will be equally embarrassed by reciprocal challenges. They point out that the Soviet Union could play at the competitive game, "making offers with no substance behind them, merely to draw the United States into dubious projects at great cost. Of course the United States could attempt the same game, but the duplicity required seems more congenial to, and plentiful in, the USSR. In short, they could perhaps play it better."

There is more to their argument, but the flavor of it is well contained in the above quotation. They also point out that it may be difficult to ensnare the Soviet Union in formalities of a joint or multilateral program since it is difficult to draw the line between aid, trade, commercial credits and "fuzzy" assistance loans.

The authors favor an "independent policy of economic assistance," one which recognizes what the Soviet bloc is doing, but which does not overtly oppose it or react to it in any specific way. They believe we should not withdraw from a country that accepts Soviet aid, but we should also not deliberately try to outdo the Soviet bloc. They believe that we may need a flexible type of assistance in particular cases, of which the Icelandic fish problem mentioned already is an example. They estimate, incidentally, that the Soviet Union has reached the point where it probably has an economic advantage in enlarged trade with

149

these areas and believe we should not dismiss their activities altogether as a short-run political experiment.

Clement Johnston, Chairman of the Board of the United States Chamber of Commerce, conducted the survey of Southeast Asia programs for the Senate Committee and reached a quite contrary view:

It would be most unfortunate if the United States were to find itself whipsawed in a competitive aid race and placed in the doubtful position of seeming to try to outbid our rivals for the privilege of giving aid away. One possible way of avoiding involvement in an aid race would be to make it abundantly clear that the United States aid program in each country has been based upon an appraisal of the total needs of the country....Each and every gift or trade arrangement from Communist sources or any receipt from any other source, either foreign or domestic, if it contributed to the meeting of this overall or total need, should make possible an immediate corresponding reduction in the total United States aid.

## 10  Relation of economic to political development

Where and how does the process of economic development impinge on American objectives in an underdeveloped country? There is one view—fortunately becoming less common—that the problem in Asia and Africa is a kind of "unrest" due to a shortfall in living standards below what people need or demand, and that economic growth will automatically reduce the "gap" between hope and realization. There is a contrary view that economic growth causes social strain—even depends for its success on a breakdown of traditions and other forces of social cohesion—and can only create instability to the discomfort of American objectives.

Abstract argument makes little progress here since there is something to be said on both sides. What is needed is a way to assess the relative weights of the forces that make growth conducive to, or antithetical to, the kind of political development that is in our interest. Some of the studies reviewed help to make progress on this question. The draft report of the House Committee reminds us that we probably do *not* have a choice between some growth and no growth. What we are faced with, according to that report, is governments determined on development, and the question is only one of our relationship to that development. The choice is rarely between quiescence and growth. More often it is between various degrees of frustration.

But whose fustration? This is a question that may help us to find, if not an answer to the fundamental question, the right point at which to hold the argument. Who in an underdeveloped country is "satisfied" by economic growth, "frustrated" by the obstacles to it, exhilarated by its success, conscious of its shortcomings?

The answer may depend on whether we are talking about 1, 3, or 10 per cent per year of growth in income per capita; and to that we shall turn in the following section. Nevertheless it is worth while to pose at this point the question of whether we have in mind the "people" of a country—the population at large—as the ones to be affected by economic growth, or the "leadership" of the country, defined narrowly or broadly. John J. McCloy told the House Committee that

if these countries could be induced to step up their investment by another 20 to 25 per cent, the marginal improvement in living standards would have a profound effect. The man in the street would be conscious of it; governments and peoples alike would gain the psychological lift that comes from an awareness that there is real hope for a better future....To get this added investment there will have to be some increase in help from abroad—perhaps on the order of $1 billion to $1.5 billion.

Millikan and Rostow expect development to promote political maturity by "posing for the leadership and the people.... challenging and constructive internal tasks which will....harness the energies of individuals throughout the society." They hope that development programs will encourage new, young, and vigorous leadership on local and national levels. They expect an increase in social and economic mobility, with the reduction of differentials between city and country, and between the sophisticated and the provincial, and a "diffusion of power." They expect with development a greater sense of confidence " as nations, and as individuals and small communities, that they can make progress through their own efforts." They emphasize that these results, which depend on the momentum of development rather than on its ultimate attainments, can be immediate rather than delayed.

Whatever the correctness of the particular expectations of Millikan and Rostow as to who in a country responds how to economic growth, it is essential to tackle the problem they have tackled, and try to identify the strategic elements in a country that does respond. It is one thing to say that the "people" will get relief from a 2 or 3 per cent rise in income—if we allow enough time to pass and if they do not get used to the rise too quickly—and another to say that political leaders will get satisfaction from statistical evidence of a 2 per cent rise that they know is due partly to their own constructive efforts. Further progress on this question is essential to the broad question of whether or not development *per se* is a force for stability and democratic values.

## 11 Significance of aid for economic development

What impact on the rate of development can an assistance program have? There is little doubt that aid programs can speed up economic development. (For some such doubt see the discussion of private investment below.) But how much difference can an aid program make? Not only must we weigh the results against the costs to see whether they are worth while. We ought also to know what to expect, to avoid disappointing ourselves in the future, and to avoid relying either too little or too much on aid in the solution of these problems.

A few of the studies contain estimates of the difference it would make to the economic progress of underdeveloped countries to provide

151

aid of perhaps $2 billion per year. It is not clear whether the estimates are all independent. Several of those who testified before the House Committee referred to the estimates of Millikan and Rostow; the estimates of the University of Chicago study are based on the same methodology as those of Millikan and Rostow. There may have been some mutual influence between the estimates.

The Chicago group is fairly explicit. Judging from the experience of India they expect that the underdeveloped countries, left to themselves, could *at best* achieve a growth of about 2 per cent per year in income per head—"better than stagnation, but not sufficient for setting in motion a genuine process of self-sustained growth in the underdeveloped countries." This 2 per cent growth rate of income per capita would correspond, they say, to saving and investment of less than 10 per cent of national income. The authors indicate that a minimum of $3 billion of assistance, combined with $1 billion of private investment, would be required to permit income per capita to rise at a rate of 3 to 4 per cent per year (assuming an average rate of increase in population of 1.5 per cent). (The aid figure would be lower if not all underdeveloped countries outside the Iron Curtain were eligible; but if some of the more favorably situated countries are excluded, so is a large part of the potential private investment that would be going to them.) Like Millikan and Rostow the authors expect part of the assistance to be met by countries other than the United States.

Both the Chicago and the M.I.T. authors emphasize that it might not be possible for the recipient countries to use much more than $3 billion effectively. In later years—in another decade or so, according to the Chicago group—the countries might be able to use as much as $5 billion per year, but their need for outside assistance is seen as declining from then on as their ability to generate internal savings increases. With the strengthening of national economies the climate for private foreign investment might improve, "a fact illustrated by the Latin American events in recent years." But all such estimates, they say, are only "illustrations of the rough order of magnitude of the amount of aid which might be required to achieve the objectives stated in this report." Expenditures on foreign aid of a few hundred million dollars per year, in their opinion, would certainly fall far short of the need; tens of billions would be wasteful. This range is a wide one.

These estimates have been criticized—for example, by the American Enterprise Association, Inc., author of one of the Senate's studies. But there are few competing estimates to choose among. On the amount of assistance, the Committee for Economic Development estimated a year ago that $.5 to $1.5 billion of additional outside capital, over and above the amount then being received by underdeveloped countries, would be needed. Various estimates in the order of $1 to $2 billion per year have been put forward as illustrative of the size of a really effective, and imaginative, program of American assistance.

Several of these estimates have been influenced by India's Second Five-Year Plan, which shows a gap between proposed investment and available financing. When transferred to the whole underdeveloped area on a per capita basis, this works out at $2 or $3 billion per year depending on what area one has in mind, what definition of "assistance" is used, and what allowance one makes for the fact that India is several years ahead of many countries in its ability to program and use foreign capital. (The "official" gap in India's program may not, of course, indicate India's estimate of the most it could actually use if more might be available.)

How sure are we that the difference between a 1 or 2 per cent rate of growth of income per capita and a 3 or 4 per cent rate, will make a real difference to the complexion of a country's society and the behavior of its government? Is 4 per cent adequate, or would 10 per cent be required? A 4 per cent growth rate would double income per capita in about a decade and a half; 3 per cent in a quarter of a century. Is this enough? This would mean that the next generation would be twice as well off as the present generation.

It would also mean that Burma in another generation would be as well off as Thailand today, not nearly as well off as Egypt is today. Pakistan in the next generation would have caught up to where Ceylon is today. Nigeria would be up to where Ghana, or Peru is today. Turkey could stagnate for fifteen years, yet India would only reach half the Turkish level of income per capita at the end of fifteen or twenty years. (These comparisons are faulty in relying on income per capita. The average income figure for Egypt or Iran overstates the "typical" income because the former includes the income of a small number of extremely wealthy inhabitants. Additionally, the estimates are in most cases exceedingly crude. Nevertheless, they illustrate the point.)

Under the best of conditions, then, the larger part of today's underdeveloped world would still be "underdeveloped" in another generation, and characterized by poverty of an acute and degrading sort.

This is no counsel of hopelessness. Project it as many years in the future as have elapsed since the end of World War I, and most of the countries will be up to the level of the poorer countries in Europe. Compound interest does great things, even if it starts rather slowly. But to a casual observer, the difference between the American standard of living and that of South Asia seems so nearly infinite that a doubling of the lower figure would hardly be noticed. But comparison between countries may give a wrong emphasis. Doubling the income of the extremely poor may be more important to their own awareness of it than doubling the income of more well to do countries. The fact that India today would only have caught up in fifteen or twenty years with the Egypt of today, under an ambitious aid program, can reflect as much on the urgency of the need as on the modesty of the target.

*Avoidance of forced saving.* There is another way to look at the problem. Accepting severe limitations on the rate of growth that could occur, let us suppose for a moment that governments are determined to achieve those maximum rates. How can they achieve them? Without assistance they must generate internally a much higher rate of saving than now occurs. How can it be achieved? We should not generalize for countries as diverse as India, Indonesia, Morocco, and Peru; nor can we assume that they would all elect to take the necessary measures. But the example of China is unfortunately available, and Russia also, particularly during the years of mass starvation in the early thirties, illustrates how it can be done.

It can be done by abandoning the less rigorous and more civilized inducements and relying instead on forced collections from agriculture, labor inducements through fear, and the expropriation of wealth wherever it is found. People can be *made* to consume much less. They cannot readily be *induced* to under a system that relies on popular consent. Foreign assistance in these cases may provide the margin of investment resources that would otherwise be obtainable only through a repressive system of "forced saving," a system that would not only be unattractive for its ruthlessness but would involve a potent ideological affinity for the *Soviet bloc.*

## 12  Size and duration of program

What is the proper magnitude and duration of development assistance? The previous question was mainly concerned with what might be accomplished if aid were available. There is still the question of whether it is $1, $2, $3, $4, or $5 billion of aid that would bring about the highest rate of growth of which the countries are capable. Here it will be recalled that the Chicago group referred to its estimates as only "illustrative." The possible error is serious. The requirement for aid is in the nature of a "residual" between the level of investment we might wish to see achieved and the level that is likely to be financed by the country's own resources. In the case of India this residual was estimated at no more than 20 per cent. (Again, this estimate appears to rely greatly on India's official program rather than on an estimate of the most India could actually make use of.) But the basic "absorptive capacity" that may ultimately limit the rate of growth, is essentially an estimate of the total investment program that India could manage, given its technical and management skill, the capacity of its government, and the flexibility of productive resources in India. A 20 per cent error in that estimate of absorptive capacity could more than double the need for aid or wipe it out altogether.

This potential error in the aid figure might not be as large for other countries, since indigenous investment in India is large relative to the total absorptive capacity that the M.I.T. and Chicago groups have estimated for it. Nevertheless, errors in the investment estimate would have a high leverage on the errors in our aid estimate. Furthermore, in a country like India the aid requirement depends a good deal on what portion of the rise in income over the next several years would be diverted to additional investment rather than consumption (or military strength). If it turns out that the proportion is 15 or 20 per cent rather than 25 per cent—Millikan and Rostow have estimated 25 to 50 per cent—the difference may be several billion dollars, all falling into the residual to be financed by an aid program.

It can be hoped that the effect of these errors is to reduce the requirement; but there is probably more leeway on the side of higher consumption, lower taxes, more serious inflation, and all the other pressures that would raise the requirement for outside aid. Additionally, there may prove to be short-run emergencies and crises that call for nondevelopment financial assistance. Whether or not we treat these in a separate program, they may prove to be a competing claim on the funds available in a total program.

*Duration.* In addition to the annual size of these programs there is the question of duration. Most American aid programs have been inherently temporary. The Marshall Plan originally had a four-year schedule, while Lend-Lease, UNRRA and other postwar relief programs, and even the equipping of European forces under NATO, were related to situations or objectives that were terminable even if no date could be exactly forecast.

Can a development assistance program similarly be tied either to a defined span of years or to some process that necessarily comes to a close? The question can be subdivided. First, will the reasons for assistance disappear, or the objectives of assistance be achieved, so that the programs would come to a natural close? Second, does embarkation on an enlarged program of assistance to development commit us indefinately, so that we cannot readily stop even if we change our minds or develop urgent competing needs in the future?

The answer to the first question must surely be no. Point Four or the World Bank is the appropriate historical model, not the Marshall Plan or Lend-lease. Development is a continuing process. At some stage a country can outgrow its reliance on outside capital—when it reaches what Millikan and Rostow call " self-sustained" growth—but the M.I.T. and Chicago authors indicate that the elapsed time will be decades, not years, even for those in which the development process is now well under way. It must also be kept in mind that the estimated limits to how much aid could be used in the near future reflect the unreadiness of many countries to use it yet. As these countries reach the point where they can effectively use larger amounts of capital, they may offset any countries that have by then progressed to where they could drop out of the program.

The program is thus potentially very long term. It is probably of such duration that it makes no sense now to try to see where it ends. In a decade, if the program lasts that long, the character of the world will be quite different, even if only the economic growth of America and Western Europe is taken into account. Perhaps the way to formulate this conclusion is that the program potentially extends further into the future than it is worth while to plan and predict. But this conclusion does not imply that the fruits of a program are only in the far future. As most of the studies have emphasized, the process of successful development itself and our relationship to that development—

155

not just its ultimate attainments—may be the principal objective on which to focus.

## 13 Types of loans and grants

What kinds of loans or grants are appropriate to development assistance? Most of the studies recognize that grants are appropriate for defense support and for certain "crisis" situations in which financial aid must be given without regard to possible repayment. For the most part technical assistance is expected to continue on a grant basis ("on much the present basis" according to Secretary Dulles). But it is otherwise almost uniformly accepted that development assistance should be loans, not grants. The stated reasons for the most part are not to get our money back, but to provide assistance in a businesslike way, with formalities that emphasize that money is scarce and that the program is aimed at capital formation, not relief. Within the category of loans, however, there are several possibilities; and opinion is not uniform.

The Citizen Advisers state that loans "repayable in the inconvertible currencies of foreign nations are undesirable, and the practice of granting them should be terminated." (They make no exception for sales of agricultural surpluses, which they propose be disposed of by price reductions rather than by easy loan terms; in any case they are skeptical whether much of the surpluses can be disposed of without damage to world markets.)

Secretary Dulles did not mention how the loans of his proposed Fund would be repaid, but he did state that they should be "repayable on a basis subordinate to the claims of the World Bank, the Export-Import Bank and private lending agencies." Since there are no formal bankruptcy procedures for these situations, "subordinate" presumably means that the United States development fund would be the first to waive payment if the country had difficulties.

Several witnesses have doubted whether completely "hard" loans could be relied on, and suggest that "local currency" loans be considered, at least in some cases, i.e. loans the repayment of which would be accepted in the country's own currency. It is sometimes proposed that the United States could eventually find use itself for such currencies, perhaps for purchasing goods for third countries under aid programs to the latter. But it seems usually assumed that something like the present agricultural-surplus procedure would be used, or like some of the "counterpart-currency" revolving loan funds under E.C.A. —that is, repayment in local currency that will be lent again to the same country. Here the operation is a loan in its initial formalities, perhaps treated like almost any other loan in the receiving country's fiscal procedures, but is recognized as ultimately a grant from the point of view of the lender—or, at least, potentially a grant if the terms of repayment are left to the lender's discretion.

There is a real dilemma here. On the one hand there is the desire—quite aside from wanting our money back—to conduct the program with loans for the benefit of superior discipline and better understanding. On the other is a recognition that many of the countries will find it difficult to make repayment, that some of them will even still need aid when repayment begins to be made, and that it can be embarrassing to the United States to be a "hard" creditor to poor and struggling debtor countries at a time when past favors are forgotten in the midst of current financial problems.

The solution is not easy. Eventually it might involve finding some device whereby the United States can make loans but not remain a creditor. Perhaps earmarking the funds in advance for third countries would help to identify the beneficiary as someone other than the American lender. Possibly the World Bank or some international fund will eventually be in a position to assume the creditor's position when it becomes embarrassing for the United States. In any case, getting the money back should be the least of the considerations, if the program is really as important as the President and others have implied.

"Getting the money back" does raise one technical issue, however, that may be of some domestic importance in the United States. There is occasional evidence of confusion whether a program based on loans would be inside or outside the United States budget. Marshall Plan loans were "inside" the budget. They were appropriated funds, and their expenditure was treated like any other expenditure, the difference being only that a repayment claim went on the balance sheet. Export-Import Bank loans are outside the United States budget, as are Commodity Credit Corporation crop loans (until such time as a loss is recorded and made up by an appropriation to "restore capital").

There is probably some choice of treatment here if it is decided to have a separate "Fund." The economic difference to the United States is nil, but the difference in budgetary appearance is great. The choice may be narrowed, however, by the fact that an extrabudgetary "fund" probably could not be reconciled with "fuzzy loans." Foreseeably bad debts will probably not be permitted to go on the balance sheet of an ostensibly "sound" banking type of institution.

## 14 Effect of aid on private investment

Will government loans defeat their own purposes by reducing private foreign investment in the underdeveloped countries? It was remarked earlier that the Randall Commission was concerned about the effect of our aid programs on the welcome or hostility that underdeveloped countries extend to private American capital, or private capital from any other sources. One of the studies for the Senate Committee, "American Private Enterprise, Foreign Economic Development, and the Aid Programs," by the American Enterprise Association, Inc., bases its opposition to development assistance for the most part on this relationship:

157

Nations which feel that they have at least an outside chance of obtaining large-scale development aid from the United States Government are unlikely to take many steps to encourage increased private foreign investment, since interest and dividends on such investments are often regarded by them as a net drain on their development resources (thereby necessitating more aid).... In short, development aid and private foreign investment are more often competitive rather than complementary.

Later the authors qualify this conclusion:

The point is not that American grants and loans will compete with private capital. In general, most United States Government agencies and international organizations like the International Bank for Reconstruction and Development have sought to avoid competition with private capital in fields that would be attractive for private investors. The point is rather that governmental loans carrying especially easy terms as a kind of gift will create misunderstanding in the borrowing country about the rate of return on private loans or investments that is appropriate and commensurate with the risk.

They add the further qualification that their objection does not apply in the case of aid for the provision of "genuine" public service facilities such as roads, which they expect the countries to get from the World Bank.

The authors are fairly optimistic about the prospects for overseas investment in the underdeveloped countries, on the important conditions that the recipient countries themselves take the kinds of steps that would make investment there attractive. "Most of the obstacles to expanded private foreign investment are found in the less-developed countries themselves." They have in mind both general disincentives such as inconvertibility of currencies, and the more specific disincentives such as nationalization and confiscation, discriminatory taxation, discriminatory exchange controls, restrictions on the nationality of ownership and of management, and direct prohibitions on private enterprise in particular sectors of the economy.

The authors do not necessarily argue that a dollar of government assistance will reduce private investment by a dollar. A substantially lesser impact on private investment would still cause them concern. The reason is that they consider private investment to play an important role in supplying initiative and organizing ability, in transferring skills, encouraging modern marketing procedures, broadening local capital markets, improving commercial attitudes in the countries concerned, and generally promoting the benefits of an economy less dependent on government finance, government initiative, and government management. (Their discussion of the role of private investment, and the influences affecting it, is excellent, and a valuable addition to the available literature.)

They are also skeptical of the process of forced development generated by public expenditure. They are doubtful both whether it can occur and whether it could occur without extreme social disturbance.

They prefer a less rapid rate of growth based squarely on private rather than government enterprise.

Yet it is doubtful whether most of the other authors could disagree with the study at specific points, except in terms of emphasis and degree. If there are fundamental differences between the premises of that study and those of most of the others, they are two: First, their approach is at complete variance to that of the draft House Committee Report, on a point already quoted, but that bears to be quoted again:

Although we have justified economic assistance on a number of grounds, the most important reason is that nations are determined to develop. Only by participation in that process will we have an opportunity to direct their development along lines that will best serve our interests.

Second, the study is unique among those under review in making no reference to the communist threat, the cold war, or the exigencies of diplomacy and military policy. In both these respects, it assumes a wider range of options available to the United States.

*Antidotes to socialism.* Finally, it also disagrees with most of the other authors—certainly with the Chicago group—on what is the best antidote to socialism, or for that matter on the question of how important it is to the United States that other countries avoid socialism. Government assistance may, by reducing either the scarcity of foreign exchange or the scarcity of investment resources in a country, permit a relaxation rather than a tightening of direct controls in a country. This must certainly have been true of the Marshall Plan, even though it appeared superficially that the United States government, by requiring a careful screening and rationing of imports, promoted direct controls. The strongest economic forces toward direct controls are inflation and foreign exchange difficulties.

The United States government may also be in a stronger position to influence countries in the direction of freer economies if it engages with them in a programming process than if it confines its interest to bargaining over the terms to be accorded to private American investors. On this point the IDAB report believes that "economic assistance .... provides a major channel for mutual understanding and influence, perhaps the most important channel available.... Economic cooperation—working together in common purpose—offers, we believe, the most durable bridge for linking our objectives and theirs for economically and politically free societies." (The record, incidentally, will show striking enthusiasm for free enterprise in the administration of American aid programs.)

Finally, as mentioned earlier, for most of these countries the critical question is not one of government management versus private management. It is whether totalitarian methods will eventually be resorted to in order to increase the level of saving. A crude distinction among "communism," "socialism," and "capitalism," might be made, with the grave possibility of winning the fight against socialist

159

enterprise and losing the final decision to communist techniques in providing the indigenous capital for economic growth.

*Areas of public financing.* In assessing the relative roles of private and government capital, the CED said in an earlier statement (on Economic Development Abroad, February, 1956) that

even after all practical measures are taken to increase private foreign investment from the United States and other industrial countries, it seems probable that most of this shortage of capital will remain until development has proceeded well beyond its present stage. For this shortage is, in the main, an unfilled need for funds to invest in transportation and other basic economic facilities—fields of investment which are not likely to be attractive to private foreign investors.

It should also be kept in mind that, though "aid" usually is extended to governments, not private business, the net impact is not necessarily restricted to government projects. Aid-financed government investment may reduce the government's domestic financing, thereby releasing resources for private investment. Or the proceeds of an aid program can be channeled into loans to private business, farming, housing, etc. In areas where capital markets are still rudimentary, intergovernmental loans may be an important contribution to the financing of private investment.

## 15 Individual projects vs. comprehensive programs

Should American aid be related to individual projects, or to some over-all program of development for the country? This question should be divided. First, is there any logical way of deciding on the amount of aid for a country, or on the allocation of investment among sectors of the economy, except on the basis of an over-all program of investment and sources of finance? A second question is whether it makes sense, in the administration of an aid program, to relate the aid closely to specific, identifiable projects, rather than just to underwrite some residual deficit in the investment resources of a country.

On the first question the logic is clear. There may be tactical reasons for never discussing with a country its total requirements, and limiting our aid to a narrow range of activities. But for intelligent analysis what matters is not whether we finance only "sound" projects, in the "right" industries. If the country is financing unsound projects in the wrong industries with its own resources, and is doing so because we have taken care of the sound projects and the right industries, the net effect of our program is to make possible the unsound projects and the wrong industries. This is the same point that was recognized in the Marshall Plan. If one buys all of a country's necessities for it, its own resources are free to be spent at the country's own discretion on lesser priority goods. Only by a comprehensive review of the resources available, and some understanding of how they will be applied, is it possible to judge the net effect of an aid program. This is true whether the country's main shortage is foreign exchange or domestic saving.

When we come to the management of an aid program, though, there is a good deal to be said for the project approach. One useful effect of an aid program—and this has been important with the World Bank—is the educational process that goes into the "projects." High standards of analysis, planning, consideration of costs and alternatives, and careful consideration of whether the technical and management skills are available to handle the project once built, can all be encouraged by a well-conducted project procedure.

*Comprehensive "programs" and controlled economies.* Another issue sometimes arises under this question. Does an over-all "programming" approach induce governments to "plan" their economies more than they otherwise would, and to control them more as a result of the planning process? It is sometimes argued that it is "socialistic" to map out the allocation of total investment in a country, private as well as government, and that it would be better to restrict the government planning to those particular projects that are going in any case to be financed by the government. The American Enterprise Association, Inc., in its study for the Senate Committee, remarks that

the granting of aid is often tied to the formulation of development plans and programs, which envisages substantial government investment or compulsory saving, or other forms of governmental control over the economy, and which in a number of ways retard the emergence, entry and activities of private enterprise, both domestic and foreign. At times the aid is not only tied explicitly or implicitly to the preparation of such a plan but actually takes the form of a grant for such purpose.

We should be careful not to identify "planning" with controlling everything that goes into the plan. Much of what is called "planning" is estimating or forecasting, so that the activities that do come under the purview of government are conducted in the context of an intelligently foreseen economic development. For this purpose, private enterprise itself can benefit from the effort to put together a consistent picture of what is happening in all sectors of the economy, especially in view of the interdependence among the growth processes in different sectors. Certainly the planning of a road network requires consideration to what is happening in agriculture and industry; and the decisions made in agriculture and industry can be more intelligently made if there is a picture of what is happening to the road network. The "plan" may serve as a clearing house of information. Perhaps the term "projection" that has come into use in the United States is sometimes a better term for what is called "planning" in other countries. It has the more neutral connotation of looking at the foreseeable picture, both the controlled and the uncontrolled part of the economy, rather than the apparent connotation of necessarily determining what will happen in all sectors.

More important is the educational process of "programming" itself. A serious obstacle to constructive controversy in underdeveloped countries—to realistic expectations, intelligent government, and the focus of attention on what is feasible—is lack of acquaintance with the simple arithmetic of economic development. Until one sits down with the national statistics, a pencil and paper and perhaps a slide rule, to think about what is really feasible, there may exist the wildest ideas about what could be accomplished through a little bit of expropriation, income redistribution, land reform, reorganization of business, expansion of bank credit, dissipation of foreign exchange reserves, increase in wages or decrease in wages, or any other panacea.

But when inter-agency and inter-party disagreements can be forced into the constraint of simple logic and arithmetic, where the imaginary is replaced by the feasible, there may result a more sober appreciation of what needs to be done. Demagogues may have to shut up or put up a workable alternative to what they object to. The press may be educated into a better understanding of what alternatives are actually available. The Indian Five-Year Plans, whatever else they may have done, have channeled economic controversy into constructive argument over actual alternatives within a fairly realistic picture of what can be done and what has to be done, and has eliminated much that was fanciful, unrealistic, or just destructively critical. Some of the strongest refutations of irresponsible communist claims is provided by the simple arithmetic of production, consumption, saving, and capital formation.

## 16 Multilateral administration

Should our assistance to economic development be conducted through multilateral channels? Interest in this question has died down since a year ago, when there were many proposals for channeling aid through the U.N., the World Bank, or agencies yet to be announced. With a few exceptions the studies and witnesses reviewed here are persuaded that multilateral aid decisions would be undesirable or, at least, impracticable. Two exceptions were Roy Blough of Columbia University and Norman Buchanan of the Rockefeller Foundation.

Most of the arguments both for and against multilateral aid are implicit in our earlier questions. There is a necessary correlation between one's view on this subject, and on the desirability of bilateral involvement, on the pragmatic approach vs. the new and integral program, on one's confidence in "objective" criteria and on the separability of development aid from all other aid. (The same underlying questions have an important bearing on the desirability and practicability of utilizing regional institutions for the determination or administration of aid. It should, incidentally, be kept in mind that most of the geographical "regions" outside Europe and North America do not have much economic cohesion. Their important trade is often with countries outside the region rather than with each other, with the possible exception of a region built around the industrial nucleus of Japan.)

Millikan and Rostow believe that "bilateral aid within a multilateral framework" might be a worthwhile experiment. They suggest three features: formal arrangements for consultation, full exchange of information, and some kind of technical "clearing house" that might, among other things, establish criteria by which all countries should judge development programs and aid allocations. This clearing house —which is evidently the ambitious part of their proposal—they suggest might engage in a screening process on behalf of all countries extending assistance, and provide a commonly recognized basis for judgment, or perhaps even judgment itself.

Another possibility is to distinguish unilateral decisions on the *amounts* of aid from detailed *administration* by something like the World Bank, as "agent," of amounts already decided. This arrangement might be especially useful where more than one country is extending assistance.

## 17 Legislative framework

Should development-assistance be put on a long-range basis, with permanent legislation or the establishment of a separate "fund"? The need for long-range planning is indicated by all of the studies under review. Several recommend some special legislative framework to give effect to this aspect of the program. The International Development Advisory Board has proposed the establishment of a separate International Development Fund, financed for a minimum of three years at the outset, well enough endowed to permit an immediate and substantial increase in the programs, operating mainly through loans but with flexibility left to the administrator. "The fund should not meet requirements that can be filled by private investors, the IBRD, the IFC, or the Ex-Im Bank. It should supplement these institutions and, as a matter of basic policy, it should encourage and step aside in favor of private investments."

Others have suggested that the Congress might authorize a development assistance program with permanent legislation, even though the appropriations would still be on an annual basis. The Citizen Advisers proposed that programs be presented to Congress every two years, in the first session of a Congress, to permit "more efficient planning and utilization of funds." At the same time, they say, each session of Congress could call for a review at any time that it saw fit, and no Congress would be committing, in advance, any subsequent Congress. Secretary Dulles' proposals of April 8, 1957, appear to envisage a loan fund along the lines recommended by the International Development Advisory Board.

In this connection the House Committee is a party at interest; but that may qualify as much as disqualify it to speak on the subject. The draft report makes the point that to place all subsequent responsibility

163

for these programs on the appropriations committee has disadvantages "if these programs are to be considered in the larger framework of foreign policy." The report proposes that the Committee on Foreign Affairs retain some control over them. "The Committee has handled these programs from their inception. Through testimony and travel its members have gained an understanding of their relation to other phases of our foreign policy. Under the Legislative Reorganization Act the Committee is made responsible for 'relations of the United States with foreign nations generally' and for foreign loans." Further, a permanent authorization relieves the Executive Branch of accountability, at least within the House of Representatives, for the foreign policy implications of the programs.

The report abstained from observing that the Committee on Foreign Affairs has been a good deal friendlier to these programs than the Appropriations Committee and that their different responsibilities and interests make it natural that they should be friendlier. It would indeed be a shame to lessen reliance on the authorizing committee, if it converted the whole annual Congressional cycle into just an attempt to save money.

(A similar juridsictional transfer might result from placing the military assistance and "defense support" programs in the Defense Department's budget. Heretofore the Senate Foreign Relations Committee has been at least coordinate with the Armed Services Committee in reviewing the program, and in some years has done so alone; in the House it has been the Foreign Affairs Committee that reviews the whole program. How this responsibility would be affected by Secretary Dulles' recent recommendations is not altogether clear; but it seems likely that the responsibilities of the Foreign Relations and Foreign Affairs Committees would be reduced.)

The question whether it is proper for one Congress to commit another one deserves clarification. Technically there are certainly schemes, legal and by no means unprecedented, for funding programs in advance. The IDAB proposal is an example. On the other hand, though this particular objection to long-range financing may be a quibble, there would be every advantage in assuring the longevity of the program by a display of enthusiasm in both parties, rather than by a purely legal act of putting some funds beyond recall. There are also some special problems with a large initial endowment. Under any reasonable program, the expenditure of funds would be low in the early years, rising sharply in the intermediate future. It would be unfortunate if the program were under pressure to get rid of the funds in a hurry, to avoid seeming to be overfinanced. It might also be difficult to get refunded with a proper lead-time, if when two-thirds of the funded period were over, two-thirds of the money still remained.

An alternative approach is implicit in the testimony of Mr. Collado before the House Committee. He said that "the amount of foreign aid should therefore be decided on a country basis and the total should be built up in that fashion rather than the reverse." The CED witness said that "we should move ahead with parts of our program for economic development abroad as soon as those parts can be decisively formed, rather than to await formulation of a complete program."

These remarks suggest that a "long-range funding" could be done either as the IDAB suggests, by funding a global program in advance, or by funding individual country programs as and when they reach the stage where they are ready for financing. Under the latter approach there presumably would be annual appropriations, but they would fund for several years the particular country programs presented in each year.

The latter approach has the advantage of not confronting Congress with a vague, global estimate. It also has a disadvantage. One of the strongest inducements in an underdeveloped country to do a workman-like job of analysis of its own requirements, to make the necessary project surveys, and—most important—to make the painful internal decisions that are always required on how to allocate investment resources, is the fairly sure prospect that once these costly surveys and painful decisions have been made, there will be money to finance the program. If harried governments, short on technical personnel, must cross all bridges before they come to them, reaching their development decisions before the money can even be requested of the Congress, the pace of development may be slowed at the very beginning of the process.

## 18 Evolutionary process vs. a new and integral program

Should we move ahead piecemeal, or try to develop an integral whole program? Some of the proposals, like the IDAB recommendation for a special fund, the Millikan-Rostow proposal for a worldwide "banker's approach," and the Chicago-group proposal for a nondiscriminatory development program for all underdeveloped countries, have favored a substantial departure from past practice and the development of a new concept and new basis for aid.

In contrast, the CED representative said:

We in the CED feel that our approach to the problem of a program for economic development abroad needs to be pragmatic, evolutionary, and adaptable. We shall have to deal with crises as they occur, to judge the worth of programs as they develop. The aim—to assist the momentum of development—is clear. Policy must evolve by decisions in major cases. The process of programming is in itself a policy-making function. We shall better come to grips with the problems that arise in making decisions on those policies, rather than in abstract, advanced debate.

The difference between these two approaches is fundamental.

The pragmatic, country-by-country approach involves less of a break with the past, less of an impact—or at least a less immediate impact—on public opinion abroad, and in all likelihood a speedier start, than the effort to develop an integral concept of development

165

separate from other aid programs, politically neutral, and conducted under well-defined ground rules.

Many of the issues discussed above are correlated with this question. If assistance programs are incapable of divorcement from the rest of foreign policy, if one's preference for separation from military or "crisis" programs has to be compromised, if "objective" criteria cannot be found that are beyond the criticism of either the countries that get the aid they expect or those that do not, and if one believes the next half-dozen years will be as unpredictable as the last, one inclines toward the pragmatic approach of the CED.

If one believes that our programs will be self-defeating unless we can demonstrate clean hands and a break with the past, and can state the rules by which we will operate and abide by them and convince both aid-receiving countries and others that this is one program that is beyond the reach of either military strategy or petty diplomacy, then it seems worth while to hold out for a program that has an integrity of its own.

The choice depends also on whether one is concerned primarily with the economic results of development assistance, or with the impact on foreign governments and foreign opinion. If India, Ghana, or Peru, will be mainly influenced by the way the program is conducted for India, Ghana, or Peru the integrity of the overall program is less important. It is more important if India is as much affected by our apparent behavior in Pakistan as by what we do for India.

*Domestic considerations.* Could Congress and the public be induced, though, to increase the money they spend on programs of this sort, unless they can be presented with a fairly ambitious concept, a sense of adventure, and a feeling that the enterprise needs a new start on a large scale to make its impact visible? Can the apathy of recent years be overcome in a "pragmatic," evolutionary process? Is it possible within the executive branch to attract, keep and motivate the people who are required to bring imagination, analytical talent, and experienced judgment to these programs?

Nobody who participated in the Marshall Plan, during the year that preceded its enactment or the year following, can fail to have been impressed with the intellectual resources and political influence that that program gathered by sheer excitement. Much of the discussions about whether an aid program is, or should be, motivated by "humanitarian" considerations, perhaps misses the point. Americans probably do not vote or work for aid programs because of a humanitarian interest in the results, but for the sheer sense of accomplishment. One's interest in whether per capita income in Indonesia has risen ten per cent will depend on whether it has risen because of something that he did.

However much the joy of accomplishment motivates the electorate and the Congress—and we should not discount that—it certainly is the principal force that keeps the most desirable personnel either in Washington or overseas, working on these programs. Even if they could be attracted by the "pragmatic approach," it might be some time before the attraction began to work on them. In sum, the impact on ourselves may belong in the balance too.

## Conclusion

Since the purpose of this essay is exploratory and provocative, the purpose may be served if the questions are allowed to stand as listed rather than compressed into an attempt at a neat and logical outline. In any case the questions discussed are only a sample. We have ignored Poland and the other satellites (as well as Finland and Yugoslavia), and important special cases like Japan. NATO has not been discussed, and it has been assumed that the Middle East is sufficiently on everyone's mind to require no further reminder in this paper. Among multilateral schemes we have ignored SUNFED, still pending before the United Nations Assembly, as well as the proportions in which our own technical assistance funds should be divided between unilateral and U.N. programs. We have said nothing about jurisdictional problems, the wisdom of continuing the Battle-Act threat of aid termination as a means of enforcing collaboration in east-west trade controls, or the appropriate degree of flexibility that the legislation should allow the President in allocating funds among countries and among purposes and in meeting crises not contemplated in the legislation.

The special roles of the World Bank and the Export-Import Bank have hardly been touched on, and we have not inquired into the prospects for aid extended by other countries than the United States. Special problems of agricultural surpluses, and the extent to which aid funds should be tied to purchases in the United States, are representative of a large number of "technical" policy questions that have been left out, together with all matters of trade policy and commodity-price arrangements or strategic materials programs. The proper role of regional arrangements has only been touched incidentally. How to select—more important, whether to select—projects for popular "appeal" or impact on the "common man" in recipient countries is another question omitted. An endless list of individual-country problems could be added.

But our purpose cannot be to solve all the problems, or even to acquaint ourselves with all the issues. It is to establish the premises on which issues are to be resolved. If the sample discussed here is adequate to evoke the underlying attitudes and principles, it should help to provide a basis for settling most of the remainder.

## Research projects and country-survey missions

The research projects and country-survey missions undertaken for the Special Senate Committee to Study the Foreign Aid Program are given below.

167

## Research projects

1. Military Assistance:
   Part A: *The Policy*. The Institute of War and Peace Studies of Columbia University, New York City.
   Part B: *The Program*. Systems Analysis Corporation, Washington, D. C.
   Part C: *Military Review and Evaluation*. Panel composed of Mr. Marx Leva, Gen. Joseph T. McNarney, Mr. S. L. A. Marshall, Maj. Gen. Gerald J. Higgins, and Adm. Robert B. Carney.
2. *The Objectives of United States Economic Assistance Programs*. The Center for International Studies of the Massachusetts Institute of Technology, Cambridge, Massachusetts.
3. *Foreign Assistance Activities of the Communist Bloc and Their Implications for the United States*. Council for Economic and Industry Research, Washington, D. C.
4. *American Private Enterprise, Foreign Economic Development, and the Aid Programs*. The American Enterprise Association, Inc., Washington, D. C.
5. *The Use of Private Contractors in Foreign Aid Programs*. Jerome Jacobson Associates, Washington, D. C.
6. *The Role of Foreign Aid in the Development of Other Countries*. The Research Center in Economic Development and Cultural Change of the University of Chicago.
7. *The Foreign Aid Programs and the United States Economy*. The National Planning Association, Washington, D. C.
8. *Agricultural Surplus Disposal and Foreign Aid*. The National Planning Association, Washington, D. C.
9. *Foreign Aid Activities of Other Free Nations*. Stuart Rice Associates, Washington, D. C.
10. *Personnel for Foreign Assistance Programs*. Louis J. Kroeger & Associates, San Francisco, California.
11. *The Administrative Aspects of United States Foreign Assistance Programs*. The Brookings Institution, Washington, D. C.

## Country surveys

1. Former Ambassador Norman Armour: *Countries*—Greece, Turkey, and Iran.
2. Mr. Hamilton Fish Armstrong, editor of Foreign Affairs: *Countries*—Lebanon, Iraq, Jordan.
3. Former Ambassador David K. E. Bruce: *Countries*—Peru, Chile, Argentina, Uruguay, Brazil.
4. Former Ambassador Jefferson Caffery: *Countries*—Portugal, Spain, France, and England.
5. Dr. John A. Hannah, president, Michigan State University: *Countries*—Korea, Japan, Okinawa, Formosa, Philippines.
6. Mr. William Randolph Hearst, Jr., president, Hearst Consolidated Publications, Inc., and editor in chief of Hearst Newspapers: *Countries*—Norway, Denmark, Western Germany.
7. Mr. Clement Johnston, chairman of the board of the United States Chamber of Commerce: *Countries*—Burma, Thailand, Cambodia, Indonesia, Laos, Vietnam.
8. Dr. Lewis Webster Jones, president, Rutgers University: *Countries*—Pakistan, India, Afghanistan, Ceylon.

9. Mr. James Minotto, former MSA Chief in Portugal: *Countries*—Cuba, Haiti, Dominican Republic, Venezuela, Panama, Costa Rica, Nicaragua, Honduras, El Salvador, Guatemala, Mexico.
10. Mr. Allan B. Kline, former president, American Farm Bureau Federation: *Country*—Yugoslavia.

## *Additional study*

*Views of Private American Citizens Abroad on the Foreign Aid Program.* Summary analysis of views received by the Committee from some thirty organizations that had forwarded to their overseas representatives a questionnaire prepared by the Special Committee.

# Final report

# of the Eleventh American Assembly

The participants in the Eleventh American Assembly at Arden House, Harriman, New York, May 2-5, 1957, on INTERNATIONAL STABILITY AND PROGRESS, reviewed as a group the following statement at the close of their discussions. Although there was general agreement on the Final Report, it is not the practice of the American Assembly for participants to affix their signatures; and it should not be assumed that every participant necessarily subscribes to every recommendation included in the statement.

## Preamble

In the mid-twentieth century, the United States finds itself in a position of unprecedented prosperity and power. It is inescapably involved in a world of rapid change which tests its institutions and basic values, and could threaten its survival.

The most pressing danger comes from Soviet power combined with Red China and the international communist movement they dominate. This threat is backed by an increasingly powerful military apparatus, and by a combination of political, military, economic, and psychological instruments.

A major challenge also arises from the emergence into independent nationhood of hundreds of millions of people in Asia and Africa. These peoples have a passion for independence and self-respect and acutely resent remnants of colonialism; they are responsive to nationalism, in some cases extreme and irrational; and they seek ways of escaping conditions of dire poverty, often aggravated by population pressure. This challenge would for formidable by itself but is intensified by Soviet efforts to subvert these nations.

171

In this situation, there is bipartisan support for the use of American resources and energies to back an affirmative foreign policy. That policy needs many instruments: diplomacy, the United Nations, military strength, alliances, international information programs, and economic measures. The actions of private business, religious and charitable organizations, universities, foundations, and individual citizens are also vitally important to the carrying out of foreign policy.

Among the instruments of foreign policy, programs of military, economic, and technical assistance have a major role. In the period since the war they have been effectively employed to meet many changing situations. They have proved a sound investment of American resources, contributing to increased strength for the free world and helping to reduce international tensions.

This year a major reappraisal has been undertaken in order to modify policies and adapt methods to the altering situations in which the United States finds itself. There is need for fresh public understanding both of objectives and methods in the situation which now confronts us and is likely to confront us in the next few years.

## Findings and recommendations

### The United States interest in foreign assistance

1. For the foreseeable future the United States must continue to employ military, economic, and technical assistance as instruments of foreign policy. In view of the continuing military threat of Soviet and Red Chinese imperialism, the most immediate national interest involved and the one responsible for the magnitude of the program is the security interest. Foreign assistance serves other major and enduring interests—political independence, stability, and economic progress, especially in the new nations of Asia and Africa. Such independence, stability, and progress will reduce the danger of international conflict and permit the evolution of these new nations as peaceful and constructive members of the world community. These programs will also serve to expand international trade and private investment and thereby help our own nation as well as others. It is thus clear that foreign assistance is based on the positive interests of the United States. At the same time it accords with the humanitarian impulses of the American people.

### The role of military assistance

2. Military assistance accounts for the great bulk of our current foreign aid expenditures. Arms alone constitute well over half the total. Other support for foreign military efforts ("defense support") represents an additional one-quarter. Yet military assistance altogether is less than one-tenth as large as our domestic defense expenditures.

172

3. The United States needs formal allies and prospective military associates to deal with the danger of general or of limited war. Notwithstanding weapons developments, collective arrangements will remain an indispensable part of the effort to deter and if necessary to defeat aggression. The maintenance of overseas bases is now one of the essential elements of this common defense.

4. Assistance both in arms and in defense support is well justified, adding more to collective free world strength than could a similar additional expenditure for our national defense establishment.

5. In some less stable countries the support through American assistance of an adequate military force may be essential to the achievement of reasonable political stability as well as defense against external aggression. In addition, useful by-products of military assistance and training may be the development of skills, both mechanical and administrative, and the improvement of basic facilities. At the same time, measures must be taken to meet situations where military forces divert so large a portion of local resources as to create serious political and social problems and retard economic development. Where the forces cannot safely be reduced, defense support assistance should be used to supplement the local resources, but the possibility of reducing force levels without jeopardizing security should also be carefully explored.

6. Apart from strengthening weak countries and providing an additional deterrent to limited and general war, military assistance can, in exceptional cases, be used in aid of other foreign policy objectives, such as forestalling Soviet infiltration or subversion. Care must be taken not to encourage local armaments races or to aggravate regional international tensions.

*Governmental assistance for economic development*

7. Expenditures designed directly to promote economic development now account for less than one-eighth of total foreign aid expenditures, apart from special agricultural commodity programs.

8. Orderly economic progress in independent underdeveloped countries accords with the political, security, and economic interests of the United States. Such progress serves as a bulwark against international communism, and in the long run will help to assure that the role of the new nations in world affairs will be increasingly constructive. While no nation has an inherent right to assistance from the United States merely because it is underdeveloped, the promotion of sound economic development should be an accepted element of American foreign policy.

9. Development is a highly complex and necessarily slow process. Nations are at many different stages of political, social, and economic evolution, and the needs and opportunities for promoting their development vary accordingly. Ultimately, the success of development programs depends in large part upon the execution and administration by the government and institutions of the underdeveloped countries. In

173

some cases, technical assistance in education, public health, agricultural and industrial skills, or in public and private administration merits the top priority. In others, capital requirements are urgent and exceed the capacity of local savings or normal foreign borrowing; the development of a pool of skilled and professional manpower, however, tends to encourage the accumulation of local savings, even though perhaps inadequately at the start. In still others, the needs for financial capital are being adequately met from private sources. An effective program requires a general definition of objectives and criteria, but must then be built up in the light of the actual conditions in each country being considered for possible assistance.

10. Alliance with the United States should not be a prerequisite for development assistance; the important thing is the will of a nation to develop its resources and defend its independence. The present uncommitted countries include some of the most important nations of Asia, whose orderly evolution and long-run orientation are crucial to American interests. Hope in these countries for achieving economic and social progress in a reasonable time and within a constitutional framework is among their dominant political objectives. It would be folly for the United States to leave totalitarianism as their only apparent way out of poverty and hopelessness, or the Soviet bloc as their only source of assistance. The fact that a country has undertaken the additional obligations involved in the alliance system is a proper element to be taken into account in determining the amount and character of the assistance.

11. Any United States assistance program must be geared to the long run. It takes years to carry out an economic development program; it may take several years to complete individual projects. The prospect of continuing outside support may encourage leadership in the countries involved to make the difficult decisions required for an effective process of development. For these reasons, the legislative and administrative arrangements for development assistance should give assurance of continuity. The American Assembly strongly favors the establishment of some kind of development loan fund, with an authorization covering several years. On condition that arrangements are made to ensure that such a fund is managed as an integral part of our foreign assistance program, there are several alternative possibilities for its fiscal administration. These could include existing institutions like the Export-Import Bank or new institutions of corporate character. At the very minimum, there should be a clear declaration of congressional intent on continuity, coupled with authority to make commitments covering several years on individual projects.

12. Since successful economic development is wealth-producing, assistance for such development should, over a period of time, create the ability to repay. It should normally be on a loan basis. On the other hand, many underdeveloped countries are unable to anticipate with assurance the ability to repay on usual terms. Development assistance should, therefore, be sufficiently flexible to permit loans on long

terms or with repayment in local currency. While such repayment poses some problems, the loan technique has some advantage in encouraging the use of economic standards in planning development projects. The terms of development assistance should complement and strengthen the possibilities for loans on normal terms and for private investment, and not compete with or undermine them.

13. If the United States continues to generate agricultural supplies beyond the demands of normal markets, they should be used in conjunction with other assistance for promoting foreign economic development, with continued care to avoid disrupting normal markets.

14. Formal declarations of political alignment should not be made a condition of receiving development assistance. On the other hand, it is both proper and necessary to negotiate conditions concerning the soundness of individual development projects or economic policies required for the success of the program.

15. Presently available evidence suggests that the magnitude of development assistance should certainly be no lower and probably higher than present expenditure levels for this purpose (now roughly $500 million per annum including the estimated share of "defense support" contributing to these objectives). More reliable estimates of the needs would have to be based on a country-by-country review. The United States should be prepared to provide a substantially higher amount in future years if it can be effectively used for these purposes.

16. It is likewise not possible to set in advance a fixed duration for development assistance, but it will certainly be necessary in some form for many years to come. No country should be led to expect development assistance in perpetuity. Certain countries are now at a stage where little beyond technical assistance could be usefully employed, and conditions permitting true development programs may evolve only after several years. In other cases development has already sufficiently progressed so that a rapid reduction of such assistance can be envisaged in the near future. In each case the planning should look to the earliest possible tapering off of such assistance through the creation of conditions conducive to broadly based domestic saving and investment and normal foreign capital financing.

## Economic assistance for special purposes

17. Apart from defense support and development assistance, economic assistance in limited amounts is also justifiable for other purposes—for example, to secure some specific advantage to the United States, to meet political crises, or to cope with natural disasters. Experience has shown that the timely provision of such assistance in adequate amounts can be critical to the continued independence of friendly nations. Requirements for such assistance cannot always be foreseen accurately; consequently considerable flexibility must be given the Administration in the management of resources provided for these purposes.

175

18. In cases such as Yugoslavia and Poland the fact that the regimes are communist should not preclude the giving of assistance where this might help increase the independence of such countries or the degree of human freedom within them.

## Technical assistance

19. Technical assistance expenditures, both bilateral and through the United Nations, now amount to about $150 million per year. The value of a well-conducted technical assistance program has been fully demonstrated. Such programs should be continued and expanded, especially in the newly emerging nations. More satisfactory arrangements should be made in order to attract to these activities qualified administrative and technical manpower in sufficient numbers, with suitable personal qualities and training and aptitudes for working in various environments as effective representatives of the United States. The United States should be prepared to employ suitably qualified foreign nationals in these programs. Technical assistance through the United Nations and its specialized agencies has several advantages, notably the ability to draw on a larger manpower base. We should encourage the gradual expansion of these United Nations programs and be prepared to continue sharing in their cost and seeking improvements in their administration.

## Countering Soviet initiatives

20. In the last few years, the Soviets have sought to counter our programs by themselves using trade, loans, and military and technical assistance as important instruments of their foreign policy. The best general means of minimizing the effectiveness of these moves is a constructive program of our own. It would be unwise to invite blackmail or attempts to induce the United States to bid against the Soviet Union. The United States should, however, have the ability to deal with such moves by counter measures in particular cases.

## The role of private enterprise

21. Private enterprise already plays a major part in promoting foreign economic development and strengthening the international economic order through trade, investment, patent licensing, management contracts, and other means. The United States government is also making substantial use of private business and educational and other institutions in the aid program. These trends should be encouraged. With respect to foreign investment, tax incentives and guarantee arrangements are of real value. One possibility in connection with a developmental fund lies in further expanding joint public and private financing arrangements, both in the United States and in the recipient countries; this should be carefully explored. Moreover, while not

176

making revision of foreign governmental attitudes toward private enterprise a condition of economic assistance, much greater efforts should be made, both by government and by private organizations, to encourage an appreciation that progressive private enterprise methods offer the best long-range prospects of sound economic development, while strengthening the democratic foundations of societies.

## Organization and administration

22. Proposals now being put forward by the Administration seek a sharper distinction between military and economic assistance, in order to clarify at home and abroad the objectives of the program. This purpose is sound. At the same time, it must be recognized that in underdeveloped countries receiving military assistance, any line drawn between "defense support" and "development assistance" is necessarily arbitrary. More important, it must be recognized that political, military, and economic developments in any country are inter-related and that American policy and programs must be an integrated whole. It is therefore essential to strengthen the decision-making and coordinating arrangements within the United States government, especially if military assistance and defense support are transferred to the defense budget, and to ensure that all aspects of foreign assistance, both in programming and in execution, conform to a consistent line of foreign policy.

23. Efforts should be made to ensure maximum participation by other advanced countries in promoting economic development in underdeveloped countries. Where circumstances make it desirable, regional coordinating arrangements involving both supplying and recipient countries should be encouraged.

24. The administration of the assistance programs in the United States government requires a new sense of purpose and a new spirit of drive, energy, and imagination as well as clarification of objectives and methods. No fresh approach will be meaningful without this spirit in its administration. Only thus can persons of exceptional qualifications be attracted to the program. Nor can its administration be successful over the long term without a corps of properly trained personnel with real career opportunities, including status in the Foreign Service.

## United States costs and benefits

25. Foreign assistance as a whole accounts for only about one per cent of our gross national product today, as compared with over two per cent in the peak year of 1949. Moreover, three-fourths of the total is for military purposes and must be appraised in terms similar to those of our domestic defense program. The program as a whole does not impose unreasonable strains on our total resources or on any important segment of the American economy. The contribution of foreign

177

assistance to export markets, to increasing raw material supplies, and to the general strengthening of the world economy constitutes at least a partial offset to the direct economic costs.

26. At the same time, national security costs as a whole, including those for foreign assistance, are mainly responsible for a total national budget and corresponding tax burden which bear heavily on the American people. The main hope of lightening these burdens lies in promoting world conditions which would permit a reduction of military expenditures; foreign assistance is one of the most important means of bringing about such conditions. Meanwhile, no unnecessary expenditure can be permitted and no opportunity should be lost for tightening up methods of program-making and administration to eliminate any avoidable waste. The objectives and methods of foreign assistance can be clarified, and competent administration assured. The benefits of these programs to American interests greatly outweigh their cost. That cost is part of the inescapable price of an American foreign policy calculated to promote our deepest interest as a nation.

# Participants in the Eleventh American Assembly

Dillon Anderson
Former Special Assistant to the
  President for National Security
  Affairs
Houston

George W. Ball
Washington, D. C.

William Benton
Publisher
Encyclopedia Britannica
Southport, Connecticut

Jonathan B. Bingham
Secretary to the Governor
State of New York

Thomas C. Blaisdell, Jr.
Bureau of International Relations
University of California
Berkeley

Roy Blough
Professor of International Affairs
Columbia University

Robert Blum
President
The Asia Foundation
San Francisco

Courtney C. Brown
Dean
Graduate School of Business
Columbia University

Arthur F. Burns
Professor of Economics
Columbia University

Harlan Cleveland
Dean, Maxwell Graduate School of
  Citizenship and Public Affairs
Syracuse University

John Cowles
President
The Minneapolis Star & Tribune
Minnesota

Philip K. Crowe
Ambassador to Ceylon
New York

179

William Diebold
Council on Foreign Relations
New York

Douglas Dillon
Deputy Undersecretary of State
  for Economic Affairs

James Terry Duce
Vice President
Arabian American Oil Company
New York

Marriner S. Eccles
Chairman of the Board
First Security Corporation
Salt Lake City

Lamar Fleming, Jr.
President
Anderson, Clayton & Company
Houston

Edwin T. Gibson
President
Eisenhower Exchange Fellow-
  ships, Inc.
Philadelphia

Brigadier General Sidney F. Gif-
  fin
Vice Commandant
Air War College
Alabama

Lincoln Gordon
Professor of Economics
Harvard University

Edward S. Greenbaum
Brigadier General, USA (Ret'd)
Greenbaum, Wolff & Ernst
New York

Allen Griffin
Editor
Monterey Peninsula Herald
California

Mrs. J. Ramsay Harris
International Childrens Emer-
  gency Fund
Denver

Henry J. Heinz, II
President
H. J. Heinz Company
Pittsburgh

Francis Hickman
Editor
Cotton Trade Journal
Memphis

Benjamin Higgins
Center for International
  Studies
Massachusetts Institute of Tech-
  nology

Paul G. Hoffman
Pasadena, California

Edward F. Holter
President, Farmers & World Af-
  fairs
Lecturer, The National Grange
Washington, D. C.

Donald W. James, Jr.
Harriman Scholar
Columbia University

Philip C. Jessup
Hamilton Fish Professor of In-
  ternational Law & Diplomacy
Columbia University

Clement D. Johnston
Chairman of the Board
U.S. Chamber of Commerce
Roanoke, Virginia

Eric A. Johnston
President
Motion Picture Association of
  America
Washington, D. C.

180

Sam H. Jones
Former Governor of Louisiana
Lake Charles, Louisiana

Robert J. Kleberg, Jr.
King Ranch
Texas

Allan B. Kline
Former President
American Farm Bureau Federation
Western Springs, Illinois

Walter J. Levy
Economic Consultant
New York

George C. McGhee
Former Ambassador to Turkey
Washington, D. C.

William W. Marvel
Carnegie Corporation of New York

The Reverend Dr. Kenneth L. Maxwell
Department of International Affairs
National Council of the Churches of Christ
New York

Abe Mellinkoff
City Editor
San Francisco Chronicle

James A. Michener
Tinicum, Pennsylvania

Melvin S. Moyer
Harriman Scholar
Columbia University

Paul H. Nitze
President
Foreign Service Educational Foundation
Washington, D. C.

F. Taylor Ostrander, Jr.
The American Metal Company, Ltd.
New York

Norman D. Palmer
Wharton School of Finance and Commerce
University of Pennsylvania

Gardner Patterson
Director
International Finance Section
Princeton University

Herbert V. Prochnow
Vice President
First National Bank of Chicago

Whitelaw Reid
Chairman of the Board
New York Herald Tribune

Walter W. Rostow
Center for International Studies
Massachusetts Institute of Technology

Dean Rusk
President
Rockefeller Foundation
New York

Thomas C. Schelling
Professor of Economics
Yale University

Forrest W. Seymour
Editor
Telegram-Gazette
Worcester, Massachusetts

Lauren K. Soth
Editor of the Editorial Pages
Des Moines Register and Tribune
Iowa

Ib Eric Sundt
Harriman Scholar
Columbia University

Wayne C. Taylor
Former Undersecretary of Commerce
Heathsville, Virginia

Max W. Thornburg
Bahrain, Persian Gulf

Frank N. Trager
Head
Southeast Asia Program
New York University

John M. Vorys
Congressman from Ohio
Washington, D. C.

Edward W. Weidner
Chairman
Department of Political Science
Michigan State University

Howard Whidden
Foreign Editor
Business Week
New York

David J. Winton
Chairman
Winton Lumber Company
Minneapolis

C. Tyler Wood
Assistant to the Director for Evaluation
International Cooperation Administration
Washington, D. C.

# The National Policy Board
# of the American Assembly

183

Oveta Culp Hobby
President
The Houston Post
Houston, Texas

Grayson Kirk
President
Columbia University
New York City

Allan B. Kline, *Chairman*
Former President
American Farm Bureau
   Federation
Chicago, Illinois

Leonard F. Mc.Collum
President
Continental Oil Company
Houston, Texas

Don G. Mitchell
Chairman of the Board
Sylvania Electric Products Inc.
New York City

William I. Myers
Dean
New York State College of Agri-
   culture
Ithaca, New York

Herschel D. Newsom
Master
National Grange
Washington, D.C.

Jacob S. Potofsky
General President
Amalgamated Clothing Workers of
   America
New York City

Charles Sawyer
Attorney and former U. S. Sec-
   retary of Commerce
Cincinnati, Ohio

Henry M. Wriston
Director
The American Assembly

# The American Assembly

•

Henry M. Wriston, Director

Clifford C. Nelson, Associate Director

James L. Malfetti, Associate Director

---

Room 401, Graduate School of Business Building, Columbia University

New York 27, New York

Telephone UNiversity 5-4000, Extension 795

Arden House, Harriman, New York, Telephone TUxedo 4-0367